Morality, Reason, and Power

Morality, Reason, and Power

American Diplomacy in the Carter Years

Gaddis Smith

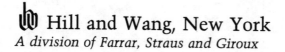 Hill and Wang, New York
A division of Farrar, Straus and Giroux

Library of Congress Cataloging-in-Publication Data
Smith, Gaddis.
  Morality, reason, and power.
  Bibliography: p.
  Includes index.
    1. United States—Foreign relations—1977–1981.
2. Carter, Jimmy, 1924–   I. Title.
E872.S66 1985   327.73   86-317

Preface

Historians ought not to shy away from the recent past. Americans have very shallow memories. The rush of today separates most of us from what occurred only a few years ago. Indeed, there may be a particular fog covering those decades between what was formally learned in most history courses and the present—say, from the 1950s to the 1980s. People of college age are especially prone to this phenomenon because generally they have no usable direct recollections of political events before they came into their teens. Thus, Jimmy Carter's foreign policy is as inherently unfamiliar to someone entering college in 1986 as the Paris Peace Conference of 1919—both need to be described and explained.

Such thoughts constitute my first reason for this foray into recent history. My second reason is a fascination with the events themselves. As I hope this book will demonstrate, American diplomacy during the Carter Presidency was like a prism in which many of the basic ideas, dilemmas, and policies of the twentieth century are reflected and illuminated. President Carter, perforce, is the central character. But this is not a study of his personality. The focus is, more broadly, on ideas in their historical context and on American foreign policy as a whole.

The sources for this book are all public. The archival record for the 1970s will not be available to historians for decades. But it is my conviction that the Carter Administration was unusually open about its purposes and activities. Members of the Administration at the time spoke candidly and in detail to the press, to congressional committees, and to the public. The President, Secretary of State Cyrus Vance, and National Security Adviser Zbigniew Brzezinski have all published informative memoirs. This book could not have been written without them or without the excellent monographs which have appeared on such subjects as relations with Iran, Soviet-American relations, negotiations for arms control, and the treaties with Panama—all duly noted in the notes and bibliography.

I owe a special debt of gratitude to Arthur Wang for his encouragement, patience, and careful editing; to Robert Schulzinger, fellow diplomatic historian, for reading the manuscript and offering his usual incisive criticism; and to my wife, Barclay, for listening to me read the draft manuscript and tolerating a rather messy author-at-work.

G.S.

August 1985
New Haven, Connecticut

Contents

Morality, Reason, and Power

Purpose and Prologue

Judged by the scoreboard of Presidential elections, the Carter Administration was a failure. Not since Herbert Hoover in 1932 had an incumbent President been as thoroughly defeated as Jimmy Carter was by Ronald Reagan in 1980. Four years later, in 1984, Reagan was still running more against Carter than against his real opponent, Walter Mondale—just as Democrats for decades after 1932 ran against the image of Hoover. But electoral victory or defeat has no necessary connection with significance. The purpose of this book is to argue that the four years of the Carter Administration were among the most significant in the history of American foreign policy in the twentieth century. One may deplore or applaud the objectives, methods, and results of those years. But to ignore or forget them is to block from memory a period when a fundamental debate about how the United States should behave in international affairs was waged with unusual clarity; when the President and his highest advisers tried more intensively than at any time since 1945 to grapple with and relieve the terrible insecurity of the nuclear age through negotiated arms control; when an effort was made to think in terms of a lasting world order beneficial to all people rather than to make every decision on the basis of short-term calculation of American advantage over the Soviet Union; when leaders tried consciously and explicitly to discover and apply an effective combination of morality, reason, and power in the conduct of American foreign policy.

The uniqueness of the Carter Administration's foreign policy lies in the intensity and multiplicity of the issues addressed, not in the novelty of the issues themselves. Every idea, every objective, every achievement, and every failure was tied to previous American experience and international events. Thus, as this book seeks to demonstrate, one cannot understand the Carter years except in the long context of the twentieth century. Conversely, one can understand the sweep of American foreign policy in the twentieth century better after a close examination of how perennial themes and problems were expressed or confronted in the Carter years.

Those who have the responsibility for conducting foreign policy seldom have the time or temperament to ponder questions of human purpose and ultimate values. Nor do they normally try to envision the distant future. Reacting to this year and next, or perhaps to the period between now and the next election, is about all they can handle. But there are implicit assumptions about the nature of people and nations beneath even the most overtly unphilosophical behavior. Because President Carter and several of his advisers tried harder than is customary among officials to think about values and about the longer future, the Administration provides an exceptionally good case study in the intellectual roots of foreign policy. This theme is laid out more fully in chapter 1.

Since 1945, the existence of nuclear weapons has thrown all traditional assumptions about the pursuit of national security into doubt—at least in the minds of those who have been willing to think deeply on the matter. But most leaders, whether in the United States, the Soviet Union, or in other nations possessing or hoping to possess nuclear weapons, have seldom been willing to think deeply. The enterprise is too unsettling, too subversive of familiar institutions and ways of acting. Really to contemplate nuclear weapons and the almost certain consequences of their use is too sickening for most leaders to do—at least not for long or very often. To devise ways of reducing or eliminating the danger is conceptually difficult almost beyond the capacity of the human mind. And then to win domestic and international political agreement for an effective program is a task daunting beyond any ever attempted. Thus, most leaders since the beginning of the atomic age have averted their gaze. They have warded off psychological nausea and mental paralysis by speaking not of reality but of numbers, acronyms, abstractions deliberately drained of human meaning. Or they have simply denied that nuclear weapons make a difference and have gone on using the old guidelines.

President Carter and some of his advisers were readier than any of their predecessors to stare directly at the reality of nuclear weapons. They disagreed among themselves over what could and should be done, disagreed with the Soviet Union, and failed to win strong public and congressional support. The results of their efforts—an unratified treaty which changed the status quo only marginally, and programs for new and more powerful weapons—were tragically short of or contrary to President Carter's initial hopes. But the full and open discussion and the prolonged efforts at the highest level left a record which illuminates the problems of the nuclear age.

Related to the problem of nuclear weapons and almost as difficult to assimilate into the conduct of foreign policy are the issues of the long-range human condition. Will there be enough energy to sustain a humane standard of living, or even life itself? Will the air and water be fouled and poisoned by thoughtless misuse of resources? Will violence and the armaments with which the world is afflicted multiply until it is a smoking maze of armed camps? Will nuclear weapons be acquired by dozens of nations, even by private criminals and terrorists? None of these questions was answered satisfactorily by the Carter Administration. But they were raised more explicitly than ever before. The story of what was attempted by way of solutions, however limited and ineffective, is nevertheless an important part of the historical record, with some usefulness, perhaps, for those who will again raise the same questions.

Historians and policymakers share the problem of how best to organize and present information. On a given day the President, or Secretary of State, or National Security Adviser may deal with dozens of issues, but at any moment must concentrate on one. Records, memory, continuity are preserved more by issue—SALT, the Panama Canal, hostages in Iran—than by units of time. Imagine the chaos of a file system set up only by date, with all subjects mingled together. To write in an absolutely chronological fashion about many people concerned with many issues would be equally chaotic. This book, therefore, follows the practitioner. Chapters deal with topics, not days, weeks, or months. But compartmentalization also creates a problem, because everything is connected with everything else. Policymaker and historian must, even while dealing with one thing at a time, be aware of all the developments which fill the week, the month, the year. What are the larger patterns, the broad changes in the United States and in the world, and the multiple interconnections which affect the way each particular issue is played out? As prologue, therefore, let us begin with an overview, a high-altitude survey as it were, of the chronological landscape of the four years of American foreign policy—January 1977 to January 1981—of the Administration of President Jimmy Carter.

1977: *FAST START*

The election of Jimmy Carter in 1976 was a consequence of the defeat of the United States in the Vietnam war. His lack of experience in foreign policy was an asset which he skillfully exploited during the campaign. He promised to lead the country in a new direction, openly, morally, and with an absolute commitment to human rights. No longer would an obsession with the Soviet Union and communism shape every policy. The United States would recognize the distinctive problems of every nation and would work for a more humane world order, not simply for a position of strength against one adversary. Proposed military solutions would be viewed skeptically. A sincere effort would be made to reduce the sale of arms to developing countries, curb the proliferation of nuclear-weapons technology, and above all, by negotiations with the Soviet Union, reduce the danger of nuclear war.

Secretary of State Cyrus Vance agreed with this approach. National Security Adviser Zbigniew Brzezinski was less enthusiastic, but during 1977 he muffled his doubts. Vance had substantial influence in selecting the middle-level people who would develop and carry out the specifics of policy. They for the most part shared his and Carter's initially reformist, non-military assumptions. The Administration began by trying to address almost every issue simultaneously and quickly. A comprehensive proposal for deep cuts and extensive controls over strategic nuclear weapons was presented to the Soviets—who rejected it emphatically. But the Administration was only momentarily discouraged. By the autumn of 1977, the general shape of a possible agreement was in sight.

Efforts to bring peace between Egypt and Israel and to solve the problems of the Middle East more broadly were energetically pursued. Panama was successfully engaged in drafting treaties to provide for the relinquishment of American control over the Canal. The Administration hoped this would open a new, happier era of relations with all of Latin America. Overtures were made to Cuba and Vietnam for the establishment of diplomatic relations. With United Nations Ambassador Andrew Young as spokesman, the United States embraced the concepts of majority rule and racial equality as guidelines for policy toward Africa. The President cancelled production of the B-1 bomber and announced that American ground troops would be withdrawn from Korea. And the banner of human rights was waved as a rebuke to Soviet treatment of dissidents and the abuses of authoritarian regimes everywhere, but especially in Latin America. The sheer level and range of activity, if not the results, suggested a foreign-policy equivalent of the domestic activity of the first year of Franklin D. Roosevelt's New Deal.

1978: HARVEST OF ACHIEVEMENT

The Carter Administration's principal formal achievements occurred during 1978. In March and April, the Senate, by the narrowest of margins, approved the treaties with Panama. Carter invited Anwar Sadat of Egypt and Menachem Begin of Israel to Camp David in September. The three leaders produced the accords which led to a peace treaty and Israeli withdrawal from Egyptian soil. Carter and many observers considered Camp David the high point of four years of foreign policy. The United States and the People's Republic of China established full normal relations at the end of the year, and the United States severed its formal ties with Taiwan. The hope of completing the SALT II agreement during 1978 was repeatedly dashed and revived, but by the end of the year only a few details remained before Carter and Soviet leader Leonid Brezhnev met, as they did in Vienna in June 1979, to sign the treaty.

But achievements during 1978 were more than balanced by portents of trouble. A revolution erupted in Iran and by the end of the year the Shah's days as a ruler were numbered. The Administration was divided over how to react. Brzezinski advocated doing whatever was necessary to keep the Shah in control. Others believed it was more consistent with American values to urge reform and to place no obstacle in the way of the Shah's departure from the country. Then the United States should try for amicable relations with the successor revolutionary regime. During 1978, President Carter cancelled the development of the neutron bomb, a battlefield nuclear weapon intended for Europe, and thereby exacerbated relations with the major NATO partners, especially

Germany. Cuban troops, seen as proxies of the Soviet Union, became more active in Angola and Ethiopia. Liberals did not fare well in the midterm congressional elections, and as the trauma of Vietnam receded, public-opinion polls indicated that the American people were becoming more supportive of military expenditures, readier to support a more muscular foreign policy.

1979: *RETURN TO MILITARISM*

The character of the Carter Administration's foreign policy changed radically during 1979, continuing and completing a shift which had begun in 1978. The peace treaty between Egypt and Israel, delivering less than the Camp David accords had seemed to offer, was an anticlimax. President Carter had exhausted himself through detailed personal attention to the various aspects of the Arab–Israeli conflict. After the spring of 1979, he left it up to subordinates to continue unproductive negotiations over the status of the Palestinians. The SALT II treaty, too long anticipated, was another anticlimax. Rather than a cause for rejoicing, the signing was followed by a grim and finally unsuccessful effort to gain Senate approval.

The Administration paid in advance for Senate votes, which were never cast, by proposing the full development of the MX missile system and a higher overall defense budget. The United States and its NATO partners also agreed that intermediate-range cruise and Pershing II missiles would be deployed in Europe unless the Soviets agreed to withdraw much of their theater nuclear arsenal. Soviet behavior around the world was now interpreted in the most ominous possible light. The relationship with the People's Republic of China was increasingly described both in Washington and in Moscow as a strategic alignment against the Soviet Union. All possibility of a peaceful accommodation with Vietnam ended when the United States tacitly supported (even while denying any support) China's invasion of Vietnam.

In the case of the supposed Soviet "combat brigade" in Cuba, the alarm was tolled for a threat that did not exist.

Andrew Young was fired—ostensibly because of his unauthorized conversations with a Palestinian leader, but more generally because his philosophy was contrary to the Administration's new direction. African policy now reflected more concern with meeting Soviet influence and less with African issues per se. Cuba, with troops in both Angola and Ethiopia, was seen to be the link between a communist threat in Africa and Latin America. In 1979, the corrupt right-wing regime of Anastasio Somoza in Nicaragua collapsed. The Carter Administration was happy to see Somoza go, but not happy at the triumph of the left-wing Sandinistas, whose leaders openly admired Cuba as model and mentor.

The Soviet Union had nothing to do with the Iranian revolution, but that revolution contributed to the shift of American policy toward a greater emphasis on military force and containment of the Soviet Union. The fall of the Shah ended the American alliance with Iran, meant the loss of electronic listening posts tuned in on Soviet missile tests, led to a doubling of oil prices and the most acute phase of the energy crisis, which Carter considered more threatening than anything except nuclear war. The President's inability to persuade Congress to pass the energy legislation he desired filled him with a bleak sense of frustration and discouragement. He spoke of a crisis of spirit in the nation itself, but the crisis, or malaise, was primarily within himself. Midsummer 1979 was the lowest point of the Presidency.

The seizure of the American Embassy in Teheran and the captivity of the hostages, beginning in November, intensified the public's impression that the United States was powerless and in retreat. The answer, self-evident to Carter in terms both of international events and of what was necessary for him to retain domestic political support, was to subordinate all other foreign-policy considerations to the rebuilding of military power. The Soviet invasion of Afghanistan at the end of December did not bring about a change; it emphatically confirmed and seemed to justify what had already occurred.

1980: AN ADMINISTRATION HELD HOSTAGE

The final year, 1980, was sad for Carter and his supporters. The fifty-two hostages held captive in Teheran seemed to symbolize the ineffectiveness of the President and of the United States under his leadership. Carter's application of economic and political sanctions against the Soviet Union in response to the invasion of Afghanistan, his request that the Senate suspend consideration of the SALT II treaty, his assertion of the "Carter Doctrine" promising to use armed force in the Middle East if American interests were threatened, even his endorsement of a new strategic doctrine for fighting and trying to win a nuclear war all testified to the increasingly confrontational and military character of American policy. Those measures were unhappy evidence of the almost complete failure of the aspirations of the first year of his Administration. The failed attempt at a military rescue of the hostages in April did serve, strangely enough, to reduce the intensity of attention to the plight of the captives—but it increased the Administration's reputation for ineptitude. It was also a last straw of disagreement for Secretary of State Vance. He told the President that he would resign, whether or not the mission succeeded.

Jimmy Carter did gain renomination as the Democratic Party's candidate in the November election, thanks largely to the mistakes of challenger Edward Kennedy. The Republicans nominated Ronald Reagan, who began an exuberant campaign. Reagan's victory was no surprise. All that remained now was eleven "lame duck" weeks during which the only issue was whether or not the hostages would be returned before Jimmy Carter left office.

1

Echoes of History

American foreign policy during the four years of Jimmy Carter's Presidency (1977–81) was a whirlpool of disagreement over the fundamental nature of national and world security. President Carter, his advisers, supporters, and critics attempted to define that security and set an appropriate course for the United States. During some past Administrations, a single current of thought and action had prevailed, allowing policy to glide on a smooth stretch of consensus. For example, during the early years of the Cold War, the nation was agreed on the "zero-sum game" approach to the Soviet Union. Whatever made the United States stronger and the Soviet Union weaker was good. But during the Carter years a combination of world events, political developments within the United States, and decisions by the Administration brought multiple currents more visibly into conflict than at any time since the United States became a world power.

A quartet of philosophical problems pervaded the foreign policy of the Carter Administration and tied those years to the broad sweep of history. The problems were not new. They had been confronted repeatedly by Americans during the twentieth century. As long as nations compete with or threaten each other, these problems will never be ultimately resolved.

First, is preservation of moral principle or enhancement of material power the primary objective of foreign policy? Which is the end and which the means? Should moral principle be sacrificed when questions of power are at stake? Always? Sometimes? Never? Is the United States ever justified in using methods abroad which would be immoral or illegal at home? Should the moral character of foreign leaders and nations influence American decisions to extend or withhold support? Or is the only test of a relationship whether the other nation can be of material benefit to the United States? Conversely, should the United States ever make a sacrifice for moral principle? How great a sacrifice, and on whom, specifically, should it fall? And if these questions have no clear answers, what rules of reason should a government follow in seeking a viable balance? Should those rules be spelled out in advance, perhaps by Congress, or should the President and his advisers make decisions case by case?

Second, is foreign policy dictated by external threats which are real and undeniable; or are alleged external threats merely the excuse for actions driven by internal forces? Throughout American history, all commentators on and makers of foreign policy have been primarily externalists or internalists in their analysis of what is wrong and what needs to be done. Externalists emphasize the hostile intent of other nations. President James K. Polk was an externalist in 1846 when he said that Mexico had shed American blood on American soil. Franklin D. Roosevelt was an externalist in 1941 when he said that the defense of all nations under attack by Germany was vital to the United States. Ronald Reagan was an externalist in 1982 when he said the Soviet Union was the source of evil in the modern world. Externalists are usually people in power and their supporters.

Internalists, on the other hand, have generally been critics outside of government or politicians trying to win office (if they do win, they often become externalists). They argue that foreign policy is too often the result of unworthy internal forces—e.g., selfish economic interests, ruthless politicians putting personal advantage over the general welfare—and is therefore wrong and even immoral. Internalists offer an easy solution: Americans need only repent, reform, and throw out the rascals. The democratic process will solve all problems. Internalists have been relatively ill informed about conditions outside the United States, but confident that externalists misrepresent and exaggerate foreign threats. Abolitionists who said the greed of slaveowners for more territory caused the war with Mexico, isolationists who said Roosevelt in 1941 wanted to become the supreme ruler of the world, and most opponents of the Vietnam war were internalists. The voice of reason would suggest that externalists and internalists are both right and wrong. The nation has faced real external threats and has acted against other countries for inappropriate internal reasons. But can reason tell, case by case, where lies the dividing line between appropriate and inappropriate internal motives, between real and concocted threats?

Third, should it be a rule for the United States to abstain from foreign quarrels unless vital interests are clearly threatened; or should the presumption be on the side of intervention lest an unfavorable development, no matter how remote, grow into a threat? Was George Washington's warning against entangling alliances useful advice only for a young, weak nation, or was it wisdom for all time? Is the world a seamless web with no limit to or prioritization of American interests, or is it a collection of zones and spheres, some of which have little or no meaning for American security?[1] At one end of this debate stood outright isolationists, and at the other the advocates of the "domino theory"—i.e., the fall of any nation to unfriendly influence could lead to the fall of all, including the United States itself. The strict isolationist position became untenable after Pearl Harbor in 1941, and the extreme interventionist position fell into disrepute after the United States lost the war in Vietnam. It was the task of the Carter Administration to try to find solid ground on shifting terrain. In an unstable world, both abroad and at home, this task proved beyond the Administration's intellectual and political means.

Fourth, should the United States be concerned primarily with prevailing over particular hostile nations, specifically the Soviet

Union? Or should an enlightened foreign policy focus on universal problems of the human condition: violations of human rights, the shortage of energy and other resources, the threat of proliferating arms, both nuclear and conventional? Should foreign policy, like a football game, be controlled by "the logic of conflict" or by an effort to create a more beneficial world order?[2] Is the traditional objective of maintaining a favorable balance of power permanently valid? Or is the old objective part of the problem in that it obscures deeper dangers, such as the worldwide spread of armaments, uncontrolled technology capable of producing nuclear weapons, inadequate sources of energy, the maldistribution of wealth, damage to the environment? Advocates on one side of this debate said that the failure to attend to global problems could make the earth uninhabitable. Traditionalists, on the other hand, said that a failure to contain the Soviet Union would render the United States powerless to save itself or the world. The world-order advocates generally stressed the priority of North–South relations over those of East and West. They said it was more important to ask if a nation was rich (the North) or poor (the South) than to inquire if it was in the political sphere of the United States (the West) or the Soviet Union (the East). This division ran like a fault line through the Carter Administration and all discussion of the wisdom or folly of its particular decisions.

THE GHOST OF WOODROW WILSON

In 1917, six decades before Jimmy Carter was inaugurated, President Wilson made military power the servant of moral principle when he led the nation into war against Germany, not to protect specific American interests, but "for the ultimate peace of the world and . . . for the rights of nations great and small and the privilege of men everywhere to choose their way of life." He said the United States had "no selfish ends to serve . . . We are . . . champions of the rights of mankind." But any government denying those rights, any autocratic government, "could not be trusted to keep faith . . . or observe its covenants."³ Arching over Wilson's thought and program was the conviction that the moral injunctions of Jesus Christ were equally applicable to nations as to individuals. Whatever was sinful for a person was sinful for a nation.

Wilson's principles contained an irresolvable contradiction and a cluster of political problems. How could the United States pledge to respect the right of every nation to determine its own way of life and at the same time insist that such a way of life imitate American ideals of human rights? If human rights were violated within another nation, must the United States abandon the principles of non-intervention and self-determination in order to rectify or punish that violation? Must the United States be invariably hostile to "autocratic" governments, refusing to seek a range of mutual interests, lest recognition and negotiation taint moral principle? Must the United States expend resources without limit in a crusade for a morally perfect world? Was there any room for choice of policy when the nation was faced with a moral issue? And if so, who would decide what the choice was? The President alone? The Congress?

The role of weapons and military force was ambiguous in Wilson's world view. In the ageless discussion over whether weapons are a cause of insecurity or neutral instruments capable of either furthering or deterring aggression, Wilson seemed to come down on the side of those who saw weapons as evil in themselves. He adhered to the international equivalent of support for domestic gun control. He would have disagreed with the implication of the slogan, favored by those who oppose control, that "guns do not kill people; people kill people." The fourth of Wilson's "Four-teen Points" of January 1918 called for "Adequate guarantees given and taken that national armaments will be reduced to the lowest point consistent with domestic safety."⁴ On another occasion, he advocated "that moderation of armaments which makes of armies and navies a power of order merely, not an instrument of aggression or selfish violence."[5] But when one nation's "order" seemed "selfish violence" to another, who could distinguish between weapons of peace and weapons of aggression? Wilson assumed that issues of right and wrong would always be clear and that if any nation was guilty of wrongdoing it would be punished by the collective, democratic will of mankind as interpreted under American leadership in the new League of Nations.

Wilson assumed that democracies by their nature had no selfish purposes. They would always respect human rights and act peacefully. When he said the United States was going to war to make the world "safe for democracy," he meant as well safe through democracy. He believed that wars were plotted by autocrats or small groups of conspirators to advance their selfish purposes against the true interests of the people. Democracy would reject the use of spies, secrecy, lying, war itself.

The great irony is that the President who exalted the democratic process as inseparable from a moral foreign policy was defeated by that process. In 1919, the United States Senate refused to approve American membership in the League of Nations on Wilson's terms. In 1920, the American people agreed with the Senate's decision and elected Republican Warren G. Harding. It was the opinion of the majority, expressed through democratic means, that the United States should make no permanent commitments to other nations or to a world security system, moral or otherwise, and should remain free to decide every course of action in terms of the nation's interests in each case.[6]

Wilson died in 1924, and the remnant of Wilsonian true believers dwindled in number and influence until, by the early 1930s, there was close to a national consensus in favor of isolationism, defined as almost total non-involvement in the political affairs of nations outside the Western Hemisphere. The defeat of Wilson's vision was also a victory for an enlarged congressional role in foreign policy, and Congress during the 1920s and 1930s put severe limits on Presidential power. Isolationists were vehement internalists. They denied that other nations had the capacity to injure the United States, as long as the United States refrained from intervening in their affairs. They asserted that the United States had gone to war in 1917, not to make the world safe for democracy and from autocracy, but to serve the interests of bankers and munitions makers who had an investment in a victory for Great Britain, France, and Russia over Germany. As the historian and political activist Charles A. Beard argued, it should be the obligation of the American government to establish the "open door" of equal opportunity for all Americans at home, rather than intervene around the world to protect the "open door" to trade and investment profits for selfish interests.[7]

But the outbreak of the European war in 1939 made it increasingly difficult to argue that the United States faced no external threat. Isolationists found themselves on the defensive, and after the Japanese attack on Pearl Harbor, they were quite undone. The American people were virtually unanimous in approving the nation's entry into war against the Axis (Germany, Japan, and Italy). Never before or since has there been such support for a cause: the complete defeat of the enemy.

COLD WAR "REALISM"

The death of isolationism did not, however, mean the rebirth of Wilsonian moralism. Although political leaders after 1941 paid graceful tribute to Wilson's memory, those who provided the new guiding assumptions for American foreign policy were more fundamentally anti-Wilsonian than the isolationists. As adherents to the newly embraced assumptions of "realism" and "geopolitics," they agreed that the United States should be involved in world affairs, but the reasons involved power, not morality. In the words of Nicholas Spykman, an influential academic exponent of the new geopolitics, nations should make the "preservation and improvement of their power position" the primary objective of foreign policy. "The statesman who conducts foreign policy can concern himself with values of justice, fairness, and tolerance only to the extent that they contribute to or do not interfere with the power objective. They can be used instrumentally as moral justification for the power quest, but they must be discarded the moment their application brings weakness."[8]

The "realist" view of the world guided American leaders during the Second World War, easing the pain of sending men to their deaths and of inflicting enormous casualties on the enemy. The decisions to develop atomic bombs and drop them on Japan were made in that spirit. "Realism" also facilitated the transition from war against the Axis to Cold War. The principles of geopolitics ordained that the alliance between the United States and Great Britain on the one hand and the Soviet Union on the other was an expedient and temporary measure directed against Hitler. Geopoliticians argued that, after the destruction of German power, it was inevitable that the two remaining great powers, the United States and the Soviet Union, would come into conflict. The fact that the Soviet Union was a grim totalitarian state, with many characteristics reminiscent of Nazi Germany, added intensity to the perception of inevitable hostility. Even those who, in the euphoria of victory over the Axis, dreamed of resurrecting a Wilsonian world order through the United Nations or some form of world government were converted to an anti-Soviet position because of the Soviet Union's use of the veto in the United Nations and its patent violations of human rights. The creation of an ideal world would have to wait until Russia ceased to be simultaneously powerful and totalitarian.

The philosopher of the "realist" attack on Wilsonian moralism was the theologian Reinhold Niebuhr. In 1932, Niebuhr published *Moral Man and Immoral Society*, a closely reasoned critique of the assumption, so dear to Wilson, that moral standards for individuals and for nations could be the same. Niebuhr said that an individual could, by an act of supreme moral selflessness, sacrifice his or her interests, even life itself, in service to a higher good. But nations existed to protect their members. They could not act except in terms of their interests, interests which often conflicted with those of other nations and which made strife inevitable. Twenty years later, at the height of the Cold War, Niebuhr applied this argument specifically to American foreign policy. In *The Irony of American History*, his most widely read book, he stressed the tragic necessity of making "conscious choices for the sake of good. If men or nations do evil in a good cause; if they cover themselves with guilt in order to fulfill some high responsibility; or if they sacrifice some high value for the sake of a higher or equal one they make a tragic choice. Thus the necessity of using the threat of atomic destruction as an instrument for the preservation of peace is a tragic element in our contemporary situation."[9]

Niebuhr and some of his more thoughtful contemporaries warned that the United States must not become so obsessed with fighting the evils of communism that it decided that any weapon was justified. In this way, said Niebuhr, Americans could become as ruthless as the enemy. But this warning was a minor note in the orchestrating of American power against the Soviet Union. The major theme, by the late 1940s, was containment through military means, resting on economic strength.

The makers and spokesmen of Cold War foreign policy were all externalists. Their creed began with the conviction that the principal, proper, and necessary obligation of the American government was to maintain and be prepared to use military superiority against the foe. No other obligation could be allowed to interfere. The foe, the Soviet Union, was an aggressive, totalitarian force bent on world domination, oblivious to any reasoned appeals, responsive only to force. Conflict between the United States and the Soviet Union was irreconcilable and would continue until one side prevailed, with or without general war. Fundamental cooperation between the two nations was impossible, although each might adopt a transient cooperative posture for tactical reasons, but in the end the Soviets could never be trusted. The only way for the United States to deter war or mitigate its worst consequences was through the maintenance of military superiority. The existence of nuclear weapons reinforced and in no way invalidated this principle. To accept limits on American armed force because of a desire to avoid offending the Soviet Union was naïve and dangerous. Arms-control agreements were also dangerous unless they clearly increased the relative power of the United States over the Soviet Union.

Those who believed in this creed were so sure of their own righteousness and so convinced of the utter evil of the Soviet Union that they denied there was any danger of corrupting American ends through the use of immoral means. The issue was explicitly addressed in early 1950 by the authors of National Security Council document 68–NSC-68, as it is generally known. This long memorandum, written principally by and under the guidance of State Department official Paul Nitze and formally approved by President Harry S. Truman, is the single most important statement of the creed of containment and the "zero-sum game" approach to the Soviet Union. Although the actual text remained secret until 1975 (largely because of information in it on atomic weapons), the ideas were proclaimed by the government on every occasion and used as guides for policy. NSC-68 called for subordinating all other concerns to increasing American power and diminishing the relative power of the Soviet Union. Did that mean the United States should be prepared to use any means? The answer is yes, said NSC-68. "Our free society, confronted by a threat to its basic values, naturally will take such action, including the use of military force, as may be required to protect those values. The integrity of our system will not be jeopardized by any measures, covert or overt, violent or nonviolent, which serve the purposes of frustrating the Kremlin design, nor does the necessity for conducting ourselves so as to affirm our values in actions as well as words forbid such measures, provided only they are appropriately calculated to that end and are not so excessive or misdirected as to make us enemies of the people instead of the evil men who have enslaved them."[10] Despite the weak closing qualification, the statement was a justification for employing any means—secrecy, lying, covert interference in the affairs of other nations, sabotage, assassination—for a self-proclaimed end; in short, for doing all those things which Woodrow Wilson once thought could never be done by a democracy.

Indeed, the philosophy of NSC-68 was fundamentally anti-democratic and skeptical of the capacity of American society to survive unless it accepted limits on free discussion. As the document said: "The democratic way is harder than the authoritarian way because, in seeking to protect and fulfill the individual, it demands . . . that he exercise discrimination: that while pursuing through free inquiry the search for truth he knows when he should commit an act of faith; that he distinguish between the necessity for tolerance and the necessity for just suppression. A free society is vulnerable in that it is easy for people to lapse into excesses— the excesses of a permanently open mind wishfully waiting for evidence that evil design may become noble purpose, the excess of faith becoming prejudice, the excess of tolerance degenerating into indulgence of conspiracy."[11]

"Suppression" meant not only a voluntary act by the individual; it meant something the government was justified in doing to individuals and groups. Senator Joseph R. McCarthy achieved national attention in February 1950, just as NSC-68 was being drafted, with his public crusade to suppress communists and other dangerous thinkers in America. The sophisticated men who wrote and approved NSC-68 considered McCarthy and his methods crude and malodorous. But the difference between McCarthyism and the arguments of NSC-68 were matters of tone and style, not substance.

If the Cold War "realists" harbored doubts about the viability of democracy in the United States, how viable was democracy in the rest of the world—where Wilson had once said that only democratic nations were qualified for membership in the community of the righteous? In the Cold War climate of 1950, the diplomat-historian George F. Kennan had an answer to that question. During a tour of Latin America, he concluded that liberal leaders in countries without a tradition of strong democratic government appeared to lack the capacity to resist communism. This meant, said Kennan in a report to Secretary of State Dean Acheson, that the United States ought not insist on fulfillment of democratic niceties. "We cannot be too dogmatic about the methods by which local communists can be dealt with . . . Where the concepts and traditions of popular government are too weak to absorb successfully the intensity of communist attack, then we must concede that harsh governmental measures of repression may be the only answer; that these measures may have to proceed from regimes whose origins and methods would not stand the test of American concepts of democratic procedure; and that such regimes and such methods may be preferable alternatives, and indeed the only alternatives, to further communist successes."[12]

For two decades, from the late 1940s until the late 1960s, the foreign policies of the men (and they were all men) who followed the creed of NSC-68 enjoyed almost total support from Congress and the people. Whether a Democrat or a Republican was in the White House made no fundamental difference. There was an overwhelming consensus behind the policies of reviving and rearming Western Europe, organizing a string of anti-Soviet alliances around the world, fighting the Korean war, maintaining a hostile face toward communist China, and forever building superiority in nuclear weapons over the Soviet Union. The secret aspects of these policies were known in broad outline to those attentive to foreign affairs: the overthrow with CIA assistance of Mossadegh in Iran (1953) and Arbenz in Guatemala (1954), manipulation of elections in other countries, bribery, spying, perhaps assassination. Such operations were criticized only when they failed—as with the attempt to overthrow Fidel Castro of Cuba through the ill-fated Bay of Pigs invasion of 1961. The attitude of Congress during these years was that the President knew best; the responsibility of Congress was to provide the money and ask no embarrassing questions. The historically minded believed congressional restrictions on foreign policy during the 1930s had made German aggression easier and thus had contributed to the Second World War. Few congressmen wanted to make that mistake again.

"The best and the brightest" (to use David Halberstam's phrase)[13] of those years considered themselves moral beings. Some of them read Reinhold Niebuhr. They believed they were capable of avoiding excess while accepting the tragic necessity of doing evil in a good cause. But the sense of restraint—slight as it had been early in the Cold War—eroded. Suppression of the truth became more common, and so did covert action against other governments. Bonds were strengthened between Washington and harsh, repressive dictators. And the United States entered the Vietnam war.

VIETNAM

The steps by which the United States became involved in Vietnam illustrated the reigning assumptions of foreign policy during the Cold War.[14] The French, who had conquered Vietnam in the nineteenth century and who were in turn defeated by the Japanese, returned to the country in 1945 to confront a powerful independence movement led by Ho Chi Minh, a communist. American idealistic opposition to colonialism at first inhibited the United States from supporting the French directly in their widening war. But in 1950, in the same spring that NSC-68 was approved, Secretary of State Acheson decided the United States should send military aid to the French. He knew the French cause was morally impure, but the lesser of evils was to back colonialism if it would stop communism. Four years later, after the surrender of French forces at Dienbienphu to Ho Chi Minh's army, and in spite of heavy American military aid, the French accepted defeat and Vietnam was partitioned along the 17th parallel, pending nationwide elections. The United States, however, did not accept this result. Policymakers in both the Eisenhower

'ministrations believed Americans could do
—especially with a combination of covert
ɪg of anti-communist Vietnamese in counter-
ɪe, and political guidance of the government in
ɪɪtal of South Vietnam. In 1963, that guidance led to
ɪɪassination of South Vietnamese President Ngo Dinh Diem
ʋy rivals who had been encouraged by the United States to stage
a coup (although not to kill Diem). Three weeks later, in an
unconnected tragedy, President Kennedy was also assassinated.
There were at that time about sixteen thousand American troops
in Vietnam.

The evidence that the United States was doing no better than
France in the effort to impose a friendly, anti-communist government on Vietnam was there for all to see. But through 1964
scarcely a single difficult question was asked in Congress. In
August 1964, the House (unanimously) and the Senate (with two
negative votes) passed the Tonkin Gulf resolution, which granted
the President a free hand to use any method, including military
force, to prevail in Vietnam. President Lyndon B. Johnson held
back until after winning the election of 1964. He then doubled
and redoubled American forces until their number exceeded
500,000 in early 1968. The number of American dead and wounded
mounted proportionately, and the consensus over foreign policy
crumbled.

The critics of the American entanglement in Vietnam divided
roughly into disillusioned externalists and passionate internalists.
The disillusioned externalists were generally people of long experience in foreign affairs, such as Senator J. William Fulbright,
chairman of the Foreign Relations Committee. They had supported every major American initiative in the world since 1941,
including the early steps in Vietnam. They still believed in the
soundness of past policies, but beginning in 1965, they saw the
huge commitment to Vietnam as the result of an incorrect understanding of the external world and especially of a propensity
to make invalid comparisons between Vietnam and previous events

such as the Nazi conquest of Europe and the North Kor؟ invasion of South Korea in 1950. The internalist critics were, f؟ the most part, impatient with close analysis of international relations and fine points of history. Their focus was on the alleged immorality of American leaders—Lyndon Johnson, Richard Nixon, Henry Kissinger—or on the inherent aggressiveness of the American system. They were believers in a negative version of American omnipotence: all troubles were the result of American wickedness. The internalists were vehement, loud, often radical. They commanded attention and changed the political landscape.

The growing disillusionment with Vietnam on the part of old externalist Cold Warriors and the vehemence of the internalist anti-war movement persuaded Lyndon Johnson in 1968 not to run for reelection; in effect, to abdicate. Richard M. Nixon was elected President in 1968 because Democratic candidate Hubert Humphrey, Johnson's Vice President, could not put sufficient distance between himself and "Johnson's war." Nixon reduced the number of American ground troops in Vietnam but escalated the air war, including secret bombing of neighboring Cambodia.

Congress, as distinguished from a few individual members such as Fulbright, was slow to abandon its acquiescence in Presidential prerogatives in foreign affairs. But in the early 1970s it adopted a new assertiveness, repealed the Tonkin Gulf resolution, limited the President's powers to commit troops to combat without congressional approval (the War Powers Act of 1973), conducted investigations of the misdeeds of the Central Intelligence Agency (with particular attention to the overthrow and death of the duly elected left-wing President of Chile, Salvador Allende), and demanded that American foreign policy show a commitment to human rights.[15]

The illusion that "peace was at hand" in the fall of 1972 contributed to Richard Nixon's reelection by a wide margin over George McGovern, an internalist critic of the war. For a brief moment it appeared that Presidential authority had been reestablished. But the Watergate scandal, unfolding from the spring of

1973 onward, revealed Nixon's contempt for law and morality. It seemed to confirm the internalist view that the basic problem was sin. Public and congressional outrage forced Nixon's resignation in August 1974. Had he not resigned, he would have been impeached. Four months later, an obscure governor of Georgia named Jimmy Carter announced that he was a candidate for the Democratic nomination for President in 1976.

JIMMY CARTER: THE INTERNALIST CANDIDATE

Jimmy Carter, born in 1924 near Plains, Georgia, had no significant experience in foreign affairs before announcing his candidacy. He entered the United States Naval Academy in 1943, graduated in 1946, and remained in the Navy until 1953. His concerns at that time were with the professional and technical work of a young officer, including his brief employment in the nuclear-submarine program under the direction of Admiral Hyman Rickover. His 1975 autobiography says nothing about his attitude, if any, toward the early Cold War; it displays no awareness of the world historical events through which the author was living. Carter left the Navy in 1953 for farming and business in Plains. He entered and rose in local politics: county school board, state senate, and the governorship of Georgia in 1970.[16]

In 1972, he made his private decision to seek the Presidency, driven by ambition for the office itself and not by commitment to particular policies, domestic or foreign. He began then to study foreign affairs, less as something important in itself, and more as necessary preparation for the public announcement and campaign for the nomination. Meanwhile, President Nixon resigned in disgrace and President Gerald R. Ford undermined his effort to restore a sense of integrity to the Presidential office by pardoning Nixon in advance of any possible trial, thus protecting him from criminal prosecution. In the spring of 1975, the government of South Vietnam collapsed. The communists won complete control of all Vietnam, and the last Americans retreated by helicopter from the embassy in Saigon (soon to be renamed Ho Chi Minh City).

The discontent of millions of Americans with Presidential leadership following the disaster of Vietnam and the squalor of Watergate made possible the otherwise implausible nomination and election of Jimmy Carter. He made an asset of his inexperience. Having never held national office, he bore no responsibility for the past and carried no burden of old commitments. His knowledge of the United States and his commitment to moral principles were, he said, the best qualifications for correcting past mistakes and restoring the United States to moral leadership. Enough voters in the Democratic primaries in the spring of 1976 either accepted this argument or divided their ballots among other candidates so that Carter was assured of the nomination before the July convention. The Republicans then nominated President Ford, although Ronald Reagan, the conservative former governor of California, came close to gaining the prize.

Carter's lack of experience, his own deep religious feelings, and the national mood after Vietnam and Watergate provided an ideal opportunity for an internalist approach to the campaign. Carter and his political advisers saw the opportunity and seized it. Carter the campaigner presented himself as a quintessential internalist, moralist, neo-Wilsonian. In his hundreds of speeches and interviews during 1975 and 1976, he said very little about the behavior of other nations, while reiterating themes of reformation, repentance, and restoration. "We've lost the spirit of our nation," he said. "We've seen a loss of morality . . . and we're ashamed of what our government is as we deal with other nations around the world, and that's got to be changed, and I'm going to change it . . . What we seek is . . . a foreign policy that reflects the decency and generosity and common sense of our own people."[17]

Carter often mentioned Reinhold Niebuhr, but only to repeat one short quotation: "The sad duty of politics is to establish justice in a sinful world." He forgot or never understood Niebuhr's fundamental arguments that political leaders cannot bind themselves to standards of individual morality but must often do evil in pursuit of good. Carter, on the contrary, declared: "I don't ever want to do anything as President that would be a contravention of the moral and ethical standard that I would exemplify in my own life as an individual."

He proclaimed his belief in the primacy of moral principle over power in foreign policy, his disapproval of intervening in the affairs of other nations, and his intention to focus on problems of world order and broad international collaboration rather than confrontation. Here is a representative sampling of his campaign statements:

> The question, I think, is whether in recent years our highest officials have not been too pragmatic, even cynical, and as a consequence have ignored those moral values that had often distinguished our country.

> We must move away from making policies in secret; without the knowledge and approval of the American people.

> But military strength alone is not enough. Over the years, our greatest source of strength has come from those basic, priceless values which are embodied in our Declaration of Independence, our Constitution, and our Bill of Rights: our belief in freedom of religion—our belief in freedom of expression—our belief in human dignity.

> These principles have made us great and, unless our foreign policy reflects them, we make a mockery of all those values.

> We have often been overextended, and deeply entangled in the internal affairs of distant nations. Our government has pursued dubious tactics, and "national security" has sometimes been a cover-up for unnecessary secrecy and national scandal.

We stumbled into the quagmires of Cambodia and Vietnam, and carried out heavy-handed efforts to destroy an elected government in Chile.

Our people have now learned the folly of our trying to inject our power into the internal affairs of other nations. It is time that our government learned that lesson too.

Never again should our country become militarily involved in the internal affairs of another country unless there is a direct and obvious threat to the security of the United States or its people. We must not use the CIA or other covert means to effect violent change in any government or government policy . . . The CIA must operate within the law.

I would never . . . openly or covertly, legally or illegally, support nations who stand for principles on which their people violently disagree and which are completely antithetical to what we believe in.

Candidate Carter promised to take effective action to curb the proliferation of nuclear weapons, to seek genuine reductions in the level of strategic weapons, and to reduce the transfer of armaments to the developing world—no longer would the United States be the world's leading arms merchant. He would support the principle of majority rule in Africa, stand behind the security of Israel while working for peace in the Middle East, and cooperate closely in a "trilateral" relationship with the democracies of Western Europe and Japan. He would appoint ambassadors on the basis of talent, not on the basis of political campaign contributions. He would consult Congress. He would create "a government as good as the people."

A major ambiguity in Carter's campaign positions concerned the Soviet Union. On the one hand, he put heavy emphasis on the need to reduce nuclear weapons and called for Soviet–American cooperation in "dealing with such world problems as agricultural development and the population crisis." On the other hand, he condemned the Soviet Union for violating the 1975 Helsinki accords on human rights and said the Ford Administration had simply looked the other way. His statement that other nations would have to respect human rights if they wanted American friendship, echoing Wilson's dictum that the United States could not deal with non-democratic regimes, sounded like a hardline threat.

When President Ford blundered during their televised debates by saying that the Poles did not consider themselves dominated by the Soviet Union, Carter suggested that Ford try to convince Polish-Americans of that fact. He accused Ford of weakness in dealing with the Russians and of apparently accepting the so-called doctrine of State Department official Helmut Sonnenfeldt that the United States should recognize a natural Soviet sphere of influence in Eastern Europe. Carter also criticized Ford for refusing to see the anti-Soviet novelist Alexander Solzhenitsyn and promised that he, as President, would issue an invitation. Although tough criticism of the Soviet Union was a secondary theme in Carter's campaign, directed at Jewish voters and those of East European descent, it is possible and ironic that he gained more votes by calling Ford soft on the Soviet Union than he did from his larger theme of removing immorality from American foreign policy.

In November, Carter won the Presidency by a narrow margin. Ford had been closing the gap, according to public-opinion polls, and might have won had the election been held a few weeks later. That in itself was not an auspicious sign for Carter. Had he and his advisers reflected on the historical pattern of elections, they would have had another cause to be concerned. There had been ten previous elections in the twentieth century in which foreign policy was a significant issue and in which the people perceived differences between the candidates (1916, 1920, 1940, 1948, 1952, 1956, 1960, 1964, 1968, and 1972). In each case, one candidate was seen as more likely to keep the United States out of war or extricate the country from an unpopular entanglement. The peace and non-entanglement candidates won half the time (Wilson in 1916, Harding in 1920, Eisenhower in 1952, Johnson in 1964, and Nixon in 1968). But, in every election, one candidate was perceived as more likely to maintain or increase American military power. The strength candidates won every time (Wilson in 1916, Harding in 1920, Roosevelt in 1940, Truman in 1948, Eisenhower in 1952 and 1956, Kennedy in 1960, Johnson in 1964, Nixon in 1968 and 1972.) The peace candidates won only when they were simultaneously the strength candidates. But Carter broke the pattern. He was unquestionably the peace and non-entanglement candidate, but as a critic of excessive military spending and an advocate of reducing both nuclear and conventional arms he allowed Ford to campaign as the strength candidate. Thus, for the only time in the century, the peace candidate beat the strength candidate. In 1980, the traditional pattern was restored. Carter was still perceived as the candidate of peace and relative weakness, despite his militant response to the Soviet Union's invasion of Afghanistan. He lost to Reagan, the strength candidate. That outcome was repeated in 1984, with Mondale as the peace candidate losing to Reagan, who was again the strength candidate.

In January 1977, Jimmy Carter took the oath of office. The biblical text he wished to use in his inaugural address was an explicit call for repentance and reform—II Chronicles 7:14: "If my people . . . shall humble themselves, and pray, and seek my face, and turn from their wicked ways; then will I hear from heaven, and will forgive their sin, and will heal their land." But at the urging of aides who claimed some listeners might think that Carter was equating himself with Solomon and condemning all Americans as wicked, he chose instead Micah 6:8. The message was similar, although muted: "What doth the Lord require of thee, but to do justly, and to love mercy, and to walk humbly with thy God?"[18]

If the words of a new President alone could determine the

nature of American foreign policy, Carter's inauguration fore-tokened radical change. He and the nation had inherited two legacies sixty years after Woodrow Wilson asked Congress for a declaration of war against Germany. Jimmy Carter promised to be guided by the first legacy, moral principle. He would use the legacy of power with restraint and only as an instrument in the service of principle, not as an end in itself. But fulfillment of this apparent promise would depend on the behavior of other nations, on currents of American domestic politics, and on the attitudes and performance of the people Carter picked to advise him and carry out his instructions in foreign affairs.

2

People and Policies

For his personal White House staff and for confidential domestic political advice, President Carter turned to fellow Georgians who had been with him since his days as governor or before—his wife Rosalynn; Jody Powell, appointed press secretary; Hamilton Jordan, his selection as White House chief of staff; and Bert Lance, the new director of the Office of Management and Budget and the President's most trusted senior adviser.

Lance, who was forced to resign in September 1977 because of his questionable banking practices in Georgia, had no discernible influence over foreign policy. Powell and Jordan viewed foreign policy primarily through the prism of Carter's political fortunes at home—although Jordan, almost by accident, played a major role in the diplomacy of the hostage crisis with Iran. Rosalynn Carter was more involved with foreign policy than any Presidential spouse since Eleanor Roosevelt. Mrs. Roosevelt's role had been that of independent conscience, prodding her husband in liberal directions, but not eagerly consulted by him. Jimmy and Rosalynn Carter, in contrast, appear to have discussed every problem and decision in detail. She was a partner in the Presidency, dealing heavily with domestic political fence-mending, but also leading a substantive diplomatic mission to Latin America and another to Thailand in connection with the refugee problem.

She was intelligent, perceptive, and had firm, quickly formed opinions.[1]

But these people had no more direct experience or deep knowledge of world affairs than the President himself, which meant almost none. For informed advice on foreign policy, the President had, thus, to go outside his inner circle of Georgia friends. In selecting Zbigniew Brzezinski as National Security Adviser and Cyrus Vance as Secretary of State, he drew from two traditional pools of talent. Brzezinski was representative of the post-1945 breed of university-based foreign-policy specialists with a taste for power like McGeorge Bundy, Walt and Eugene Rostow, and most notably Henry A. Kissinger. Vance was a New York lawyer who had moved throughout his career between corporate practice and government office in the same manner as former Secretaries of State Elihu Root, Charles Evans Hughes, Henry L. Stimson, Dean Acheson (whose law practice was in Washington rather than New York), and John Foster Dulles. Vance and Brzezinski had recommended each other, and each appointment in isolation seemed excellent. But differences in temperament and policy proved, in the end, to be far deeper than President Carter or either of the men believed at the start. The difficulties between the two would ultimately be crippling for the Administration. They were both a cause and a result of the President's and the nation's inability to find a stable balance among morality, power, and reason.

ZBIGNIEW BRZEZINSKI

Zbigniew Brzezinski, son of a pre–World War II Polish diplomat, came to North America as a youth, was educated in Canada and at Harvard (where he and Kissinger were graduate students at the same time), and rose to prominence as an activist scholar of international relations during the Cold War. While Kissinger was gaining tenure at Harvard, Brzezinski was doing the same at Columbia. Although Brzezinski wrote on a variety of subjects—

the Soviet Union, Africa, Japan, the impact of high technology on international relations—he shared and never abandoned the conventional wisdom of the 1950s. He deplored the moralism of Woodrow Wilson and extolled the primacy of power, especially military power. He did indulge in fashionable speculation about the emergence of a global intellectual elite, communicating in electronic computer language about "what it is about man's life that we wish to safeguard or to promote."[2] But as an intellectual child of the 1950s, he held fast to the view that the nature and the very existence of Soviet power were the primary obstacles to the creation of a stable world. His imaginative leaps drew attention, but old doctrine shaped his policies.

In 1962, during the Cuban missile crisis, Brzezinski sent a telegram to Arthur Schlesinger, Jr., then a member of President Kennedy's staff, that "any further delay in bombing missile sites fails to exploit Soviet uncertainty."[3] In 1963, he wrote that it was "absolutely essential to maintain American military superiority over the Soviet Union, since even parity could tempt Soviet leaders to engage in brinksmanship on the assumption that our society would be more likely to yield to nuclear blackmail."[4] On a Voice of America broadcast a year before Carter's election, he speculated on how the United States could have a constructive influence over the inevitable collapse of Soviet power. "My hope would be that after the disappearance of the Soviet state, a combination of residual socialism and internationalism would mitigate the power-oriented ambitions of extreme Russian nationalism . . . It has to be our objective to promote . . . that more acceptable alternative."[5] His taste for dramatic military action and his views on the nature of the Soviet Union and the necessity for American military superiority remained unchanged in 1977. In facing a choice between inflicting pain and trying reassurance as an approach to changing Soviet behavior, Brzezinski came down on the side of inflicting pain.

In the preface to his memoir *Power and Principle*, Brzezinski stated that the central question of foreign policy was "whether it is possible to blend a concern for moral principle with the imperatives of national power."[6] He did not ask whether it was possible to blend a concern for power with the imperatives of moral principle. For Brzezinski, as for Nicholas Spykman in 1942 and the authors of NSC-68 in 1950, power was the goal and morality was an instrument to be used when appropriate, abandoned when not. World politics is "not a kindergarten," Brzezinski remarked to Carter when trying to overcome the President's reluctance to see blood spilled in Iran through military action.

The previous American leader whose thinking Brzezinski most closely resembled was Dean Acheson, Secretary of State and principal architect of foreign policy for President Truman. Acheson believed in "negotiation from strength"—which meant, in practice, never negotiate with your adversary when you are weaker, and when you are stronger, you can get what you want without negotiation. President Truman accepted Acheson's advice.[7] Truman was Brzezinski's favorite former President.

Brzezinski was an outspoken critic of the foreign policies of the Nixon–Ford Administration and of the presiding genius of those years, his arch-rival Henry Kissinger. His criticism did not focus on participation in the Vietnam war or on any excessive readiness to employ immoral means. Brzezinski's charge was that Kissinger placed too much reliance on manipulating the triangle of the United States, the Soviet Union, and the People's Republic of China, while neglecting another triangle, that which linked the economically developed democracies of the United States, Western Europe, and Japan. He also charged, somewhat unfairly, that Kissinger's penchant for diplomatic spectaculars concealed an absence of "architecture."[8]

In 1972–73, Brzezinski, Chase Manhattan Bank chairman David Rockefeller, and a few others founded the Trilateral Commission—a group of business, political, and academic foreign-policy elite from Europe, Japan, and the United States, dedicated to strengthening economic, political, and strategic relations within the triangle of America, Europe, and Japan. Brzezinski became the commission's first director. The commission's insiders were New Yorkers. They wanted regional diversity for the American membership and were especially interested in the South. Some advisers in Atlanta recommended Governor Jimmy Carter. In the spring of 1973, Carter was asked to join and accepted.[9]

During the next three years, Carter attended Trilateral Commission meetings, read the commission's reports, and exploited to the full the opportunity to make contacts among people prominent in international affairs. At the same time, Brzezinski, betting on a long-shot candidate for President, became candidate Carter's principal foreign-policy adviser, supplying memoranda, briefings, and drafts for speeches. Several other members of the Trilateral Commission would eventually be recruited for Carter's Administration—including Secretary of State Vance, Secretary of Defense Harold Brown, Director of the Arms Control and Disarmament Agency Paul C. Warnke, and Secretary of the Treasury W. Michael Blumenthal—but none threw their support to Carter so early or provided advice as extensively as Brzezinski.[10]

The internalist analysis of what was wrong with American foreign policy and the campaign theme of repentance were Carter's own, an astute reading of the public mood of the moment. Much of the knowledge of specific nations and problems which Carter acquired came from Brzezinski. Remarkably, the internalist-moralist candidate and this externalist acolyte of power remained compatible. Brzezinski's hostility to the Soviet Union reinforced Carter's emphasis on opposing violations of human rights. His flashy observations about the problems of a new global age were exciting. Fundamental differences between the primacy of power and the primacy of principle were muted. After Carter's election, Brzezinski was appointed to the position for which he yearned: National Security Adviser.

Pervading every aspect of foreign policy during the Carter years was the institutional rivalry between the Department of State and the National Security Council staff—the several dozen people who worked for the National Security Adviser. Brzezinski's staff was young, highly trained (many had Ph.D.s in their areas of expertise), and loyal to their chief. David Aaron, the deputy, had been Vice President Walter Mondale's staff adviser on foreign policy when Mondale was in the Senate. Aaron specialized in matters relating to arms control and consultations with Europe. The staff itself was divided into regional and functional offices. Robert Pastor for Latin America, Michel Oksenberg for China, and William Quandt for the Middle East were especially active and influential. The smallest regional office, with only one person, covered United Nations affairs and South Asia—a reflection, perhaps, of Brzezinski's ranking of what was important. The largest group dealt with defense coordination. Its staff grew in step with the Administration's increasingly military approach to foreign affairs.[11]

The rivalry between State and the NSC staff was in part the bureaucratic reflection of the differences in philosophy and personality between Secretary of State Vance and Brzezinski. It was also a continuation of a long tradition going back to the days of Woodrow Wilson and Colonel Edward M. House, the first equivalent of a national security adviser and an intriguer, who delighted in the political impotence of Secretary of State Robert Lansing. A similar situation prevailed when Franklin D. Roosevelt used Harry Hopkins for important diplomacy and ignored Secretary of State Cordell Hull. Henry Kissinger's consolidation of power at the expense of State and every other department during the Nixon years was an instant legend. Brzezinski—all disclaimers to the contrary—sought to perpetuate the Kissinger tradition, although in less blatant form.

Brzezinski and his staff had three built-in advantages over the Secretary of State and his department. They were housed in the White House and the adviser had instant access to the President. They were a small, cohesive group—not an organization of thousands. And they could concentrate on selected issues without the burden of a mass of routine matters. Vance, on the other hand, was constantly abroad on diplomatic missions, had the responsibility for a large department, and was supposed to be the country's principal spokesman, after the President, on foreign policy. It was impossible to do these three things and be the President's premier adviser.

CYRUS R. VANCE AND THE DEPARTMENT OF STATE

Cyrus R. Vance was a pillar of the New York foreign-policy establishment. After graduating from Yale College and Yale Law School and after wartime service as a gunnery officer on destroyers in the Pacific, he began a successful legal career. In the 1950s, he served as counsel to Senate committees dealing with defense issues. In 1961, he became chief counsel to the Department of Defense under Robert McNamara in the Administration of John F. Kennedy. In 1962, he was appointed Secretary of the Army, and in 1964, Deputy Secretary of Defense. President Lyndon B. Johnson recognized Vance's talent for negotiation and used him repeatedly as a peacemaker and troubleshooter—in Panama after the anti-American riots of 1964, in the Dominican Republic in 1965, in Vietnam in 1966, in Detroit following racial violence in 1967, in Cyprus in 1967, in Korea in 1968 after the seizure by North Korea of the U.S. naval vessel *Pueblo*, and in Paris in 1968–69 for peace talks with the North Vietnamese.

Vance agreed with President Carter that the United States had made many mistakes and that fundamental reforms were necessary in the conduct and content of foreign policy. Although he had supported military escalation in Vietnam in the mid-1960s, he now believed that the intervention had been a mistake, but not the result of a moral flaw. He accepted that repentance was good for the soul, but hardly provided answers to specified real problems. Vance's philosophy was that of the traditional diplomatist, who, in an imperfect world where good and evil are forever mingled, seeks to reduce the level of conflict and to discover areas of mutual interest through quiet bargaining with adversaries. Patience and persistence were his hallmarks.

After decades of experience in both the administration of military power and the resolution of conflict, Vance was wary of idealistic and ideological absolutes. He accepted military force as an inevitable ingredient in international relations, but he was deeply skeptical of its utility in most situations. He realized that a resort to force usually altered the situation and the nation's goals in unintended and unfortunate ways. Vance rejected the myth of the omnipotence of both the United States and the Soviet Union and the belief that either nation could carry out a grand design for the world. He believed that most local conflicts in the world had local causes and local solutions and were not the result of masterful planning and diabolical intent in Moscow. He applauded a concern for human-rights considerations in foreign policy but did not believe that such a concern could be "absolute" as President Carter said in his inaugural address.

The threat of nuclear war was the dominant element in Vance's outlook. He believed that the reduction of that threat must be the overriding mutual interest of both the United States and the Soviet, and that it should be pursued independently of other issues. Disagreements with the Soviet Union would never disappear, but they should never be used as an excuse for turning away from the goal of arms control. Conversely, the possibility of accepting or rejecting arms control should not be used as a lever to induce the Soviet Union to alter its behavior in other areas. Vance recognized that the element of coercion could not be totally removed from an adversarial relationship, but in seeking a balance between affecting Soviet behavior through intimidation and confrontation or through reassurance and the lessening of anxiety, he came down on the side of reassurance.

Carter, Vance, and Brzezinski were all aware of the differences between the two principal advisers. Carter saw Vance and Brzezinski as balancing each other—with the former providing an element of caution, the latter stimulating innovation and action.

Vance, while discreet in published comments, said in his memoirs that Brzezinski was afflicted with "visceral anti-Sovietism."[12] Brzezinski in his memoirs was the most outspoken. He was kindly, although condescending, toward Carter and applauded the President for moving under his guidance and the pressure of events toward a proper appreciation of the "centrality of power."[13] But he was close to contemptuous of Vance and all the things that, in Brzezinski's mind, Vance represented. Brzezinski gave Vance credit for a grasp of detail and a talent for negotiation in a supporting role, but "when diplomacy yielded to power politics," he would "shy away from the unavoidable ingredient of force in dealing with contemporary realities." Why? Because Vance was, said Brzezinski, a "quintessential product of his own background: as a member of both the legal profession and the once-dominant white, Anglo-Saxon, Protestant elite, he operated according to their values and rules, but those values and rules were of declining relevance not only in terms of domestic American politics but particularly in terms of global conditions." For example, Brzezinski deplored what he saw as Vance's tendency to place the lives of the American hostages in Iran ahead of Brzezinski's definition of national honor. "It bothered me . . . that the one to speak up for American honor was a naturalized American. I wondered what this indicated about the current American elite and whether we were not seeing here symptoms of a deeper national problem."[14]

Brzezinski's attitude toward Vance and power is illuminated by his admiration for historian Crane Brinton's *The Anatomy of Revolution*, a book widely read in the 1950s. Brinton wrote of the "striking failure of rulers to use force successfully" against revolutions and attributed that failure to the "general ineptness and failure of the ruling class," characterized by a loss of faith in military virtues and "no confidence, no desire for action."[15] In Brzezinski's eyes, Vance's views reflected a Brintonian paradigm wherein the defects of membership in a decadent ruling class were intensified by the paralyzing experience of the Vietnam war.

When Henry Kissinger had been National Security Adviser to President Nixon, he had used his position and his talent for bureaucratic warfare to render Secretary of State William P. Rogers powerless. Carter, Vance, and Brzezinski all agreed at the beginning of the Administration that the Kissinger pattern would not be repeated. And for some months Brzezinski followed the script. The Secretary of State was the government's spokesman, under the President, on foreign policy. Vance drew the headlines and Brzezinski stayed behind the scenes, directing the staff of the National Security Council, organizing information for the President, setting out options, and making no attempt to dominate. But the differences between him and Vance were too profound to be contained indefinitely. For the middle two years of the Administration, until Vance resigned in April 1980 because of his disagreement over the attempted rescue of the hostages in Iran with military force, the conflicting philosophies of the Secretary and the National Security Adviser affected every major policy and decision. Vance and Brzezinski denied with tiresome frequency that there was a personal rivalry between them. In one sense, the denials were true. The conflict between the two men was merely a surface manifestation of the deeper unresolved conflict within the entire Administration and, beyond that, within all of modern American foreign policy.

The professional diplomats in the Department of State admired Vance as someone who respected their talent and taste for working doggedly at a problem for years if necessary, avoiding the temptation for dramatic quick-fix gestures, never showing anger, proceeding on the assumption that talking was almost always better than killing. Vance had nearly a free hand in filling policy positions in the Department of State. As his deputy he selected Warren Christopher, a lawyer who shared Vance's attention to detail and his imperturbability. Christopher managed the department during Vance's many trips abroad and took special responsibility for human rights and during the hostage crisis. He remained as Deputy Secretary of State during the eight months of Edmund Muskie's secretaryship following the April 1980 resignation of Vance. Muskie, a Democratic senator from Maine and onetime contender for the Presidential nomination, did not have enough time in office to make an impact—especially since the Administration was entangled in the hostage crisis and then defeated at the polls.

Vance's third-level appointments were a mixture of career officers and younger people who had gained prominence as critics of the Vietnam war. Two important career officers were Under Secretary David Newsom, a hardworking troubleshooter, and Harold Saunders, Assistant Secretary for Near Eastern and South Asian Affairs. Richard Holbrooke (Assistant Secretary for East Asia), Richard Moose (Assistant Secretary for Africa), Anthony Lake (director of the Policy Planning Staff), and Leslie Gelb (director of the bureau of Politico-Military Affairs) were all young, with experience both inside and outside of government, articulate, and members of the anti-Vietnam generation.

American ambassadors, appointed by the President, and reporting to the Secretary of State, were on balance a well-qualified group during the Carter years. Jimmy Carter, as campaigner, had attacked "the disgraceful . . . policy of appointing unqualified persons to major diplomatic posts as political payoffs. This must be stopped immediately."[16] Although the political payoff did not entirely disappear, Carter's record was good. Former Senate majority leader Mike Mansfield went to Japan and former United Auto Workers president Leonard Woodcock went to China. Robert Goheen, once president of Princeton, went to India, and Kingman Brewster, once president of Yale, went to the United Kingdom. Ambassadors appointed by Nixon or Ford were retained in several instances: Malcolm Toon in the Soviet Union, Hermann Eilts in Egypt, Walter Stoessel in the Federal Republic of Germany.

Ambassadors with particular qualities were sometimes assigned as a way of signaling a foreign-policy attitude. Thus, career officer William Sullivan, fresh from a successful tour dealing with the authoritarian Ferdinand Marcos in the Philippines, was sent in 1977 to keep the Shah of Iran happy. In 1979, Malcolm Toon resigned as ambassador to the Soviet Union because he had been ignored in the SALT process. He was replaced by Thomas J. Watson, Jr., former head of IBM. The appointment was a sign that the Soviet Union could look forward to acquiring computer technology from the United States—if Soviet-American relations improved. In Nicaragua and El Salvador, career officers with strong reputations as defenders of human rights were appointed, to express the Administration's hope of humane, democratic reform in Central America.

BROWN, TURNER, AND MONDALE

Secretary of Defense Harold Brown was, after Brzezinski and Vance, the President's most important adviser. He was a distinguished scientist and administrator who had long been involved at a high level in the development of nuclear weapons. He had served as deputy to Secretary of Defense Robert McNamara in the Kennedy and Johnson years and had gone on to become president of the California Institute of Technology. Brown spoke and wrote clearly, succinctly, and colorlessly.[17] He avoided involvement in personal and bureaucratic feuds and did not seek a close friendship with Carter or others in the Administration. He was cool, discreet, aloof, professional. The officers on the Joint Chiefs of Staff respected him. In 1977, he saw no need for a substantial increase in defense spending or for new programs for nuclear weapons. But, much to Brzezinski's delight, he changed his mind, and by 1979 had become a powerful advocate of greater military effort.[18]

The President's choice to head the Central Intelligence Agency, a position which on occasion in the past had been very influential, was Theodore Sorensen, once close adviser and speech writer for John F. Kennedy and now a liberal lawyer, with no experience working in the clubby atmosphere of the "intelligence community." Sorensen came under immediate and severe attack—specifically because he had used classified documents in writing his book on Kennedy and had revealed this fact in order to help in the defense of Daniel Ellsberg when the latter was on trial for having released the classified "Pentagon Papers." To his critics, Sorensen symbolized the worst of the naïve, liberal, apologetic approach to intelligence and covert action. President Carter never gave Sorensen the chance to prove or disprove this stereotype. The nomination had stirred an ideological hornets' nest—and the President retreated instantly.

The nomination was withdrawn and the name of Admiral Stansfield Turner submitted instead. Turner, at the moment commander of NATO forces in southern Europe, was a Rhodes Scholar, a seagoing intellectual who had reformed the curriculum of the Naval War College, a critic of sloppy thinking and inefficiency, but no radical. He and Carter had been classmates at the Naval Academy, but they did not know each other well.[19] "The balance is slowly tipping against us," Turner had just written in an article on the Soviet and American navies. In the same article, he called for the most accurate intelligence possible on the strength of the other side. "Great and wasteful wars have broken out in our century partly because of misperceived comparisons of armed forces."[20] The Senate confirmed Turner with no difficulty.

But the admiral was not a major influence on foreign policy. He was not able to gain ready access to the President, nor were he and Brzezinski congenial, especially after Brzezinski tried to make Turner and the CIA a scapegoat for alleged intelligence failure in Iran in 1978.[21] He refrained from offering purely political judgments, and was outspoken on only one issue: the necessity for maintaining the American capacity to verify Soviet compliance with arms-control agreements. He had far greater interest in the gathering of intelligence through high technology than he did in covert espionage and operations, aspects of the CIA's activities which were at a comparatively low level during the Carter years. He was unpopular within the Agency because of his dismissal of many old hands who had, in his opinion, outlived their usefulness.

It is a ritual of American politics for an incoming President to declare that the Vice President will be given genuine, unprecedented responsibility. Jimmy Carter made the expected promise and then carried it out. Vice President Walter Mondale participated in crucial meetings on most important policy decisions. He was a regular member, along with Vance, Brzezinski, and Secretary of Defense Harold Brown, at the President's weekly foreign-policy breakfast. He traveled often as a special envoy, discussing real issues, not just stepping through the ceremonial paces. He attended the Camp David meetings on peace in the Middle East. He loyally supported President Carter in public, although behind the scenes he disagreed on several issues—for example, he opposed the policy of withdrawing American ground troops from Korea, and he disapproved of the grain embargo imposed against the Soviet Union after the invasion of Afghanistan. As a protégé of Hubert Humphrey and a veteran of the Senate, he had far more national political experience than Carter. His advice usually put considerable emphasis on the domestic consequences of decisions. He believed, for example, that the Administration was too critical, on occasion, of Israel. Mondale was not dogmatically attached to any single philosophy of foreign affairs. Sometimes he was Vance's ally—for example, on the necessity of combating racial inequality in Africa, rather than being obsessed with what the Soviet Union might be doing on that continent. On other occasions, he was on Brzezinski's side—for example, on the usefulness of forming a strategic relationship with the People's Republic of China.

THE CONVERSION OF CARTER

Brzezinski and Vance held fast to their philosophies, but President Carter wavered and then moved into Brzezinski's camp. A philosophy of repentance helped him gain the White House. It guided his Administration's successful negotiation of the treaties with Panama (one of the few goals and achievements on which Carter, Vance, and Brzezinski were in full agreement). It prompted a satisfying litany of criticism directed against violations of human rights in the Soviet Union, Latin America, and by whites against blacks in Africa. It led to more open diplomacy, a reluctance to take covert action against unfriendly regimes, and new guidelines designed to limit the sale of American weapons to Third World countries.

But a philosophy of repentance and internal reform did not produce the deep cuts in nuclear arms for which Carter yearned, or prevent a virulently anti-American revolution in Iran, or free the hostages in Teheran during a 444-day ordeal, or solve the energy crisis then perceived as threatening to strangle the industrial world. Nor did it make Carter immune from stinging political criticism that he was weak, indecisive, and ineffective as a guardian of American national security.

The breadth of this criticism cast doubt on Carter's ability to be reelected, perhaps even to be renominated. He had the good fortune to ride into office on the waning hour of a vaguely anti-military tide of public and congressional opinion and the bad luck to take office just as that tide turned. With each passing year of the Administration, the public became more demanding of a reassertion of American strength. By the time of the hostage crisis and the Soviet invasion of Afghanistan in late 1979, the new tide was flowing at full strength. Carter abandoned the philosophy of repentance and reform, in the face of adversity at home and abroad. Under Brzezinski's daily tutelage and without substantial knowledge and experience of his own, Carter underwent a rapid mutation from an internalist to a militant externalist, blaming the Soviet Union for almost everything that was going wrong, saying very little about human rights as an absolute principle of foreign policy, advocating higher defense budgets and the development of new nuclear weapons and the creation of new military units capable of being rapidly deployed for action anywhere in the world.

In April 1980, Vance resigned because of deep philosophical differences with the President and Brzezinski—although his disagreement with the military attempt to rescue the hostages in Teheran was the immediate reason. Brzezinski had triumphed, with an assist from the Ayatollah Khomeini and the Soviet Union's decision to invade Afghanistan. Brzezinski's verdict was that President Carter now combined the best qualities of Wilson and Truman—which meant "recognizing the importance of principle as a long-term beacon but also power as the necessary tool of effective policy."[22]

Precisely how and why this change occurred and how it affected relations with particular regions and nations is the subject of the following chapters. But the change also worked against that focus on global issues of human welfare which the President, at the outset, hoped would be a distinguishing mark of his Administration. Before going further, a word about those issues.

HUMAN RIGHTS

Jimmy Carter believed that a foreign policy dominated by the traditional struggle for power between the United States and the Soviet Union was dangerous both for the great powers and for the entire world. The obsession had led the United States down the disastrous road in and out of Vietnam. It could incinerate the world. Although he knew the struggle would not entirely disappear, he believed it was essential to direct American attention and the attention of all governments and peoples to broad global problems which transcended bilateral jousting for transient interests. What distinguished the Carter Administration from its predecessors more than anything else was the way it endowed these global issues with special importance. Whether or not the Administration would be as creative and different from its predecessors as its rhetoric promised would depend on the degree to which these broad concerns were translated into policies that produced real changes.

Jimmy Carter's emphasis on making the protection of human rights everywhere in the world a foundation of foreign policy reflected his own sincere moral beliefs and the accurate perception that the issue was good politics in the immediate aftermath of the Vietnam war. An articulate and effective human-rights lobby already existed in Congress. It had secured passage of the 1976 law declaring that it was "a principal goal of the foreign policy of the United States to promote the increased observance of internationally recognized human rights by all countries." The law ordered the Secretary of State to submit an annual report on the human-rights record of all countries receiving American assistance and declared that no assistance should go to any country engaging "in a consistent pattern of gross violations" of human rights.[23] Carter joined the crusade and made it his own.

It was easy to declare in his inaugural address that "our commitment to human rights must be absolute." It was not easy to translate that commitment into specific, effective action in foreign policy.[24] The insoluble philosophical problem was that foreign policy by its nature required that every move must be justified in terms of national advantage. In a sinful world, no leader could endanger the survival of the nation by blind adherence to an absolute moral standard. But moral issues by their nature are not susceptible to the calculus of selfish advantage. The moral person refrains from theft or murder, not because crimes do not pay (they can "pay" very well indeed if one is not caught), but because they are wrong absolutely. Should a nation's foreign policy follow the same standard, even if the moral course should strengthen an enemy and endanger the national security? To answer yes is to assert that under some circumstances a leader must decide on the suicide of the nation. To answer no is to stand on the slippery slope where the end justifies the means.

A related difficulty involves the difference between what a

nation itself does—for example, engaging in assassination, torture, imprisonment without due process, denial of political rights—and taking a stance toward another nation's acts. What are the limits of complicity? Should one nation punish another, even to the point of war, for failure to respect human rights? Should a benefactor nation suspend aid to a violator, even if the people hurt by loss of aid are the poor and the innocent? Should one nation refuse to make agreements with a violator, even agreements which are in the human interest, such as arms control? Or should reaction be limited to protest? Loud and public? Or quietly, privately? Should policy be consistent, so that, for example, every nation which imprisons citizens without due process would be accorded the same penalty from the United States? President Carter and his advisers were aware of these questions. But devising guidelines and procedures for answering them both in specific instances and as a matter of general principle proved enormously difficult.

The first step in implementing the policy was the appointment of Patricia M. Derian as coordinator and then (August 1977) Assistant Secretary of State for Human Rights. Derian was an energetic and outspoken civil-rights leader from Mississippi without experience in foreign affairs but with a determination to be heard within the department. She and her staff, also outsiders rather than career officers, immediately encountered resistance from career officers in the regional bureaus. The career officers resented the conflict between the new and imprecise issue of respect for human rights and their responsibility for maintaining good relations with and influence over the governments within their region. The problem was particularly acute for Latin America, but it cropped up also in regard to countries in Asia, Africa, and the Middle East. Derian and her people wanted to start fast, with the imposition of stiff sanctions against violators. They regarded the officers in the regional bureaus, who generally urged long deliberation before action, as the enemy. The feuding was particularly sharp between Derian and Assistant Secretary Holbrooke (East Asia) and Terence Todman (Latin America). Holbrooke was relatively successful in excluding human-rights criteria from decisions in his area. Todman lost his fight and was reassigned as ambassador to Spain. The best working relationship between the human-rights group and a regional bureaucracy involved Africa.[25]

There was no consistency. The sanction of withdrawing aid obviously could not be applied to countries not receiving aid in the first place (e.g., Cuba, Cambodia, North Korea), although in some cases the United States could vote against loans to offending countries by multilateral lending institutions, such as the World Bank. The Soviet Union was a notorious violator of human rights, imprisoning dissidents and denying the right of emigration, but Soviet–American relations were too sensitive to permit subordinates to make decisions. President Carter himself was the human-rights coordinator when the behavior of the Soviet Union was in question. The People's Republic of China did not respect every American definition of human rights either, but the objective of improving relations with China was too important to permit the human-rights issue to interfere. No sanctions were applied and nothing was said officially about human rights in China.

The cacophony of voices arguing about human rights within the Department of State and in public was so great that Secretary of State Vance attempted in April 1977 to explain the policy and announce some guidelines. In a speech at the University of Georgia Law School, he stated that there were three categories of human rights: "the right to be free from governmental violation of the integrity of the person"; "the right to the fulfilment of such vital needs as food, shelter, health care, and education"; and "the right to enjoy civil and political liberties." In working for observance of these rights, the United States must be pragmatic. "A sure formula for defeat of our goals would be a rigid, hubristic attempt to impose our values on others. A doctrinaire plan of action would be as damaging as indifference." In deciding each case, the United States must determine if an action would be effective. It must also ask: "Have we been sensitive to genuine security interests, realizing that outbreak of armed conflict or terrorism could in itself pose a serious threat to human rights?" The Secretary's questions were sensible, but did little to help decide specific cases or produce a consensus within the government or among critics. Those who believed in an active American policy could cite his careful catalogue of rights. Those who wanted to do nothing could turn to his stricture about being sensitive to "security interests" or could argue that a particular government's use of repression was the only way to deal with terrorists.[26]

Vance assigned to Deputy Secretary of State Warren Christopher the responsibility of making the application of human-rights policies compatible with the overall objectives of foreign policy. The "Christopher group" included representatives from Defense, Treasury (which issued instructions for American voting on multilateral bank loans), and Agriculture (for its role in extending food aid). At the beginning, an important bureaucratic victory went to Under Secretary of State for Security Assistance Lucy Benson. She demanded and was granted an exemption of military-aid programs, the most important of all potential levers, from review by the Christopher group. Agriculture then won exemption for food-aid programs, on the plausible ground that food helped the needy rather than the actual violators of human rights. One consequence was that the Christopher group devoted most of its attention to American voting on multilateral bank loans, and then the human-rights advocates had to contend with the legitimate concern of the Treasury that the use of the multilateral lending banks as a weapon by the United States would undermine the effectiveness of the banks.

In practice, the United States voted against or abstained on loan proposals to Afghanistan, Argentina, Benin, Bolivia, the Central African Republic, Chile, El Salvador, Ethiopia, Guatemala, South Korea, Laos, Paraguay, the Philippines, Syria,

Uruguay, Vietnam, and the People's Democratic Republic of Yemen. The countries fell into four groups: those considered to be under Soviet control, African states with bloody rulers, Asian allies of the United States, and Latin American military regimes.

The United States reduced, suspended, or eliminated bilateral aid in several instances, most notably to Argentina, Chile, and Nicaragua. Brazil refused aid in response to what that government considered unwarranted public criticism from the United States. The severe sanction of a trade embargo was imposed against the murderous regime of Idi Amin in Uganda, but the initiative for that came from Congress, not from within the Administration. In barring trade with the Ian Smith regime in Rhodesia and prohibiting the export of arms and police equipment to South Africa, the Administration acted in conformity with international sanctions. No sanctions were imposed against Iran because of human-rights violations by the Shah's regime, but the issue was heatedly debated within the Department of State. Nor was the sanction of limiting military aid applied to the Philippines or South Korea, in spite of blatant violations of human rights by those two governments.

The Administration found many opportunities to affirm its position on human rights. In October 1977, President Carter signed two long-pending United Nations covenants—one on civil and political and the other on economic, social, and cultural rights. The United States also lost no opportunity of reminding the Soviet Europe and Eastern European countries of their obligations under the Helsinki accords of 1975. The President sent former Supreme Court Justice Arthur Goldberg to the next conference in the Helsinki process (formally the Conference on Security and Cooperation in Europe) at Belgrade in 1978 and Attorney General Griffin Bell to the 1980 Madrid meeting, and both spoke strongly about the American position and the derelictions of others. There were innumerable speeches and other public statements. And there was quiet diplomacy—for example, Carter's private remarks to the Shah of Iran.

What did the Carter human-rights policy accomplish? At the verbal level, the official position of the United States was loud and clear. The victims of those who trampled on human rights were acknowledged and their plight publicized: dissidents in the Soviet Union and throughout Eastern Europe; those who had been murdered, tortured, and imprisoned in Latin America; opposition leaders sentenced to death in Pakistan and Korea; blacks denied freedom under the South African regime of apartheid; hundreds of thousands murdered in Cambodia. The immediate costs to the violators varied and were usually slight. But the victims who survived and who had enough freedom to speak out applauded the American policy and believed that conditions would have been far worse had the United States remained silent.

Americans who believed that all questions should be subordinate to the conflict with the totalitarianism of the Soviet Union attacked Carter's human-rights record. Jeane Kirkpatrick's critique was both representative and the most widely noticed. In a 1979 article entitled "Dictatorships and Double Standards," she charged that the Administration "actively collaborated in the replacement of moderate autocrats friendly to American interests with less friendly autocrats of extremist persuasion." She argued that instead of criticizing Somoza in Nicaragua and the Shah in Iran, instead of upbraiding them for a failure to follow an American model of democracy and human rights, the United States should have accepted them as traditional authoritarians, as the kind of leaders necessary to hold their societies together and prevent the triumph of the totalitarianism of the left. Her argument that Nicaragua and Iran were "lost" because of the human-rights policy could not stand up under close examination, but its superficial plausibility was appealing to those who hoped that the policy and the Carter Administration itself would soon be replaced.[27]

THE ENERGY CRISIS AND
ECONOMIC FOREIGN POLICY

The Carter Presidency overlapped the dizzy rise of oil prices which began with the response of the Arab oil-producing nations to the Yom Kippur War of 1973 and which reached a new high plateau during the revolution in Iran in 1979. The price of crude oil increased nearly fifteenfold during the 1970s, from under $3 per barrel to $40. At the same time, American domestic-oil production remained stable while consumption and imports rose.

Where would it end? With oil at $300 a barrel? Or with all the world's oil wells sucked dry? How could an industrial economy survive and what violence might result from the desperate efforts of failing nations to gain control of what remained of a vital resource? The United States and much of the industrial world was suddenly swept by doomsday predictions. The message was that, unless heroic action was taken, the world would run out of energy and civilization would come to an end. Carter, with his penchant for exaggerating both the good and the bad, believed the message and was exhilarated by the challenge.[28]

"With the exception of preventing war," the President told the nation in April 1977, "this is the greatest challenge that our country will face during our lifetime . . . Our decision about energy will test the character of the American people and the ability of the President and the Congress to govern this Nation. This difficult effort will be the 'moral equivalent of war,' except that we will be uniting our efforts to build and not to destroy." The domestic components of his program involved conservation, the decontrol of prices to encourage new oil exploration, the creation of substantial reserve supplies, and the use of coal and solar energy—all aimed at reducing imports and attaining energy independence and freedom from the "fear of embargoes."[29]

The energy crisis affected virtually every phase of foreign policy. It was a driving force behind American efforts to make peace between Israel and her Arab neighbors. It was the fundamental reason that the revolution in Iran came as such a shock. It was the reason the United States tried to get other nations to conserve their oil consumption and imports. Its greatest impact, however, was psychological—on the American people and on Carter himself.

Congress, instead of joining in a "moral equivalent of war," refused the legislation the President wanted. Imports of oil remained high. Conservation measures were slow and halfhearted. The halt in Iranian production, caused by the revolution sweeping that country in 1979, left Americans with insufficient gasoline for their automobiles, left them gnashing their teeth in long lines outside the few gas stations that were open. July was the worst month, and much of the people's resentment seemed directed at the President. Carter had just signed the SALT II treaty with Leonid Brezhnev, but he felt no sense of accomplishment. In frustration, he repaired to Camp David, fired several of his Cabinet members, and then lectured the nation on its "crisis of spirit."

> We are at a turning point in our history. There are two paths to choose. One is a path I've warned about tonight, the path that leads to fragmentation and self-interest . . . It is a certain route to failure . . . All the promises of our future point to another path, the path of common purpose and the restoration of American values. That path leads to true freedom for our Nation and ourselves. We can take the first steps down that path as we begin to solve our energy problem. [30]

Within months, the hostages had been seized in Iran and the Soviets had invaded Afghanistan. Fighting the energy crisis and confronting the Soviet Union now became the same thing for President Carter. Now he said it was imperative to equate "energy security with our Nation's military security; there's no way to separate the two."[31] Focusing on the external threat of the Soviet Union meant a return to the traditional foreign policy which he had once sought to transcend, but that focus was more psychologically appealing than the internal self-criticism concerning a "crisis of the spirit" he had voiced in July. The moral equivalent of war had turned into something very close to preparing for war itself.

The policies directed at alleviating the energy crisis were part of the Carter Administration's general economic foreign policy. Another element received less attention in the headlines because it was a familiar story without doomsday implications—the effort, pursued by all Administrations since the 1940s, to encourage a worldwide lowering of tariffs and other barriers to trade. Carter decided in 1977 to commit his Administration to persevering with the so-called Tokyo Round of multilateral talks being conducted in an often desultory fashion since 1974 under the auspices of the General Agreement on Trade and Tariffs (GATT). Patience paid off, and in April 1979 in Geneva a lengthy, useful, and often quite technical set of agreements was reached. The emphasis was on a code of behavior to regulate non-tariff barriers to trade. Congress approved the Tokyo Round agreements in July. The Administration also sought to relieve the American trade deficit by encouraging Japan and the Western European nations to increase domestic demand for goods, particularly American exports. This, too, was an old story.

A unique issue which linked economic policy with the Administration's emphasis on global approaches to human welfare involved the resources of the deep ocean seabed. The nations of the world had been meeting on and off since 1958 and intensively since 1973 in an effort to draw up a new law of the sea. The most difficult and contentious issue on the agenda when the Carter Administration inherited the talks was the disposition of the mineral resources on the ocean floor beyond the shallow continental shelves and outside the claimed jurisdiction of individual nations. There were minerals there in the form of nodules of manganese, also containing nickel, copper, and other metals. In some locations the nodules, ranging in size from golf balls to basketballs, nearly covered the seabed.

Some writers said the nodules represented wealth unlike anything to be found on dry land. The idea took hold that here was "a common heritage of Mankind" which could lift the resource-poor nations of the world out of poverty. President Carter appointed Elliot L. Richardson, a prominent liberal Republican, as head of the American delegation to the Law of the Sea Conference. Richardson and his staff spent the better part of four years trying to reconcile the dreams of limitless wealth to be distributed from the "common heritage of Mankind" with such practical questions as who would pay to develop the necessary and very expensive technology. No capital would be invested, the United States argued, unless there was a reasonable chance of a return. Finally, in 1980, a series of compromises was negotiated that balanced power to be granted to an international seabed "Authority" with protection of American interests. A comprehensive treaty on many aspects of maritime law, including the seabed provisions, was almost ready for signature when the Reagan Administration began. President Reagan decided the United States would not sign the treaty. Carter's gesture toward meeting Third World aspirations was aborted.[32]

THE PROBLEM OF
NUCLEAR PROLIFERATION

The expectation of wealth for the Third World through the mining of minerals from the deep seabed was largely an illusion. The dream of self-sufficiency in energy through the reprocessing of plutonium and the use of fast-breeder reactors was not an illusion—although the economic costs were debatable. The fast-breeder reactor was to regular atomic-power generation what a hydrogen bomb was to an original atomic bomb—immensely more powerful and dangerous. The fast-breeder reactor employed plutonium and promised to free nuclear-power generation from dependence on large quantities of expensive, scarce, and unevenly distributed uranium. But when plutonium was produced for generating electricity, it was available also for nuclear weapons. Jimmy

Carter, the first President with a technical understanding of nuclear engineering, considered this danger almost as great as the strategic arms race between the United States and the Soviet Union.[33]

More than one hundred nations had signed the Non-Proliferation Treaty of 1968 in which the nuclear-weapon powers pledged not to transfer technology for weapons to non-nuclear nations. The latter pledged not to acquire weapons and to accept "safeguards" regulating peaceful uses of atomic energy to ward against diversion for weapons. But Carter considered the safeguards inadequate in dealing with plutonium. There was the further problem that several nations, including Argentina, Brazil, Pakistan, Israel, South Africa, and Egypt, had not adhered to the treaty. India did more than decline to sign; she detonated a test bomb in 1974.

President Carter acted quickly on the domestic front. In April 1977, he announced the indefinite deferment of all commercial recycling and reprocessing of plutonium in the United States and cancellation of plans for a demonstration fast-breeder reactor on the Clinch River in Tennessee. He also asked Congress to pass new legislation tightening controls on American exports of technology. Congress complied with the Nuclear Non-Proliferation Act of 1978. Simultaneously, the Administration sought to block the use of reprocessing technology around the world—and thereby collided with the long-maturing plans and expectations of many nations to solve their energy problems with precisely that technology. The Administration was only days old before it was involved in a public effort to prevent Brazil from importing the technology for breeder reactors from the Federal Republic of Germany. The episode bruised American relations with both countries. Japan also was told that its plans interfered with what the United States considered safe. The problem of how to apply pressure and what pressure was delicate. The United States, with relatively abundant access to uranium and substantial non-nuclear sources of energy, was vulnerable to the charge of being the dog in the manger—denying to others something which it did not need itself. And how far did Washington want to go in damaging bilateral and alliance relations in pursuit of this one goal?

After the opening and rather heavy-handed episode with Brazil, the Administration turned to quieter diplomacy. There were mutually satisfactory discussions with Japan and inconclusive negotiations with India. The only country to suffer a loss of aid, under the provisions of the 1978 law, was Pakistan. The activities of South Africa, a country in which the United States had little leverage, were carefully watched. South Africa may have tested a small nuclear device at sea in September 1979, but the available evidence is inconclusive.

The United States also was the prime mover behind the International Nuclear Fuel Cycle Evaluation conference which convened in Washington in 1977 and developed a sheaf of complicated guidelines. On balance, it is impossible to say if the Administration's campaign for non-proliferation made a difference. Brazil and Germany did cancel their agreement eventually—but for economic reasons, not because of American pressure. For strategic reasons connected with the Soviet invasion of Afghanistan, the United States lifted the sanctions against Pakistan—without gaining a pledge that Pakistan would refrain from developing weapons. Overriding strategic reasoning also led the Administration to refrain from applying significant pressure on India. On the positive side, no new nations tested nuclear weapons—with the possible exception of South Africa.[34]

CURBING THE SALE OF ARMS
TO THE THIRD WORLD

In 1947, at the very beginning of the Cold War, a special committee of State, War, and Navy Department officials addressed the question of the international trade in weapons. The committee noted that only the United States and the Soviet Union had the capacity to produce arms on a large scale for other nations.

"If, through inability to obtain the equipment and supplies from the United States, they turn to the Soviet Union or its satellites they will provide the Soviet Union with a political leverage potentially dangerous to U.S. security interests. The same leverage, possessed by the United States, could be made to serve the interests of international peace and security."[35]

During the next three decades, the reasoning of 1947 supported a vast program of military assistance to dozens of countries. At first, the assistance was largely through grants or subsidized loans. But in the 1970s the sale of American arms, often to countries with new wealth from oil, became more important than grants or loans. During the Nixon Administration, the arms sales were encouraged for their impact on the balance of trade. Also, a solid flow of orders from overseas meant high employment, profits, and more research in the weapons industry. The arms-manufacturing companies were eager participants in the process. Their salesmen traveled the globe with enticing descriptions of the latest plane or vehicle or rocket. The results of governmental encouragement and the industry's energy were extraordinary. In 1970, sales of arms were less than $2 billion. By 1975, they were over $15 billion. The United States was the largest arms exporter, but the Soviet Union was close behind, and France, Germany, and Great Britain were heavily in the game.[36]

President Carter put the subject on the agenda for the first National Security Council meeting immediately after his inauguration. He then announced that "very tight restraints" would be imposed on "the efforts by arms manufacturers to initiate sales," and he personally would give final approval on all proposed transactions. Carter ordered a comprehensive policy review and the development of a set of guidelines. Four months later, the guidelines were announced:

1. The dollar amount of weapons transferred under government programs would be reduced from the levels attained in the last year of the Ford Administration.

2. The United States would not be the first to introduce new,

more advanced weapons into a region—and thus would reduce the motivation for local arms races.

3. Development of advanced weapons solely for export would be banned.

4. There would be significant restrictions on the manufacture of weapons under American license abroad.

5. There would be restrictions, amounting virtually to denial, on the transfer of American weapons from a recipient to a third country.

6. The sales activities of American companies would be closely supervised and there would be no promotion of sales by the government itself.

Henceforth, said the President, arms transfers would be viewed "as an exceptional foreign policy implement. . . We will continue to utilize arms transfers to promote our security and the security of our close friends. But in the future the burden of persuasion will be on those who favor a particular arms sale, rather than those who oppose it." The restrictions would apply to all countries except members of NATO, and Japan, Australia, New Zealand, and Israel. But even for Third World countries, the guidelines could be waived whenever the President determined it necessary.[37]

The Administration also held a series of meetings on conventional-arms transfers with the Soviet Union and discussions with other suppliers. The results were meager. Worldwide transfers continued to grow throughout the Carter years. The Administration claimed that American sales declined under its program, but thanks to exceptions and to what a Senate Foreign Relations Committee report called "mathematical manipulation," the figures were deceptive. According to a leading student of the subject, "in reality, total U.S. arms sales increased . . . from $12.8 billion in 1977 to $17.1 in 1980."[38] And yet, without the new policy, the amounts might well have been higher. The Administration did approve huge sales of advanced fighter planes in the Middle East, but it also claimed to have rejected 614 requests, amounting to over $1 billion, during its first fifteen months. The guidelines did introduce more orderly procedures. But, overall, the policy, like all the global objectives of this Administration, was oversold.

Jimmy Carter during his campaign in 1976 had promised that foreign policy in his Presidency would deal with broad global issues of human rights, the fair and judicious use of energy resources, and the curbing of weapons of destruction, both conventional and nuclear. He hoped that it would be possible to confront those issues directly and with a minimum of compromise. The hope held during his first year in office and was fully expressed in his Notre Dame speech of May 1977: "We can no longer separate the traditional issues of war and peace from the new global questions of justice, equity, and human rights."[39] But, to his regret, the four Carter years saw the resurgence, despite every good intention, of a traditional focus on military power and confrontation with one foe, the Soviet Union. The global concerns were never completely forgotten—and Carter would return to them in his farewell address in 1981—but time and again they had to be subordinated to questions of power and national security, defined just as every President had defined them since the beginning of the Cold War. In theory, a commitment to human rights and other goals for humanity as a whole could be "absolute." In practice, when that commitment conflicted unambiguously with traditional security concerns, security had the greater weight in determining what the United States did.

3

Nuclear Weapons and the Soviet Union

Once upon a time, American policy toward the Soviet Union was very simple. In the interval between the end of the Second World War, when Russia ceased to be an ally, and the late 1950s, when she had acquired both nuclear weapons and the means to deliver them on the United States, American leaders defined the Soviet Union as the source of all evil and American purpose and righteousness in terms of the necessity of combating a totalitarian menace on every front. The United States confidently played a zero-sum game. Whatever made the United States and its allies stronger was good without question. Every misfortune befalling the Soviet Union was also good, just as anything which increased Soviet power and influence was bad. With that clear yardstick, decisions in foreign policy were comparatively simple to make: build weapons in order to maintain superiority, extend foreign aid in order to make friends who shared an anti-Soviet posture, intervene in Korea lest American credibility be doubted and the dominoes begin to fall.

But once the Soviet Union acquired, as was inevitable, the capacity to destroy the United States with nuclear weapons, the yardstick ceased to work. The Soviet Union seemed no less evil, no less an expansionist threat to the "Free World." But now, with neither side able to attack the other without inviting retaliatory destruction, cooperation was essential. But how does one cooperate and at the same time contend with an enemy? Does one accept coexistence as a necessity and seek formal or tacit agreement on how far each side can intrude on the interests of the other? Or does one take a long view that there will be no security until the opposite system is dismantled or permanently transformed into something passive and benign? And which long view do Soviet leaders entertain about their nation's relations with the United States? Do they accept the necessity of coexistence, or are they bent on dismantling American power? Such questions have bedeviled every American and Soviet leader since the end of World War II and the beginning of the Cold War.[1]

The contradictions and ambiguities in Soviet–American relations were particularly deep during the Carter years. In his inaugural address, the President spoke of the ultimate goal of eliminating nuclear weapons from the earth. In the most often quoted words of his most important early Presidential speech on foreign policy, at Notre Dame in May 1977, Carter said: "We are now free of that inordinate fear of communism which once led us to embrace any dictator in that fear." He also said: "For too many years, we've been willing to adopt the flawed and erroneous principles and tactics of our adversaries, sometimes abandoning our values for theirs."[2] Three admonitory assumptions were implicit in those words. First, nothing is more important than working with the Soviet Union toward the goal of eliminating nuclear weapons. Second, the United States should not let an obsession with the Soviet Union dictate all its behavior, especially if that meant contravening moral principles. And third, the Soviet Union remains the epitome of evil against which American virtue should be defined and preserved. President Carter tried to act on these three assumptions simultaneously. It could not be done.

The Soviet leadership reacted to Jimmy Carter's election with misgiving and puzzlement, not knowing what to make of this almost unknown local politician who came to the White House innocent of experience at the national or international level. On the one hand, Carter seemed to call for a less assertive, less interventionist, less military policy for the United States. But, on the other, he had criticized Nixon and Kissinger for conceding too much to the Soviet Union while pursuing detente, and he was quick to denounce alleged Soviet violations of human rights. Kremlin experts on the United States considered the appointment of the virulently anti-Soviet, Polish-born Zbigniew Brzezinski as ominous—as well they might. Brzezinski was not content with the status quo. He believed the United States could weaken the Soviet empire by encouraging increasing independence by Eastern European nations. Carter made an official state visit to Poland in December 1977 as a quiet expression of this view.[3] Brzezinski also believed that Soviet leadership was rigid, unimaginative, and vulnerable in time of crisis. Before the four years of the Carter Administration were over, Brzezinski would be urging American war planners to focus on how, during a war, military means could be used to catalyze the breakup of the U.S.S.R.[4]

THE HUMAN-RIGHTS ISSUE

From the outset, the Administration focused public attention on Soviet violations of human rights. Carter, who had criticized President Ford for refusing to receive the anti-Soviet novelist Alexander Solzhenitsyn in the White House, welcomed the exiled human-rights leader Vladimir Bukovsky to the White House and replied warmly to a letter from physicist Andrei Sakharov, the most prominent critic of the Soviet regime. "I am always glad to hear from you," the President wrote; "you may rest assured that the American people and our government will continue our firm commitment to promote respect for human rights not only in our country but also abroad."[5] Moscow retorted that the United States was violating the principle of non-interference in the internal affairs of other countries and was conducting a campaign of provocation under the false banner of "human rights."[6]

The dialogue of accusation and petulant rebuttal continued for four years—in speeches, diplomatic exchanges, and *Pravda* ar-

ticles. For example, in September 1977, President Carter raised
the case of Jewish dissident Anatoly Shcharansky in a meeting
with Soviet Foreign Minister Andrei Gromyko. According to Carter,
Gromyko deprecated Shcharansky as "a microscopic dot who is
of no consequence to anyone."[7] (Shcharansky was subsequently
tried and convicted of espionage.) In May 1978, when the Soviets
put another dissident, Yuri Orlov, on trial, Secretary of Health,
Education and Welfare Joseph Califano canceled a trip to Russia
in protest.[8] And at Carter's only summit meeting with Soviet
President Leonid Brezhnev, in Vienna in June 1979, the pattern
was maintained. Said Brezhnev: "Human rights is a sensitive
subject for us and is not a legitimate ground for discussion between
you and me." Said Carter: "The subject of human rights is very
important to us in shaping our attitude toward your country. You
voluntarily signed the Helsinki accords, which made this issue a
proper item of state-to-state relations."[9]

And so it went. Was any good accomplished or any harm done?
Secretary of State Vance was not happy to see the subject raised
so insistently lest it impede an arms-control agreement, nor was
Marshall Shulman, his special adviser on Soviet affairs. After
noting that detente had been identified in some eyes as "callous
and cynical indifference to egregious acts of the Soviet security
apparatus," he observed that "the objective of the United States
and other democratic governments to seek to reduce the danger
of nuclear war by negotiations with the Soviet leaders is also a
moral obligation."[10] But an arms-control agreement was finally
signed, and there is no evidence that the delay reflected Soviet
resentment over the human-rights issue. Some dissidents were
allowed to leave the Soviet Union, and so were many Jewish
Soviet citizens who wished to emigrate. Carter personally believed
in raising the issue with Moscow. Politically, he had little choice,
given his general emphasis on human rights and the criticism
from American conservatives that he was harsher on abuses committed by right-wing than by left-wing regimes.[11]

SALT II: FIRST PRIORITY

President Carter's dream was a world in which American foreign policy could concentrate on the alleviation of global problems and not be obsessed with fear of the Soviet Union. But he sensed, as had a long line of Presidents, that such an ideal world would never be, as long as each superpower felt mortally insecure in the face of the other's nuclear weapons. Therefore, as much as the President and many of his advisers yearned to deal with issues of human rights, racial justice, energy, and the environment, they knew that real progress was impossible until survival of life on earth could be assured. The race for ever more numerous and sophisticated nuclear weapons had to be stopped and the remaining arsenals made more stable and less threatening. For Secretary of State Vance, this objective was the first priority, to which everything else had to be subordinated. It was a priority which, if achieved, would make all other issues easier to resolve.

The President said his ultimate objective was the complete elimination of nuclear weapons, but neither he nor any of his advisers thought that possible in the foreseeable future. What they sought was a strategic-arms limitation agreement with the Soviet Union which began the process of deep cuts in existing arsenals, limited the capacity of either side to surprise the other with a technological breakthrough, and was based on the principle of essential equivalence of strategic nuclear weapons on both sides. The pursuit of this goal on the technical level of the weapons themselves was mind-numbing in its complexity. The two sides, and even experts on the same side, could not agree on the comparative value of different weapons, numbers and sizes of weapons, and theoretical performance characteristics. Their computer-assisted imaginations could conjure up the most frightful possibilities should one side attain the slightest margin of supposed superiority, but nothing was provable and everything therefore was disputable. Would the other side, under any circumstances, start a nuclear war? If the answer was yes, how could those circumstances be prevented? And how could one side distinguish between what was provocative and what was defensive behavior on the part of the other side?

Equally difficult was the relationship of weapons, which all hoped would never be used, to the reality and perception of political power. To put it bluntly, should the United States overlook objectionable Soviet behavior in non-nuclear matters, such as violations of human rights or exploitation of turmoil in the Third World, in order to maintain the best possible atmosphere for arms-control agreements? Would the conclusions of sound arms agreements then have a beneficial influence on Soviet behavior elsewhere? Or should general good behavior by the Soviets be made an explicit condition for arms control? And what would be the reaction of American allies to a bilateral negotiation obviously affecting their security in the most profound way but from which they were excluded? It proved impossible for the Carter Administration to gain agreement within the executive branch on the answers to these questions. The problem, however, became exponentially more difficult when it came to winning Senate and public opinion. Conceptually, therefore, the effort to reach the arms-control goal had four dimensions of negotiation: within the executive branch, between the United States and the Soviet Union, between the United States and its allies, and between the President and Congress.

The historical record of efforts at strategic-arms control offered no grounds for optimism. In the years since the First World War, the United States had made four major proposals for the control of strategic weapons. The proposal at the Washington conference of 1921–22, in the pre-nuclear age, dealt with battleships—the strategic weapons of that era. The three nuclear-weapons initiatives were the Baruch Plan of 1946, the atmospheric-test ban of 1963, and the SALT I treaty and agreements of 1972. In each case, five factors, positive or negative, were at work. Without a favorable reading on all five, a successful agreement had not been achieved.

1. Consensus within the executive branch on the nature and desirability of the proposal.

2. Congressional support, or, at least, the absence of strong opposition.

3. Public support, or, at least, the absence of strong public criticism.

4. A sincere proposal designed to meet the other side's fears as well as those of the United States.

5. A conscious effort by each side to avoid provoking the other on issues other than arms control; in other words, positive linkage.

The Washington treaties of 1921–22 were the result of favorable readings on all five counts. Secretary of State Charles Evans Hughes in 1921 won President Warren G. Harding's approval for deep cuts in world battleship strength, the establishment of a ratio of tonnage among the naval powers, limits on new technology, and a ten-year freeze on new construction. Dissent among professional naval officers was limited and ineffective. Congress was enthusiastic and, indeed, had forced President Harding to act in the first place. Public support was articulate and widespread. The proposal itself met the needs and fears of all the participants and was not a case of proposing something which the other side would be forced to reject. And the major participants sought cooperation, not antagonism, in adjusting their mutual interests in China. The result was the most radical strategic-arms control agreement ever concluded: a cut of more than fifty percent in existing strategic weapons, a holiday or freeze of ten years on the construction of new weapons, and effective limits on the size and performance of existing and new weapons. The agreement won overwhelming and enthusiastic support in the Senate.[12]

The Baruch Plan of 1946 for placing all atomic weaponry and non-military atomic activity under an international authority controlled in practice by the United States failed because three of the five factors were negative. The Truman Administration was internally divided on the merits of the plan. The Soviet Union correctly saw it as a device to deny them nuclear weapons and intimidate them with the weapons of the international authority. And the United States and the Soviet Union were provoking each other on a wide range of other issues: Iran, Korea, Eastern Europe, Germany. Congressional and public support existed but was essentially irrelevant since there was no chance that the Soviet Union would accept the proposal.[13]

The atmospheric test-ban treaty of 1963, like the Washington treaty of 1921, was positive on all five counts. There were strong public and congressional pressures for relief from the hazards of radioactive fallout, the consequence of recent extensive Soviet and American above-ground tests. As a result of improved techniques of verification, the executive branch was unified behind the proposal. A few inveterate believers in security through unquestioned American nuclear superiority and mistrusters of the Soviet Union spoke against the treaty, but they were a small minority and did not sway public opinion. The ban on atmospheric tests benefited both sides, and the whole world, while giving neither an advantage. And in the aftermath of the terrifying confrontation over Soviet missiles in Cuba in 1962, both the American and the Soviet government were speaking and acting in a relatively conciliatory vein.[14]

There was no strong congressional or public demand for the SALT I agreements concluded in 1972 under the direction of President Richard Nixon and National Security Adviser Henry Kissinger, but neither was there strong opposition. Nixon was immune from criticism from the right, and liberals were for arms control in principle. The agreements certainly took the Soviet point of view fully into account and, indeed, allowed the Soviet Union a numerical advantage in land-based ICBMs. And in the era of detente, both sides made gestures of positive linkage—grain sales from the United States to the Soviet Union, and tacit Soviet assistance in the American extrication from the unpopular war in Vietnam.[15]

Other proposals in the years since 1946 were doomed because they met none of the five necessary favorable conditions. The Soviet 1946 proposal for an immediate and total ban on all nuclear weapons, but without provision for inspection and verification, was rejected by the United States as one-sided and insincere. The Soviets reacted in the same way to President Eisenhower's 1955 proposal for "Open Skies"; i.e., freedom for each side to conduct aerial reconnaissance over the other. At a time when the United States was far ahead in nuclear bombs and bombers, the idea struck Moscow as a transparent excuse for the gathering of military intelligence in preparation for possible war.[16] In 1963, the Soviets might have accepted a comprehensive test-ban agreement—prohibiting nuclear tests in all environments—but the opposition from the designers of American weapons, the military, and their allies in Congress was too great to allow the Kennedy Administration to propose such an agreement.

The Carter Administration inherited expectations created by the Soviet and American governments in the Nixon and Ford years. The SALT I treaty and its accompanying ceilings on different categories were in effect but would expire in October 1977. Ford and Brezhnev at Vladivostok in 1974 had agreed that in the next round of negotiations there would be equal limits on the strategic launchers of both sides; namely, 2,400 each, with a sublimit of 1,320 for missiles with multiple, independently targeted warheads (MIRVs). Nixon, Ford, and Henry Kissinger had been criticized from left and right. The left said that SALT I and the Vladivostok agreements were schemes for building more, not for limiting, nuclear weapons. The right said the agreements were too favorable to the Soviet Union, and that the United States had allowed its own land-based intercontinental missiles, the Minuteman, to become vulnerable to a first strike from more powerful and numerous Soviet ICBMs.

Carter agreed in part with the criticisms of both right and left. He had speculated to the Joint Chiefs of Staff, on the eve of his inauguration, that a mere two hundred weapons on either side might be enough to deter war.[17] He also believed that the vulnerability of the Minuteman was a real issue which had to be solved by a major reduction in Soviet weapons—or balanced with more modern and presumably less vulnerable American weapons. Furthermore, he had an understandable urge to propose something new, not simply to take up with the Soviets where Gerald Ford and Henry Kissinger had left off. He ordered that the United States prepare a proposal for deep cuts and far more sweeping controls and limitations than anything introduced before. Those within the Administration with the most experience in dealing with the Russians said this approach would fail. The Soviets hated surprises and would suspect a trick. Secretary of State Vance shared these doubts, but did not oppose the radical approach.

THE OPPOSITION MOBILIZES

Vance's influence was evident, however, in Carter's nomination of Paul C. Warnke as head of the Arms Control and Disarmament Agency and chief U.S. negotiator. Warnke, a Washington lawyer and a close friend of Vance, had in recent years acquired a reputation as an outspoken dove on arms control. His position, with which Vance agreed, was that both sides already had the power to annihilate each other many times over. The arms race was the mindless mimicry of two "apes on a treadmill."[18] The precise measure of overkill was meaningless and "superiority" was an illusion. If two opponents were afloat on a sea of gasoline and were threatening to light matches, would the opponent with ten thousand matches be "superior" to the other with only one thousand matches? Warnke and Vance believed that the danger was in the race itself and that the remedy was to be found in an agreement for its own sake, without excessive concern over which side got the better of the other in the negotiation. Warnke also believed that on some occasions it would be wise for the United States to show restraint in developing new weapons and then challenge the Soviet Union to reciprocate.

This attitude struck opponents of the SALT process as appeasement, and they mounted a powerful campaign to block Warnke's confirmation by the Senate. The organization leading the fight was the newly formed Committee on the Present Danger, headed by Paul Nitze and Eugene Rostow, both Democrats who had served in previous Administrations and who believed that the United States was losing the will and military power to stop the Soviet Union. Several of the committee's members, including Nitze, had served on Team B, a special group appointed by CIA director George Bush in late 1976 to challenge what he perceived as complacency in intelligence estimates about Soviet capabilities and intentions. The chairman of Team B was Harvard professor Richard Pipes, also a member of the Committee on the Present Danger. Pipes's contribution both within Team B and in the public attack on Warnke was to point out "Why the Soviet Union Thinks It Could Fight and Win a Nuclear War."[19]

Upon hearing of Warnke's nomination, Nitze wrote Senator John Sparkman, chairman of the Foreign Relations Committee, that Warnke was incompetent to make judgments concerning weapons and strategy.

> It is claimed that he is a superb negotiator. I am unfamiliar with his successes in this area. I recognize that he has certain abilities as an advocate, but at least with respect to defense matters, these do not include clarity or consistency of logic. I doubt that such advocacy has much chance of success against the strategy and tactics of the highly serious and competent Soviet negotiators.

In his formal testimony, Nitze called Warnke's views "absolutely asinine."[20] On March 9, 1977, the Senate confirmed Warnke's nomination as chief arms negotiator by a 58–40 vote. The affirmative votes fell far short of the two-thirds which would eventually be needed to approve a SALT II treaty, a fact duly noted by both sides in the debate. (His nomination as head of the Arms Control and Disarmament Agency was approved by a wider margin: 70–29.) The issue was, of course, deeper than Warnke himself or even SALT II. It was whether Carter could keep control of foreign policy unless he shifted emphatically to a more suspicious, confrontational attitude toward the Soviet Union.

THE MOSCOW FIASCO

Secretary of State Vance and the American delegation, including Paul Warnke, arrived in Moscow on March 27, 1977. Soviet Foreign Minister Andrei Gromyko opened with a proposal to base an agreement on the Ford–Brezhnev Vladivostok accords. Vance said no and responded with the American comprehensive proposal: to reduce the Vladivostok ceiling from 2,400 to between 1,800 and 2,000 launchers; to cut the number of Soviet heavy missiles from 308 to 150; to limit the number of land-based missiles with multiple warheads (MIRVs) to 550; to put severe restrictions on testing; to ban mobile land-based intercontinental missiles (ICBMs); and to prohibit altogether the development and deployment of a new ICBM.

The required reductions fell almost entirely on the Soviet side, restricting land-based missiles on which they relied, while not significantly affecting the submarine or air-launched weapons in which the United States had superiority. If the Soviets would accept the package, the United States would forego the MX (missile experimental) intercontinental missile then in the research stage. But that was the only large American concession. No one on the American side should have been surprised at the Soviet response: total, absolute rejection, and a charge of insincerity. *Pravda* called Vance's proposals "an attempt to obtain one-sided advantages for the U.S. to the detriment of the security of the U.S.S.R. and its friends and allies." *Izvestia* was self-righteous and truculent: "Trust in politics is, at the very least, firm confidence that your negotiating partner will not repudiate this morning what was agreed to last night . . . One cannot talk frivolously with the Soviet Union. The Soviet Union cannot be 'outplayed' . . . If the people in Washington understand this after the Moscow meetings . . . Vance's mission will have been completely justified."[21]

On the positive side, Vance and Gromyko did agree to meet soon again—in Geneva in May. They also agreed to establish joint working groups or regularly scheduled meetings on a broad range of subjects: a comprehensive (i.e., total) test ban, chemical weapons, prior notification of missile tests, anti-satellite weapons, civil defense, the demilitarization of the Indian Ocean, radiological weapons, conventional weapons and arms transfers to developing nations, and proliferation of nuclear-weapons technology. In the years ahead, however, progress on most of these issues was halted by the wider deterioration of Soviet–American relations.

FALLING BACK AND WHITTLING DOWN THE DIFFERENCES

Carter and Vance were originally confident that there would be a SALT II treaty before the October 1977 expiration of SALT I. It actually took almost two years longer, involving a continuous process of bargaining within the Administration and the most intensive diplomacy ever devoted to arms control. The two delegations in Geneva worked on the details of drafting, while the issues themselves were thrashed out at a higher level. Vance and Soviet Foreign Minister Gromyko met nine times. Carter and Gromyko conferred three times. There was almost continuous contact between American officials and Soviet Ambassador Anatoly Dobrynin in Washington, although the American ambassador in Moscow, Malcolm Toon, was not used as a channel, despite the Administration's efforts to have the Soviets negotiate with him.[22]

Hundreds of pages would be required to describe the intricate hairsplitting bargaining over words as well as substance, the month-by-month alternation of optimism and despair over whether there would ever be an agreement. Here, however, are the essentials. The United States abandoned the hope of a large cut in the number of launchers (land, air-launched, and submarine ballistic missiles and heavy bombers) allowed to each side and settled, on the occasion of a Gromyko visit to Washington in September 1977, for the Vladivostok limit of 2,400, to be reduced to 2,250 by January 1, 1981. Nor did the United States persuade the Soviets to dismantle any of their 308 heavy missiles. Instead, the two sides agreed to have no more than 820 land-based missiles equipped with multiple warheads. The total of land- and submarine-based MIRVed missiles could not exceed 1,200, and the total of land, submarine, and bombers equipped with multiple missiles could not exceed 1,320. No missile could have more than ten warheads, and various existing types were limited to the number of warheads with which they had been tested. If a particular missile had ever been tested with more than one warhead, all missiles of that type would be counted as MIRVed. Each side could develop and deploy one new missile, and it could have as many as ten warheads. This provision allowed the United States to proceed with the MX.

Heavy bombers, on which the United States relied but the Soviet Union did not, counted against the total number of launchers and against the sub-total for MIRVed launchers when they were equipped with cruise missiles (pilotless aircraft propelled through the atmosphere) with a range in excess of six hundred kilometers. This provision preserved an American advantage.

The treaty proscribed the testing of missiles whose deployment was not allowed. Each side agreed not to engage in measures which impeded the ability of the other to verify, through satellite photography and electronic surveillance, that tests and deployments were in compliance. Encoded transmissions from missiles being tested were banned when the coding impeded verification. Thousands of hours of negotiation went into this issue of verification, concealment, and encryption. The result was satisfactory to President Carter, but not to CIA Director Stansfield Turner or many critics in the Senate. The problem was, who could prove that successful concealment, which by definition is totally undetected, had not taken place?

The treaty was accompanied by a bundle of additional documents. There was a protocol banning, until December 31, 1981, the deployment of land- or sea-based cruise missiles with a range in excess of six hundred kilometers. After that, the United States could proceed, if it wished, with the installation of long-range cruise missiles in Europe. There was a Soviet statement that its so-called Backfire bomber was of medium range; that the Soviets had no intention of giving it long-range capability, and the rate of production would not exceed thirty per year. There were pages recording agreements on the numbers of various weapons in each other's arsenals and "common understandings" of the meaning of particular terms. And lastly, there was a joint statement, phrased in pious generalities, of the importance of proceeding with further negotiations; i.e., SALT III. This was the package which Presidents Carter and Brezhnev signed, June 18, 1979, in Vienna.[23]

SUBTRACTING AND ADDING

The SALT process was intertwined with the President's decisions on which new weapons the United States should develop or forego. Contrary to the impression conveyed in some of his campaign remarks, Carter in his first year proposed no significant overall cut in the defense budget inherited from President Ford. In subsequent years, he requested steadily larger budgets.[24] But he incurred the wrath of the hard-liners by his decision to cancel production of a new, very expensive heavy bomber, the B-1. The decision made excellent sense in terms of cost and military effectiveness against the Soviet Union. But because it was made unilaterally, without any effort to extract a reciprocal concession from the Soviets, Carter was criticized from the right as a weak, unilateral disarmer. The accusation overlooked the fact that the Soviets did not consider the B-1 a particular threat.

The B-1 was intended as a supersonic replacement for the B-52, introduced in the 1950s and still the workhorse of the bomber fleet. The time had long passed since the B-52 could count on penetrating Soviet air defenses. But the B-1 probably could do no better. The obvious answer for preserving the airborne leg of the strategic "triad" was to add cruise missiles to bombers. Since the missiles would be released a thousand or more miles from Soviet territory, the old B-52 would serve just as well as the B-1, and at a tiny fraction of the cost. As Carter wrote: "A swarm of cruise missiles, once launched, could not be intercepted short of their multiple targets. Even a fairly high attrition rate would leave a large number to conclude a successful mission."[25] The President's enthusiasm for cost efficiency was, as he contemplated the cruise missile, more evident than his repugnance over nuclear war.

Secretary of Defense Harold Brown supported the decision to cancel the B-1, for which the President was most grateful. But Carter stood alone on his second major cancellation, that of the neutron bomb, or "enhanced radiation weapon," as it was more formally known. The neutron bomb was a battlefield nuclear warhead to be fired by artillery with a range of fifteen to twenty-five miles. It was conceived for use against Soviet tanks and infantry in the event of an invasion of Germany. It produced intense, short-lived, and very lethal radiation—but less heat, blast, and long-term radioactivity than regular nuclear weapons, whose use would leave the target region uninhabitable for generations. The supposed attractiveness of the device was much exaggerated by its advocates. It was still an enormously powerful and dirty thing. A nuclear weapon by whatever name is a nuclear weapon.

There were two principal objections to the neutron bomb. One was that the concept implied a readiness to wage, win, and recover from nuclear war; therefore, the existence of the device might make war more likely. The second objection, more emotional and powerful, was that the bomb represented a peculiarly sickening inversion of values, in that it was designed to kill people but save property. Brown, Brzezinski, and even Vance were unmoved by these objections. They considered the neutron bomb an important addition to deterrence of a possible Soviet invasion of Western Europe, a compensation for Western inferiority in conventional weapons.

The President, however, had a visceral aversion to the thing. If it was to be employed, he wanted the Europeans to ask for it in unequivocal terms. But the anti-nuclear movement in Europe was resurgent and the neutron bomb was under attack. The West German government's response was crucial, for it was only within Germany that the warheads might be used. West Germany, however, was equivocal. Brown, Vance, Brzezinski, and Mondale all urged Carter to grasp the nettle, show leadership, and announce that the neutron bomb would be developed. Carter resented the pressure and on April 7, 1978, announced that production of the neutron bomb would be deferred. No other major decision of his Presidency was made so much on Carter's personal judgment and against the unanimous recommendations of his chief advisers. German Chancellor Helmut Schmidt, overlooking his own vacillation, accused Carter of betrayal. All of Carter's advisers were dismayed. And his critics on the right had another item for their indictment of Carter's softness on the Soviet Union, neglect of military strength, and overall inability to lead.[26]

President Carter's most important decision on a nuclear weapon was to go ahead with the production and deployment of the MX, an accurate new ICBM with ten warheads—the missile the United States would have foregone had the Soviets accepted the original comprehensive deep-cut proposal of March 1977. The proponents of the MX advanced two quite different arguments. The most frequently used was that the current Minuteman ICBM force in fixed silos was vulnerable to a first-strike knockout blow from newer, more accurate Soviet ICBMs. Secretary of Defense Brown in 1978 ridiculed the idea that the Soviets would risk such a "cosmic throw of the dice," which, even if it did destroy the Minutemen, would leave American air and submarine weapons for retaliation.[27] But Brown would change his mind in conformity with the developing position of the Joint Chiefs of Staff that they could not endorse a SALT II agreement unless the United States deployed the MX.

But how would the MX, even with ten warheads per missile, remedy the problem of vulnerability? The answer was some system for hiding the missiles by moving them through tunnels, trenches, or along public highways on huge trucks. But how could a system which depended on deception coexist with a SALT II agreement which depended on verification and avoidance of all measures of deliberate concealment? The solution was a basing system which allowed the Soviets to verify how many missiles were deployed but to conceal their presence in many potential hiding places. The plan ultimately endorsed by Carter called for two hundred missiles, each able to "dash" around a "racetrack" to any one of twenty-three hiding places from which it could be launched. The two hundred racetracks and 4,600 launch sites would occupy a large portion of the states of Nevada and Utah.

None of those who claimed the MX would be invulnerable to a Soviet first strike sounded very convincing, even to themselves. Invulnerability was a false issue. The real reason most supporters of the MX wanted the system was that it would give the United States in theory the same capacity to launch a silo-busting first strike against Soviet ICBMs as the Soviets in theory possessed against the United States. This capacity, said Brzezinski and other advocates, was necessary in order to maintain a "strategic balance." As Secretary of Defense Brown said, in reversing his position in April 1979, "the growing vulnerability of our land-based missile forces could, if not corrected, contribute to a perception of U.S. strategic inferiority that would have severely adverse political—and could have potentially destabilizing military—consequences."[28] The adverse political consequences were as much domestic as international. Unless the Administration embarked on the MX, SALT stood little chance of approval in the Senate.

President Carter had no enthusiasm for the MX; indeed, he found it "a nauseating prospect to confront."[29] But Brzezinski kept up the pressure, even when Carter complained that a decision was being jammed down his throat. In a showdown—June 4, 1979, on the eve of the Vienna meeting for the signature of the SALT II treaty—Carter did not repeat the neutron-bomb pattern. He yielded, accepting Brzezinski's arguments that the strategic nuclear balance was rapidly changing in favor of the Soviets. Brzezinski's concluding argument epitomized the mixed motives behind his recommendation, the confusion between whether the United States needed to strengthen deterrence or match the Soviet Union in its supposed ability and intent to fight and win a nuclear war.

> If these trends were not corrected, the United States would be able at best to wage a spasmic, apocalyptic war rather than one controlled for political purposes. Because of its potential vulnerability to a Soviet first strike, the United States would be less able to bargain stably in a protracted crisis situation, and therefore the United States might be less able in the 1980s to deter the Soviet Union from assertive behavior.[30]

The President's decision "to pursue a full-scale MX" was announced on June 8. A week later, he was in Vienna with Brezhnev.

The MX potentially could have been developed with an 83-inch diameter, big enough for the ten warheads allowed under SALT II but small enough to fit existing silos and to be launched from submarines. The alternative was a 92-inch diameter model, too big for silos or submarines and too heavy to be carried on highways. Brzezinski swayed the decision in favor of the 92-inch missile. Paul Warnke was on the mark when he commented subsequently that Brzezinski's rationale was: "The bigger, the uglier, the nastier the weapon—the better." And that his intended message to Moscow was: "Shape up, buster. We've got the ability to do you in. We're probably not going to do it—but it's an act of grace on our part."[31]

And so in June 1979 the Carter Administration simultaneously prepared to sign the SALT II treaty and present it to the Senate and decided on the largest new nuclear-weapons program since Harry Truman ordered the development of the hydrogen bomb in 1950. The connection between the two reflected conflicting views over how to deal with the Soviet Union—through reassurance and restraint or through military strength and the arousal of anxiety. In more than two years of negotiating the SALT II agreements, the Administration had failed to attain consensus within the executive branch, win strong congressional support, attract organized public backing, or avoid the impression of insincerity and of shifting the onus to the Soviet Union. On these four counts, the outlook for Senate approval of SALT II was not good. On the fifth count—positive linkage between arms control and a willingness of the United States and the Soviet Union to accommodate each other's interests around the world—the outlook was even less propitious, as the following chapters will show.

4

The Return to
Containment in Asia

The American defeat in the Vietnam war made possible Jimmy Carter's victory in the election of 1976. As President, he sought to heal some of the lingering wounds from that war and to avoid the mistakes which had led the United States into the war in the first place. That meant, above all, separating Asian policy from Soviet–American conflict. "I believed," wrote President Carter, "that too many of our international concerns were being defined almost exclusively by the chronic United States–Soviet confrontation mentality."[1]

Thus, at the outset, there was no overarching Asian policy. Particular policies toward individual nations were loosely unified by a general desire to deemphasize military considerations, emphasize human rights, and seek reconciliation with past foes. On the economic front, the Administration sought to persuade Japan to use its extraordinary productivity in ways less bruising to American interests and to work constructively with the other major industrial democracies in facing the energy crisis.

During 1977, the Administration announced its intention to withdraw American ground troops from South Korea and to move toward the establishment of diplomatic relations with Vietnam. It discussed publicly the need to improve relations with the People's Republic of China, but did it cautiously, lest too rapid or warm an embrace jeopardize the SALT II negotiations with the

Soviet Union. But by the end of 1978 the original disconnected policies had been abandoned. American troops remained in South Korea, the effort to improve relations with Vietnam was dropped, and normal diplomatic relations with the People's Republic were established in a distinctly anti-Soviet manner. In 1979, the crisis over the hostages in Iran and the Soviet invasion of Afghanistan confirmed a shift which had already occurred. Policy in East Asia at the end of the Administration was more unified than at the beginning, but it was unified around the old theme of containment of the Soviet Union, precisely what President Carter had once said should not be done.

DIPLOMATIC RECOGNITION OF THE PEOPLE'S REPUBLIC OF CHINA

The relationship of the United States to the People's Republic of China was the core of Asian policy. President Carter and his advisers agreed that it would be desirable to advance the relationship established by Richard Nixon and Henry Kissinger in 1972, moving from informal ties to full diplomatic recognition and the exchange of ambassadors. An immediate and familiar obstacle was the nature of the American relationship to the Chinese Nationalist regime on the island of Taiwan.

Peking was adamant that there could be no normalization with the United States until Washington withdrew diplomatic recognition of Taiwan, ended the U.S.–Republic of China mutual defense treaty of 1954,[2] and removed all American troops from Taiwan. The Carter Administration's problem was identical with that faced by Nixon and Ford: how could ties with Taiwan be cut without incurring the charge that the United States was betraying an old and faithful ally? During his election campaign in 1976, Carter was cautious. "I would like assurances that the people of Taiwan—the Republic of China or whatever it might be called—be free of military persuasion or domination from mainland China. That may not be a possibility; if it is not, then

I would be reluctant to give up our relationship with the Republic of China."[3]

Secretary of State Vance felt no emotional commitment to maintaining the status quo with Taiwan, but he feared that too swift a rapprochement with Peking would cause anxiety in Moscow and might be an obstruction to a strategic-arms control agreement. National Security Adviser Brzezinski, on the other hand, believed a bit of anxiety in Moscow was a good thing; it would make the Soviet leadership behave better. Brzezinski saw Moscow using the American desire for a SALT agreement as a way of blocking the move toward closer ties with Peking. He said the United States should not be so deferential to the Soviets. The Taiwan question for Brzezinski was a minor irritation which ought not to block a move that he perceived as having profound strategic significance.

President Carter remained concerned about the Taiwan issue, while supporting a modest and restrained approach to Peking. He invited Huang Chen, head of the Chinese liaison office in Washington, to come to the White House in February 1977 and heard China's position on Taiwan reiterated. He told Huang he would welcome a visit of high-level P.R.C. officials. "As long as there is a Taiwanese ambassador in Washington, this will not be possible," Huang replied.[4] Carter named Leonard Woodcock, former president of the United Auto Workers, to head the American liaison mission in Peking and said it was his wish to see Woodcock become the first ambassador. But when Brzezinski bombarded him with suggestions on how to build up a strategic relationship with the Chinese, Carter told Brzezinski that we "should not ass-kiss them the way Nixon and Kissinger did, and also be careful not to antagonize domestic constituencies."[5]

Secretary Vance visited Peking in August 1977 and conducted inconclusive conversations with Chinese Vice Premier Deng Xiaoping, the most powerful P.R.C. leader (despite his misleading title). Brzezinski, disappointed by Vance's performance, maneuvered to take charge of China policy, taking advantage of the

Secretary's immersion in other foreign-policy issues. Brzezinski urged a trip to China by Secretary of Defense Harold Brown, as a signal that a strategic-military relationship need not wait on normalization. He urged that the United States make available to China scientific technology with dual civilian and military uses and he recommended that the United States not object to arms sales to China by its European allies. Brzezinski's most direct challenge to Vance came over the matter of Brzezinski's own proposed trip to China in the spring of 1978. Vance fought the idea. The trip, he feared, would raise doubts as to who spoke for the United States. "I felt very strongly that there could only be two spokesmen, the president and the secretary of state. I was also concerned that Zbig might get into the issue of normalization before we had finished formulating a detailed position and had consulted Congress adequately."[6]

The President did not accept Vance's objections and permitted the trip. Brzezinski was exhilarated by his experience. "We have been allies before," he said at formal talks with Foreign Minister Huang Hua. "We should cooperate again in the face of a common threat . . . the emergence of the Soviet Union as a global power." When Vice Premier Deng suggested at one point that the United States was too fearful of offending the Soviets, Brzezinski replied that "my inclination to be fearful of offending the Soviet Union is rather limited . . . I would be willing to make a little bet with you as to who is less popular in the Soviet Union—you or me."[7] Brzezinski was so euphoric upon his return to Washington that Carter told him he had been seduced.[8]

It was difficult for anyone to be more anti-Soviet than Deng. He accused the United States of appeasing Moscow, and criticized the SALT talks. When a sub-committee of the House International Relations Committee visited Peking in July, they heard the same story, along with the comment that American trade and technological exchange with the Soviet Union was "feeding chocolates to the Polar Bear."[9]

After his visit, Brzezinski energetically encouraged and supervised highly secret planning within the Administration and negotiations with the Chinese, while clearly enjoying his success in taking China policy out of the hands of the Secretary of State. Thanks primarily to Brzezinski's efforts and those of Michael Oksenberg, the China specialist on the NSC staff, a formula was worked out on the Taiwan question, and accepted in Peking. The United States would reaffirm the message of the Shanghai communiqué, signed by Nixon in 1972, that there was but one China and that Taiwan was part of China; would recognize the P.R.C. as the sole government of China; would end diplomatic relations with Taiwan; would give one year's notice of termination of the Mutual Defense Treaty (rather than abrogate it immediately); and would withdraw the last American troops and all officials from Taiwan. On the other hand, the United States would continue to sell Taiwan defensive military weapons and would maintain trade and cultural relations through a technically non-governmental American Institute of Taiwan. The P.R.C., in turn, would not contradict the stated American expectation that its relations with Taiwan would be handled peacefully. But the P.R.C. did not and would not give an explicit formal pledge not to use force. The two governments agreed to a simultaneous announcement on December 15, 1978, with the date for normalization to be January 1, 1979. The Soviet Union and allied governments were informed only hours before the announcement.

The Soviet Union reacted in a predictable way. All during 1977 and 1978, the Soviet press had been denouncing the People's Republic as an enemy of peace and detente and criticizing the United States for appeasing China's aggressive intentions while trying to direct them against the Soviet Union.[10] Soviet Foreign Minister Andrei Gromyko during a September 1977 meeting with Carter warned against the "dirty game" of playing the "China card" against the Soviet Union, covertly or overtly. The President denied that such was the American intention. And the announcement of normalization brought forth a worried personal message from Soviet President Leonid Brezhnev. Carter claimed, however, that he had assuaged Brezhnev's concerns. He was wrong; no issue was of deeper concern to the Kremlin than the American move toward the People's Republic.[11]

BACKLASH AND A CONSTITUTIONAL CHALLENGE

On Taiwan, President Chiang Ching-kuo, son of Chiang Kai-shek, said the United States had dishonored its treaty commitments and "cannot be expected to have the confidence of any free nations in the future."[12] Taiwan's friends in the United States said the same thing. "Now we have our American Chamberlain. Only the umbrella is missing," said the author of a letter to *Time* magazine, probably unaware that he was echoing the Soviet line.[13] Ronald Reagan said Carter had "abandoned Taiwan to the Red Chinese";[14] Senator Barry Goldwater, Republican of Arizona, said the betrayal of Taiwan "calls into question the honor—the very soul—of America's word in the field of foreign relations."[15] The protests were loud, but not politically damaging to Carter because they came from those who already opposed him on most questions.

Senator Goldwater also led a significant constitutional challenge to the President's right to terminate the Mutual Defense Treaty with Taiwan. The Constitution (Art. II, sec. 2) provides that the President shall have the power to make treaties "provided two-thirds of the Senators present concur" and that treaties, along with the Constitution itself and federal statutes, "shall be the supreme Law of the Land" (Art. VI). But the Constitution is silent regarding the unmaking, or termination, of treaties. The President acting alone cannot repeal statutes or the Constitution. Why, then, should he have the power to repeal treaties? If he could terminate the Mutual Defense Treaty with Taiwan, he could terminate all treaties: membership in the United Nations, the North Atlantic Treaty, everything.

The Senator and twenty-three other members of the Senate and House of Representatives brought suit in the federal courts, claiming that the President's termination of the treaty was unconstitutional without the consent of the Senate or the entire Congress. The district court agreed with the senator, but the Court of Appeals in the District of Columbia overturned the decision. The Supreme Court in December 1979 agreed with the Court of Appeals and ordered the case dismissed—although the Justices advanced a variety of reasons and dissented in part with one another.[16] The action, although blurred in its arguments, sustained the Supreme Court's long predilection for avoiding direct confrontation on issues of foreign policy, especially where Presidential power was concerned.

The political weight behind the Goldwater challenge turned out to be less than the senator hoped and the President feared. Although conservatives like Ronald Reagan denounced the Panama canal "give-away" and the "betrayal" of Taiwan in the same breath, they were unable—in contrast to the Panama votes—to muster an effective challenge in Congress. Leonard Woodcock's nomination as the first ambassador to the P.R.C. passed the Senate, 82–9. Approval of the Taiwan Relations Act precipitated extensive debate, but the issue was never in doubt, even though the President worried that he might have to exercise his veto against legislation which violated his commitments to the P.R.C., "therefore leaving it illegal to deal with Taiwan in any effective way."[17] Instead, the Congress contented itself with indicating normalization of relations with the P.R.C. was based "upon the expectation that the future of Taiwan will be determined by peaceful means" and directing the President to inform Congress of any threat to Taiwan's security. Approval came at the end of March, with votes of 85–4 in the Senate and 339–50 in the House.[18]

DENG XIAOPING AND THE STRATEGIC RELATIONSHIP

The speed with which normalization had been achieved represented the first of an ongoing series of victories for Brzezinski over Vance in the struggle to set China policy. Vance wanted the United States to maintain a perfect balance between the Soviet Union and the People's Republic, granting nothing to one not granted to the other, and being especially careful not to give Moscow the impression that it was threatened by new cordiality between Washington and Peking. Brzezinski believed that the whole point of the relationship with the People's Republic was to make the Soviet Union feel threatened and, therefore, inclined to be more accommodating to the United States. He wanted the P.R.C. to be favored in every possible way.

At first, the President seemed to agree with Vance. After the Secretary of State visited Camp David between Christmas and New Year's, Carter wrote in his diary that he concurred that "the most significant responsibility we have is to balance our new friendship with the PRC and our continued improvement of relations with the Soviet Union . . . As we moved toward a most-favored-nation relationship with the PRC, we must face the need to do the same thing with the Soviet Union."[19] Vance said the same thing publicly and emphatically: "There will be no tilts one way or the other, and this is an absolutely fundamental principle and a very important one that we must always keep in mind in managing our relationship with these two countries."[20]

All that Vance won was words. The substance of policy was closer to Brzezinski's preference, thanks to some extraordinarily effective diplomacy and public relations by Vice Premier Deng Xiaoping. The Chinese leader moved quickly to accept the American invitation to visit and arrived in Washington on January 28, 1979. Before leaving Peking, he told the world, through *Time* magazine, what he would say to President Carter: ". . . It has been our view all along that since the early 1970s the U.S. has been on the strategic retreat . . . We consider that the true hotbed of war is the Soviet Union, not the U.S. . . . The first characteristic of the Soviet Union is that it always adopts the attitude of bullying the soft and fearing the strong. The second characteristic of the Soviet Union is that it will go in and grab at every opportunity . . . If we really want to be able to place curbs on the polar bear, the only realistic thing for us is to unite."[21]

Those were words to cheer Brzezinski's heart. Significantly, Deng's first engagement upon arriving in Washington was a private dinner given by the Brzezinskis in their own home. The next day was devoted to talks with the President, followed by "probably the most elegant dinner given at any time during Carter's four years in the White House."[22] Carter was enchanted and recorded in his diary that Deng was "small, tough, intelligent, frank, courageous, self-assured, friendly, and it's a pleasure to negotiate with him."[23]

Deng's general message to the President was identical with his interview in *Time*. Carter would not go so far as to favor an alliance between the two countries, but the joint communiqué issued at the end of the meetings noted that the two leaders were united in opposition to "efforts by any country or group of countries to establish hegemony or domination over others."[24] The word *hegemony* was an established term used by the Chinese in their denunciation of the Soviet Union. Vance was unhappy to see the word appear in the communiqué and suggested a follow-up statement indicating equal American commitment to improving relations with the Soviet Union. "Is that another apology?" the President asked before rejecting the idea. Brzezinski savored another victory and wrote: "I was amazed that Cy would even go to the President with such a statement. I don't think it helped to further the President's confidence in his tough-mindedness . . . and I was really relieved by the President's tough-minded decision."[25]

The Soviet Union was particularly sensitive over the prospect of the sale of arms by Western nations to the P.R.C., and Brezhnev had warned both Washington and European governments that such sales would be playing with fire. Vance was able to persuade Carter that American arms sales to China would indeed be dangerously provocative, but he lost on the question of sales by the British, French, or Germans. The American position, as urged by Brzezinski and stated by Carter, was that "our allies are independent, sovereign nations, and they would resent any intrusion by us into their weapons-sales policies." The United States would not object to whatever they decided. "The Soviets need not be concerned about this," added Carter in one of those ritualistic assertions which meant exactly the opposite of what they said.[26]

Brzezinski was able to win allies within the Administration through his influence over who would and would not make the coveted trip to China. Vice President Mondale went in August 1979, and said publicly that the basic purpose of normalization was strategic. The Secretaries of Commerce, the Treasury, and Energy and the special trade representative also made junkets. But the most important was the trip of Secretary of Defense Harold Brown, following the Soviet invasion of Afghanistan. Brown's trip led to decisions in early 1980 to sell China high-technology items and dual civilian or military support material such as trucks, communications gear, and radar—all items whose export to the Soviet Union was prohibited.[27]

Vance also lost on the question of most-favored-nation status for trade with the P.R.C. "Most-favored-nation" means that a country will not be less favored in trade than any other nation; whatever concessions are granted to any other will automatically be granted to it. The Soviet Union emphatically did not have most-favored-nation status and could not acquire it as long as it prevented the free emigration of its citizens. This condition was contained in the Jackson–Vanik congressional resolution of 1974. Emigration from the People's Republic was, of course, also tightly controlled—which created a minor problem of intellectual and legal consistency. The Administration met that difficulty with a letter from the President to House Speaker Thomas P. (Tip) O'Neill noting: "We have recently had discussions with senior Chinese officials and firmly believe that Chinese statements and the marked increase in emigration reflect a policy of the Government of China favoring freer emigration." These indications, said the President, warranted a waiver of the Jackson–Vanik provisions.[28]

At the end of 1980, a cluster of agreements further improved U.S.–Chinese relations. A civil-aviation agreement provided for direct flights by airliners between the two countries; a maritime agreement opened the ports of both to the ships of the other; a textile agreement permitted China to sell more cloth and clothing in the United States; and a consular agreement increased the number of American consulates in China from two to five.[29] These ties were not part of the strategic relationship, although they nourished and were in turn nourished by it.

VIETNAM, CAMBODIA, AND CHINA

Nothing so well illustrated the movement of American Asian policy toward a strategic emphasis on containment of the Soviet Union than the awkward position adopted toward Vietnam and Cambodia. The Vietnam war ended with American withdrawal and the establishment of a single, communist Vietnamese state in 1975. Relations between Vietnam and the Ford Administration were bad. Americans believed the Vietnamese were deliberately withholding information about prisoners of war and men missing in action. The Vietnamese government believed it had been promised reconstruction aid from President Nixon and that Ford was reneging on a commitment. President Carter and his advisers decided that these problems should be addressed immediately in the context of establishing normal diplomatic relations with Hanoi—an act which would serve to heal the wounds of an unfortunate war, and would also keep Vietnam out of the Soviet camp.

The approach to Vietnam began auspiciously. Carter appointed a prestigious commission headed by Leonard Woodcock (who would soon head the liaison office in Peking) and including Senator Mike Mansfield (who would soon be ambassador to Japan). The Woodcock commission, cordially received in Hanoi, secured the return of the bodies of eleven Americans killed in the war and concluded that there were no remaining American prisoners of war in Vietnam. The commission brought back the message that the Vietnamese government was ready to move quickly toward normalization—with talks to take place in Paris.

Carter responded and talks began with Richard Holbrooke, Assistant Secretary of State for East Asia, representing the United States in Paris. The Vietnamese insisted on a huge payment from the United States, in the neighborhood of $3 billion, as reparations for damage done during the war and in fulfillment of Nixon's ambiguous promise. President Carter said no; even if an agreement had been made, Vietnam had broken its word by the final attack on South Vietnam. The talks reached a stalemate on that issue. Perhaps Hanoi blundered. The time was ripe in the spring of 1977—before the conflict between Vietnam and Cambodia tied the issue into the larger strategic relationship of the United States to the Soviet Union and the P.R.C. When Hanoi dropped its insistence on reparations in 1978, it was too late. Although sporadic conversations on political and refugee questions took place at intervals, Brzezinski was active in assuring that they led to nothing.

The Vietnamese–Cambodian war, beginning with a Vietnamese invasion at the end of 1977, put the Carter Administration in an awkward predicament. Until 1970, Cambodia had remained neutral in the Vietnam war. Prince Norodom Sihanouk had tolerated the presence of some North Vietnamese forces inside the border and even a limited amount of American bombing of those forces. The Cambodian people as a whole were not suffering. But in 1970 Sihanouk was overthrown by the right-wing General Lon Nol. Fighting then engulfed the country with the United States supporting Lon Nol against the communist Khmer Rouge, led by Pol Pot. The Khmer Rouge won in Cambodia in the same month the North Vietnamese took Saigon—April 1975. Pol Pot then imposed a sickeningly brutal reign of terror in an effort to destroy all opposition to his particular brand of communism. A million or more Cambodians were murdered or died of starvation.[30] The Ford Administration denounced Pol Pot's atrocities in the strongest terms and also had a brief armed clash with the regime when the *Mayaguez*, an American merchant ship, was seized by the Cambodians near their coast. Candidate Carter in 1976 accepted the widespread liberal criticism that Cambodia's tragedy would not have occurred except for American immorality in encouraging an extension of the Vietnam war, and the Carter Administration had no intention of recognizing Pol Pot's regime, "the worst violator of human rights in the world today," as the President called it.[31] Meanwhile, an unresolved boundary dispute between Cambodia and Vietnam intensified—with both Pol Pot and the Vietnamese government using the conflict as a way of asserting their national power and identity.

If standards of human rights alone had prevailed, the United States should have supported Vietnam. Although Hanoi's human-rights record was not good by American standards, it was humanity itself compared to the atrocities committed by Pol Pot. But the problem was not that simple. Relations between Vietnam and the People's Republic of China had deteriorated since 1975 because Hanoi was looking increasingly to the Soviet Union for economic and military aid and also because of Vietnam's expulsion of many ethnic Chinese. Since the P.R.C. saw the Soviet presence in Vietnam as a military threat, Peking supported Cambodia in the conflict with Vietnam—even though that meant backing the odious Pol Pot regime.

"What is your reading on the border clash between the Vietnamese and the Cambodians?" a reporter asked Brzezinski in January 1978.

"I find it very interesting, primarily as the first case of a proxy war between China and the Soviet Union," Brzezinski replied.[32] Given that perception, there was never any doubt in Brzezinski's mind as to where the United States should stand: quietly behind China and in opposition to Vietnam. During the remainder of 1978, the fighting escalated, relations between Hanoi and Peking grew ever worse, and the United States normalized relations with Peking. In January 1979, the Vietnamese drove Pol Pot from the capital of Pnomh Penh and installed its own regime, headed by President Heng Samrin. A test of American policy came during Deng Xiaoping's visit to Washington the same month. The Chinese leader, having asked for a specially confidential meeting with Carter, announced that China would soon attack Vietnam, as punishment for its invasion of Cambodia and its general arrogance. Deng was as good as his word. The attack began on February 17 and lasted three weeks, whereupon the Chinese declared the punishment successful and pulled out. The cost was high. Peking admitted to losing twenty thousand soldiers and estimated that Vietnam had lost fifty thousand.

The American response was verbally correct. "We are opposed to both the Vietnamese invasion of Cambodia and the Chinese invasion of Vietnam," the State Department said.[33] But again Brzezinski tilted actual policy to favor the P.R.C. and send a message to the U.S.S.R. Vance complained that American policy was pushing Vietnam into the arms of the Soviets and suggested that the United States open direct talks with Hanoi concerning the conflict with Cambodia. Brzezinski suggested that the United States ask the Chinese first, and, as expected, Peking vetoed the idea.

The remnant of the Pol Pot regime was now in hiding in the Cambodian jungle, but still sought to retain Cambodia's seat in the United Nations. Many nations were opposed. India introduced a motion to seat the Heng Samrin government. The P.R.C. and most non-communist nations were for the Pol Pot regime as a matter of principle. The United States was in a strange position. To oppose the Pol Pot regime would mean voting on the same side as Moscow, Hanoi, and Havana. Some in the United States mission to the UN argued for such a course, on the grounds of human rights. But Secretary Vance figuratively held his nose and instructed the mission to vote for the Pol Pot regime, but to state that the vote in no way indicated "support or recognition . . . or approval of its atrocious practices."[34] The motion passed 70–35, with 34 abstentions.

When Carter and Soviet President Leonid Brezhnev met in Vienna in June 1979 to sign the SALT II treaty, Carter raised the question of Soviet intentions in Vietnam. The President, moved by the cordial atmosphere of that isolated moment, said he was satisfied with Brezhnev's assurance that "there would be no establishment of Soviet bases . . . and that the . . . use of the ports and airports is of a routine nature."[35] The remark was an echo from an earlier time—soon to be obliterated by the Soviet invasion of Afghanistan. In the final year of the Carter Administration, the assessment was quite different. In March 1980, the official line from the State Department was, in the words of Assistant Secretary Holbrooke: "Soviet ships and submarines call at Danang and Cam Ranh Bay . . . A Soviet frigate made a precedent-setting call at the Khmer port of Kompong Son, thus projecting a Soviet naval presence further into Southeast Asia. Through their increased access to these facilities, the Soviets have significantly enhanced their military capabilities, not only in Southeast Asia and the Southwest Pacific but also in the Indian Ocean."[36] Strategic concerns had taken over completely from the original hope of healing some of the wounds of the Vietnam war.

A pervasive human tragedy, transcending strategic maneuvers, was the plight of millions of refugees uprooted and brutalized by war and revolution in Southeast Asia. Several hundred thousand escaped by boat from Vietnam. Many more were caught by the fighting and the devastation of the rice crops in Cambodia. The Carter Administration's response was vigorous and consistent with its emphasis on human rights. Over 400,000 Southeast Asians were admitted to the United States—opening a new chapter in the nation's immigration history. American economic aid helped resettle many more throughout Asia, and a special effort was directed at getting famine-relief supplies into Cambodia.

THE PHILIPPINES AND INDONESIA

During the height of the Vietnam war, it was commonplace for supporters of the American military effort to say that if Vietnam fell to communism, all the other nations of Southeast Asia would follow like toppling dominoes. Five of those nations— Thailand, the Philippines, Singapore, Malaysia, and Indonesia— in 1967 banded together in the Association of South East Asian Nations (ASEAN) to coordinate their policies and work together against this possibility. They were encouraged and assisted by the United States. By the time the Carter Administration took office, ASEAN was thriving.

"The dominoes did not fall," said Under Secretary of State David Newsom in 1978. His remark reflected the desire of the Carter Administration to continue backing ASEAN as a group and its nation members individually. In 1977 and 1978, the primary American emphasis was on the importance of American economic ties with the ASEAN nations. In 1979 and 1980, the emphasis shifted to defense. One consequence of the ASEAN policy was to minimize or even overlook human-rights violations committed by ASEAN members—another example of power having precedence over moral principle.

In 1972, Ferdinand Marcos, president of the Philippines, placed the country under martial law and suspended free elections. Scores of Marcos's political critics were arrested and held for years without trial. Freedom of speech and the press was severely curtailed. Foreign journalists and missionaries who dared criticize the regime were deported. At the same time, the Philippines continued to receive substantial military and some economic aid from the United States. The country, in short, appeared to be an ideal target for the application of a policy based on commitment to human rights. The abuses of the Marcos regime were notorious and the leverage was at hand.

But President Marcos had his own powerful lever—the United States' need to maintain its huge air base at Clark Field and its naval base at Subic Bay—and he used the lever both in private negotiations and in public statements.[37] These bases had been established when the Philippines was still an American colony. They were lost to Japan during the Second World War, recaptured, and then reconstituted after Philippine independence in 1946 under mutual-defense agreements. The Carter Administration inherited a stalemated negotiation for the renewal of the bases agreement. As the negotiations progressed, the State Department and President Carter never concealed American priorities: the strategic necessity of retaining the bases would never be jeopardized by the application of too much pressure on Marcos to improve his record on human rights. Occasionally, Washington issued a polite tap on the wrist, but that was invariably followed by public affirmation of the Philippine's "strategic importance, not only for our own country but also for nations friendly to the United States in the region." The possibility of cutting back on non-military aid as a mark of displeasure was dismissed by the State Department as counterproductive. As Holbrooke testified before Congress in 1977, the rural poor were the beneficiaries of that aid and they would be hurt.[38]

In September 1977, Holbrooke went to Manila to work on details of the pending agreement. In the spring of 1978, Marcos received some high-level stroking from Vice President Mondale. In January 1979, the two governments signed the agreement. The Philippines received aid worth $500 million, primarily in the form of modern weapons, and the United States retained unhampered use of the bases for another five years. This victory of military strategy over human rights was not universally acclaimed. Marcos's critics in the Philippines and the United States accused Carter of supporting a cruel dictator. And Marcos complained that any comment at all from Washington on his human-rights record was interference in the internal affairs of his nation. President Carter squirmed. He claimed, with a touch of exaggeration, that official representations on human rights had been strong to the point of straining relations with the Philippine government;

but as a former Navy man and current Commander in Chief he knew the United States must retain the right to keep forces in the Philippines. Therefore, "I don't think that our displeasure with [President Marcos's failure in] meeting American-type standards on human rights ought to interfere."[39] Congress, after some sputters of dissent from human-rights advocates, concurred.

Indonesia, although the world's fifth most populous nation, received much less attention than the Philippines. The Suharto regime still held thousands of political prisoners jailed during the civil war against the communists in 1965. The United States expressed mild concern over the number of prisoners, but praised the government for releasing some of them. A far more tragic violation of human rights, however, involved Indonesia's war against the people of East Timor. This affair received almost no coverage in the American press and goes unmentioned in the memoirs of Carter, Vance, or Brzezinski. It represented, nevertheless, a clear case of the conflict between moral concerns and political power.

In colonial times, the three-hundred-mile-long island of Timor was divided between the Dutch and the Portuguese. The Dutch western portion became part of the new nation of Indonesia in 1948. The Portuguese colony remained Portuguese until 1974. Then, at the same time that they were pulling out of Africa, the Portuguese left, virtually without warning and with no provision for the self-determination of the 700,000 people. Two factions began to fight and Indonesia intervened in order to annex the area and squash those favoring independence. Using American weapons, the Indonesian Army carried out its slaughter, while refusing permission to any outsiders to visit the island. A few voices cried out, and some human-rights activists in the United States took up the cause. The Ford Administration did nothing. General Brent Scowcroft, Ford's National Security Adviser, recalled afterwards: "We really had no reasonable options . . . It made no sense to antagonize the Indonesians . . . East Timor is not a viable entity."[40]

Here was an opportunity for Carter to contrast his approach to that of his predecessor, but he never mentioned Indonesia or East Timor during the campaign in 1976. In 1977, low-level officials were left to reply to criticism that the human rights of the people of East Timor were being violated. We admit, said a deputy legal adviser testifying before a congressional sub-committee, that we have no evidence that the annexation of East Timor by Indonesia has been consistent with the right of the people for self-determination; but we have and will continue to accept a fait accompli—to do otherwise simply "would not serve our best interests in light of the importance of our relations with Indonesia."[41] Indonesia's military occupation of East Timor continued; famine comparable to that experienced in Cambodia descended on the people; but the United States did nothing to offend a staunch member of ASEAN.

KOREA: WITHDRAWING A WITHDRAWAL

For candidate Jimmy Carter during the 1976 campaign, the American position in South Korea was a convenient example of two wrongs which he would correct: the excessive reliance on American armed forces and complicity with a morally repugnant regime. He promised, if elected, to withdraw American ground forces from Korea and even suggested that the commitment to Korean security should be reconsidered in the light of President Park Chung Hee's "repugnant" oppression of his internal political critics. A scandal in 1976 involving a Korean attempt to bribe American members of Congress, dubbed "Koreagate" by the press, increased the temptation to criticize Park's government.

Secretary of State Vance shared the President's distaste for Park. As Lyndon Johnson's special emissary at the time of the *Pueblo* crisis of 1968, he had had instructions which included the terse command "to do what is necessary to stop Park from invading North Korea."[42] Vance considered North Korean President Kim Il Sung equally dangerous. Either headstrong leader could provoke another war. "Korea remains a trouble spot which can explode at any moment," he told Carter in October 1976. He recommended that the United States try to set up an international conference to settle Korea's long-term political problems. But he doubted that there would be much progress while Park and Kim Il Sung remained in office. Vance had serious doubts about the wisdom of withdrawing American ground troops in the immediate future—"this issue must be addressed with great care because of the way the rest of the world will perceive it."[43] He approved of raising the issue of human rights, but he did not believe the sanction of cutting back on military or economic aid should be applied.

President Carter did not follow Vance's advice on troop withdrawal. In his first press conference, on January 26, 1977, he announced that the United States would carry through with his election promise to withdraw American troops. There was consternation in Seoul. Prime Minister Takeo Fukuda of Japan was also strongly opposed, as he told Vice President Walter Mondale, then in Tokyo on a tour of touching bases with principal allies. Mondale himself was privately opposed to the withdrawal, but his instructions were to tell Fukuda that the decision was a fait accompli.

The storm over the decision intensified when Major General John Singlaub, chief of staff of U.S. forces in Korea, said publicly that withdrawal would lead to war. Carter, playing Truman to Singlaub's MacArthur, reprimanded the general and recalled him from Korea. Singlaub's statement, said Carter, was "an invitation to the world to expect an inevitable war." Carter said there was little danger. The overall American commitment remained unchanged. He added that improved relations between the United States and the Soviet Union and the People's Republic of China made for stability. And South Korea was quite capable of defending itself against North Korea.[44] As a damage-control measure, Secretary of Defense Harold Brown and Under Secretary of

State Philip Habib were sent to Korea and Japan to explain the President's decision. They made no converts.

The only high American official to support Carter was, somewhat incongruously, Zbigniew Brzezinski. Soon Carter began to bend. In April 1978, he agreed to postpone the withdrawals. In 1979, the CIA said that its earlier estimate of North Korean strength was thirty percent too low. Carter felt, correctly, that "his hand was being forced" by those opposed to withdrawal. He visited President Park in Seoul on July 1, 1979 and, after listening to a tirade on the folly of withdrawal, almost reaffirmed the decision. But on July 20, at a time when he was under fire for general weakness in meeting communist expansion and was trying to win Senate approval of the SALT II treaty, he withdrew the withdrawal. The American ground troops would remain.[45]

Three months later, President Park was assassinated by the chief of his own central intelligence agency. Secretary Vance flew to Seoul for the funeral and reaffirmed the American commitment to South Korea's security. Park's successor, Chun Doo Hwan, soon proved to be as willing to trample on human rights as Park had been. In 1980, he put the country under martial law and used murderous military force in suppressing rioting students in Kwangju. In September, a military tribunal sentenced Kim Dae Jung, the country's leading liberal politician, to death. But 1980 was not 1977. American hostages were in Teheran. The Soviet Army was in Afghanistan. The thrust of the Carter Administration was now military strength and a return to containment. Strong protests against violations of human rights were out of fashion. And so the United States issued the mildest expressions of concern. As one observer noted at the time, the Administration "was prompted by the belief that security precautions had to remain paramount and that any attempt to apply more overt pressure might backfire . . . [This] convinced Chun that he did not have to worry about any serious consequences if he largely ignored American feelings."[46]

JAPAN: TRADE AND SECURITY

Japan in the 1970s was the largest overseas trading partner of the United States, but she sold far more than she bought. American labor believed that this imbalance cost jobs—in steel, automobiles, electronics. American growers of oranges, tobacco, beef, and forest products believed they were unfairly discriminated against in the Japanese market. This situation existed before the Carter Administration came into office and would prevail long after it left. The problem was largely a matter of American inefficiency and high costs of manufacturing; nevertheless, the issue dominated Japanese–American relations.[47] President Carter and his advisers, as much as they would have preferred to concentrate on strategic-political issues, had no choice but to badger the Japanese as hard as possible to remedy the trade imbalance by restraining exports to the United States and taking in more imports.

President Carter's badger-in-chief was a notably skillful politician and negotiator, former national chairman of the Democratic Party, Robert Strauss of Texas. For two years (until he changed jobs and became a special envoy dealing with the Palestinian autonomy talks in mid-1979), Strauss worked simultaneously to get the Japanese to make concessions and to persuade American economic groups that Japan was not the enemy. He was acclaimed a genius at the job. The Japanese did respond constructively, but the trade imbalance remained.[48] Another troublesome issue was a conflict between Japan's desire to develop nuclear power plants at the fastest possible rate and the Carter Administration's non-proliferation policies, which impeded Japan from acquiring all the technology and materials she desired. This highly technical question was negotiated to the reasonable satisfaction of both sides.

On the strategic-political level, Japanese and American leaders conferred often and with relatively little friction—except for Japanese dismay over the prospective American troop withdrawal from Korea. Japanese Prime Minister Takeo Fukuda and his successor, Masayoshi Ohira, visited President Carter four times. Carter made his own official visit to Japan in June 1979, just before the Tokyo economic summit conference. Vance, Brzezinski, Mondale, and Secretary of Defense Harold Brown also visited Japan and worked at keeping the relationship in good repair. The American normalization of relations with the People's Republic of China was welcomed by Japan, and Japan's rising level of economic aid and technical assistance extended to other countries, especially the ASEAN states, was welcomed by the United States.

But in 1980, with the United States suffering the frustration of the hostage crisis in Iran and feeling the burden of trying to marshal enough military power to meet the perception of a more dangerous Soviet threat, the relationship began to fray over Japan's low military spending. Japan's post-war constitution, drafted under American supervision during the occupation, renounced the use of war as an instrument of national policy and barred Japan from developing offensive armed forces. Japan did have a self-defense force—ground troops for use in Japan only, fighter planes, and a light navy of destroyers and patrol boats. Japan also paid some of the cost of maintaining American forces in Japan. Her defense budget in 1980 was $10 billion, the equivalent of $82 per capita, compared to $550 per capita paid by Americans for defense.

The low cost of defense was politically very popular in Japan, and Americans appreciated that it was unwise to press too hard for increases. In 1977 and 1978, both sides agreed that Japan's contribution to security in Asia should be primarily in the form of economic aid. But in 1979 and 1980 the Americans changed their tune and told the Japanese they must do more on the military side. In late December, the Japanese government announced its proposed defense spending for the next year. The increase was minuscule. Secretary of Defense Brown lost his temper and excoriated Japan in words seldom addressed to an ally:

Japan is as exposed to the steady increases in Soviet military power as is NATO, Japan is even more dependent than most of the other industrialized democracies on oil from the Persian Gulf, and Japan is an economic power which could certainly afford much larger defense expenditures . . . [but] the increase contemplated in the December 29 budget proposal is so modest that it conveys a sense of complacency which simply is not justified by the facts. It falls seriously short, whether measured by the security situation, by the discussions held between senior officials of our two governments over the last year, or by considerations of equitable burden-sharing.[49]

So ended the Administration's dealings with Japan. The sour note was fortunately not representative of the four years just past. But it was an accurate measure of the transformation of policy from the 1977 emphasis on healing wounds, seeking peaceful settlement of remaining problems, and emphasizing human rights, to the dominant concern in 1980 with building military strength against the Soviet Union; in short, with returning to containment in Asia as everywhere else around the world.

__5__

Panama Success and Latin American Failure

It has long been a ritual of American foreign policy for an incoming President to proclaim his dedication to a new, more sensitive and understanding approach to Latin America. In Jimmy Carter's case, however, there was considerable substance and sincerity behind the rhetoric. During the Presidential campaign, he said "we should get away permanently from an attitude of paternalism or punishment or retribution when some of the South Americans don't yield to our persuasion."[1] For those familiar with recent history, this was a promise that the CIA would not overthrow regimes as in Guatemala in 1954 or arrange invasions as at the Bay of Pigs in 1961; the Marines would not land to force a country to follow the preferred American course as in the Dominican Republic in 1965; and the United States would not use covert power to destabilize a nation and assist an authoritarian regime to oppress the people as in Chile in 1973.

Secretary of State Vance and National Security Adviser Brzezinski shared and encouraged the President's attitude and had no deep disagreements with each other about Latin America. At an early policy-review session on Latin America, Brzezinski made the valid point that Americans might see the Monroe Doctrine as "a selfless U.S. contribution to hemispheric security; but to most of our neighbors to the south it was an expression of presumptuous U.S. paternalism."[2] Members of the Administration never used the phrase Monroe Doctrine in public.

President Carter had a personal interest in Latin America. Spanish was the one foreign language he had studied. He and his wife had traveled to Mexico and Brazil. He saw in Latin America a special opportunity to apply the philosophy of repentance and reform—admitting past mistakes, making the region a showcase for the human-rights policy, seeking to prevent the proliferation of technology which could lead to the production of nuclear weapons, and reducing the level of conventional-arms transfers. There were, however, unavoidable contradictions between his proclaimed desire to treat each Latin American country individually and his wish to abandon paternalism, on the one hand, and, on the other, the heavy-handed application of the global policy of non-proliferation and the readiness to reward or punish nations according to their record on human rights.

The President and his advisers in 1977 did not see Soviet involvement in Latin America as large or purposeful enough to warrant concern. They hoped, in fact, to reduce that involvement further by repairing relations with Castro's Cuba, the one Soviet client in the hemisphere, perhaps even establishing normal diplomatic relations. Their highest priority, however, was to conclude an agreement with Panama which would restore Panamanian sovereignty over the Canal Zone. They saw the Panamanian settlement as the foundation for a new day in the hemisphere, a demonstration that the United States had truly abandoned outmoded colonialism, and an achievement which would earn so much goodwill that other Latin American problems could be readily solved. The Panama agreement was reached. It was a major, genuine achievement, but was not the universal solvent of other difficulties which the Carter Administration had hoped. Above all, it had no impact on the spreading political unrest and military violence in Nicaragua and El Salvador—situations which would draw the Carter Administration and its successor into painful and controversial entanglement.

THE PANAMA CANAL

President Carter decided that a settlement with Panama over the future status of the canal would be the Administration's first objective in Latin America. The choice made sense for four reasons. First, negotiations had been going on sporadically for a dozen years and were at a dangerous stalemate. Vance shared the widespread opinion that Panama, if denied a settlement, might precipitate more violence and even destroy the canal. Second, the issue was bipartisan. Democratic and Republican Presidents (Johnson, Nixon, and Ford) had been committed to a settlement, in principle. Their negotiators had done much of the necessary groundwork, but larger diversions (the Vietnam war, Watergate, and Ford's fear of being outflanked on the right) had blocked fulfillment. Third, Carter believed, as already noted, that successful negotiations would have a positive impact throughout Latin America, marking an auspicious beginning for a new era. And fourth, a settlement would be, in effect, a gracious apology by the United States for past wrongdoing and thus was compatible with Carter's emphasis on the need for a moral cleansing of foreign policy.

The one argument against tackling the Panama question was the certainty of a fight with vociferous right-wingers and self-styled patriots who would follow Ronald Reagan in claiming that any relaxation of American control over the canal would be craven. If opponents of a settlement included one-third plus one of the Senate, no treaty could be approved. President Carter had discovered during his campaign in 1976 that the issue was highly emotional. For many Americans, the canal was like the flag itself, a symbol of national identity and pride. Giving it up was unthinkable. As a candidate, he had catered to this mood by saying: "I would not be in favor of relinquishing actual control of the Panama Canal or its use to any other nation, including Panama."[3] But as President he quickly learned that permanent retention of American control and a settlement were absolutely incompatible.

Panamanian discontent over the American presence in a broad corridor through the middle of the country had been building since 1903, when the United States imposed a treaty giving itself near-sovereignty in perpetuity over the canal and the surrounding zone. The 1903 treaty provided a small, ungenerous payment to Panama.[4] Since 1964, a year of riots and loss of life in the zone, the discontent had been acute. In 1965, President Lyndon Johnson ordered negotiations to begin. Presidents Nixon and Ford continued them. In 1973, General Omar Torrijos, the shrewd head of the Panamanian government, scored an international political victory by persuading the United Nations Security Council to meet in Panama City. Torrijos then maneuvered the United States into vetoing a resolution calling for fulfillment of Panama's "just demands."[5] In 1974, Secretary of State Henry Kissinger and Panamanian Foreign Minister Juan Antonio Tack agreed to a set of principles. The 1903 treaty would be abrogated and a new treaty would be negotiated with a fixed termination date and substantially increased revenues for Panama. The Canal Zone would be returned and Panama would assume full responsibility for the operation of the canal at a date to be determined. And Panama would grant to the United States the right to protect the canal.[6]

Domestic politics in both countries then produced an impasse. Panamanian nationalists wanted enormous cash payments from the United States, a treaty of very short duration, and the complete renunciation by the United States of every special privilege. In the United States, opponents of concessions to Panama rallied behind Ronald Reagan and his effort to win the Republican nomination from Gerald Ford. In 1976, Reagan made the canal a central issue. "We bought it, we paid for it, it's ours and we're going to keep it" was a rousing line which Reagan used in speech after speech.[7]

Also in 1976, the prestigious commission on Latin America chaired by Sol Linowitz, former chairman of Xerox, called the canal the most serious problem facing the United States in the region.[8] Robert Pastor, the young executive director of the Li-nowitz commission, in January 1977 joined Brzezinski's National Security Council staff as the Latin American expert. Seven Latin American presidents also warned Carter of potential trouble, in a letter sent on the eve of his inauguration.[9] The Administration had no difficulty deciding to move immediately. Vance persuaded Linowitz to join veteran diplomat Ellsworth Bunker as co-ne-gotiator, and ten days after the inauguration the Secretary of State officially reaffirmed American commitment to the Kissinger–Tack principles as the basis for negotiation.[10]

William Jorden, the United States ambassador to Panama and an important participant, has described the diplomacy of the canal settlement in fascinating detail. The substantive problems of how much money Panama would receive ($10 million a year, plus up to $10 million more from surplus operating revenues), how long the United States would retain some control over the canal (until noon, Panama time, December 31, 1999), and precisely what words would be used to describe rights the United States would retain once Panama gained full control were soluble— although only with great patience and through enormous effort by diplomats on both sides. Progress was facilitated by the wise decision to draft two treaties—one lasting until 1999 and providing for mixed U.S.–Panamanian operation of the canal; and the sec-ond, called the Neutrality Treaty, defining American rights to defend the canal thereafter. The treaties were completed on Au-gust 29 and signed in Washington at an elaborate ceremony on September 7, 1977. Brzezinski accurately described the Presi-dent's state of mind: "For him, this occasion represented the ideal fusion of morality and politics; he was doing something good for peace, responding to the passionate desires of a small nation, and yet helping the long-range U.S. national interest."[11] But there was no time for euphoria; ahead lay the battle for approval—by a national vote in Panama, and by two-thirds of the United States Senate, required for ratification.

An ultimately insoluble problem involved conflicting domestic political expectations and perceptions in both countries. General Torrijos had to present the settlement to the Panamanian people as something which would restore full, completely unfettered Panamanian sovereignty and would end forever the possibility of American intervention in Panama's internal affairs. But President Carter had to convince the Senate and the American public that the United States had the right and power to defend the canal for all time and to keep it open in all circumstances. What if an internal Panamanian situation threatened closure? Could the United States intervene?

At a meeting with Senate majority leader Robert Byrd and others, Brzezinski was asked what would happen if Panama should simply declare the canal "closed for repairs." Brzezinski's answer was that, "according to the provisions of the Neutrality Treaty, we will move in and close down the Panamanian government for repairs." Brzezinski in his memoirs took credit for winning crucial support for the treaties with this remark.[12] Had those words leaked to the press, Brzezinski could then have taken credit for assuring Panamanian rejection of the settlement, and the resulting dire consequences.

Carter and Torrijos tried to close the wide gap between the two perceptions by issuing a formal joint statement on October 14 that the Neutrality Treaty gave both countries the right to keep the canal open against "any" threat—but: "This does not mean, nor shall it be interpreted as a right of intervention of the United States in the internal affairs of Panama."[13] The contradiction remained as sharp as ever.

During the next six months, President Carter, Secretary Vance, and dozens of other officials devoted more time to explaining the treaties to the public and to persuading senators to vote favorably than to any other issue of foreign policy. There were hundreds of hours of testimony before Congress, uncounted speeches by everyone from the President to the most lowly State Department official, tons of pamphlets. Despite this effort, the American people remained opposed to the settlement. On that, all public-opinion polls agreed.[14] What counted, however, was the favorable opinion of sixty-seven senators. Carter kept a loose-leaf notebook on his desk with a page for every senator, and recorded there his tireless phone calls, personal notes, and arm twisting. A near-fatal threat came from the insistence of Senator Dennis DeConcini, a first-term Democrat from Arizona, that the Neutrality Treaty be amended to state the right of the United States to take whatever action, including the use of force, to keep the canal open. DeConcini was persuaded to accept a statement to this effect as a reservation (not requiring Panamanian acceptance, as would an amendment) to the Senate resolution of approval. But even the reservation came close to provoking General Torrijos to abandon the whole effort. In March and April 1978, the Senate approved the treaties by identical 68–32 votes. A shift of only two votes would have meant defeat. General Torrijos said afterwards that he would have ordered the canal destroyed had the vote gone the other way.[15]

Ordinarily, a President grows stronger by winning a hard political fight. But Carter's narrow triumph, while it prevented possible disaster abroad, gained him no credit at home. Ronald Reagan, his most likely challenger in 1980, stayed on the attack: "To the Communists and those others who are hostile to our country," he wrote in February 1979, "President Carter and his supporters in the Congress seem like Santa Claus. They have given the Panama Canal away, abandoned Taiwan to the Red Chinese, and they're negotiating a SALT II treaty that could very well make this nation NUMBER TWO."[16] As Carter himself sadly noted, of twenty pro-treaties senators scheduled for reelection in 1978, six did not choose to run, seven won, but seven were defeated. In 1980, another supporting senator was defeated, "plus one President."[17]

OVERTURE TO FIDEL CASTRO'S CUBA

A second specific objective of the Carter Administration in Latin America was the establishment of normal diplomatic relations with Cuba. This gesture, like the Panama settlement, was designed to heal old wounds and signal the new American approach to the hemisphere. The overture to Cuba failed—but for reasons connected more with events outside the hemisphere than with specific bilateral Cuban–American problems.

Fidel Castro came to power in 1959 after overthrowing the corrupt Fulgencio Batista, the epitome of the kind of dictator long embraced by the United States because of his ostentatious anticommunism. Castro's relations with the United States deteriorated rapidly because of his leftist political leanings. The Eisenhower Administration broke off diplomatic relations and barred Cuban sugar from the American market. The Kennedy Administration sought to remove Castro through the ill-fated Bay of Pigs invasion and assassination attempts—before pledging in 1962, as a condition of the removal of nuclear missiles from Cuba by the Soviet Union, not to attack the island. Relations remained severed and cold for the next decade and a half.

Cyrus Vance, in his long October 1976 memorandum to Carter, said he believed "the time has come to move away from our past policy of isolation. Our boycott has proved ineffective, and there has been a decline of Cuba's export of revolution in the region." If the United States lifted the embargo on food and medicine, Vance suggested, Cuba might show some restraint in Africa.[18] Carter, however, was cautious while campaigning for election. He said he was opposed to normalization in the immediate future and he condemned the presence of Cuban troops in Angola.[19] There were no votes to be won, and many to be lost, by indicating friendliness toward Castro.

But, after the inauguration, Carter reversed himself and said it was appropriate to seek normal relations with all countries, including Cuba. He also removed restrictions on travel to Cuba by Americans. In March 1977, the two countries began discussions on the location of their common maritime boundary and, in April, signed a fisheries agreement. In May, they agreed to open "interest sections" in third-country embassies in each capital. "This is a step well short of diplomatic relations," said the Assistant Secretary of State for Inter-American Affairs, "but one that will facilitate communications between the two governments and make it easier for both to address the many problems we face."[20]

Castro, in turn, indicated he welcomed improved relations. In a five-hour interview with Barbara Walters of ABC News on May 19, 1977 (portions were broadcast on June 9 as a special entitled "Fidel Castro Speaks"), he noted and praised the suspension of spy-plane overflights of Cuba and said he would release some American prisoners from jail in Cuba. He said that normal relations could not be established overnight, perhaps not until Carter's second term, but "the first steps have been taken. And I consider them positive."[21]

But the accomplishments of 1977 were not sustained. The United States rejected Castro's contention that Cuban troops were in Angola at the request of the Angolan government, for the purpose of defending the country against South Africa, and in early 1978 condemned him for sending troops to Ethiopia after that country had been invaded by Somalia. In May 1978, President Carter and Brzezinski accused the Cubans of responsibility for the invasion of the Shaba region of Zaire by rebels based in Angola—although hard evidence for the accusation was lacking.

A brief crisis erupted in October 1978, when a memorandum by Secretary of Defense Harold Brown concerning the delivery of Soviet MIG 23 planes to Cuba leaked to Rowland Evans and Robert Novak, two conservative journalists, who suggested that the presence of the planes violated the 1962 Soviet agreement not to place offensive weapons in Cuba. The Carter Administration studied the planes' characteristics and raised the question with the Soviets—and then concluded that no violation had occurred.[22]

A far more serious crisis occurred in the summer of 1979, when the Senate was considering the SALT II treaty. After the MIG 23 affair, Brzezinski ordered more intense intelligence surveillance of Cuba. This activity soon produced a report that the Soviets had recently introduced a combat brigade into Cuba. Actually, the brigade had been there since 1962, but the erroneous report caused consternation, seriously damaged the possibility of the President's winning Senate approval for SALT II, and damaged Soviet–American relations. The 1977 hope of a rapprochement with Castro, severely damaged by the continued presence of Cuban troops in Africa, was now dead.[23]

NO MIDDLE WAY FOR NICARAGUA

The relationship between the United States and the Central American country of Nicaragua followed the pattern, so fervently deplored by President Carter at the beginning of his Administration, of embracing "any dictator who joined us" in opposing communism. Ever since the 1850s, when an American adventurer named William Walker had briefly ruled the country, the United States had exercised a dominant influence—sometimes through control of finances, sometimes with the Marines, sometimes with military aid. The official American purpose in the twentieth century was "peacekeeping." In practice, that translated into excluding the left from political power. One of those excluded was a guerrilla leader named Augusto Sandino. In 1934, Sandino was murdered by order of the head of the national guard, Anastasio Somoza, and in death left a name which would be powerfully evoked in another generation.[24]

Somoza became president in 1936 and remained in power until assassinated in 1956. He was succeeded by his son, also named Anastasio. The Somozas, father and son, were very acceptable to Washington. They proclaimed their anti-communism loudly and looked to the United States for political support and military equipment—duly received. In 1972, an earthquake devastated Nicaragua, especially the capital city of Managua. The United States and other nations were generous with relief—but Somoza skimmed off much of the money for his personal advantage, greedily muscling out many businesses which were trying to recover. Soon the Somoza gang owned most of the profitable enterprises in the country. The president's excesses stimulated the opposition. The most radical element called themselves Sandinistas, after the murdered martyr of 1934. And the Church, business, teachers—almost everyone but a small sycophantic circle around the president—agreed that Somoza was an abomination.

During the first year of the Carter Administration, Nicaragua plunged into civil war. Somoza's National Guard responded to guerrilla attacks with the indiscriminate bombing of villages, mass arrests, torture, and executions. The Administration's comments, however, put more emphasis on deploring Cuban support for the Sandinistas than on Somoza's violations of human rights. It took prodding by liberals in Congress, led by Congressman Ed Koch of New York and Senator Edward Kennedy of Massachusetts, to get the Administration to hold back on some economic aid. This was a very small slap on the wrist for Somoza's atrocities. But aid was released to him almost immediately when Somoza made a cosmetic gesture toward easing repression.[25]

The year 1978 opened with the murder of Pedro Joaquín Chamorro, the liberal editor of Nicaragua's leading newspaper and a critic of Somoza. The murder served to rally business opposition and provoked a general strike against Somoza—who responded with more repression. American policy was a grim comedy of mixed signals: diplomatic pressure to curb atrocities and accept mediation of the civil war; withholding and restoring aid; and personal congratulations from President Carter to Somoza over insubstantial concessions. Despite his theoretically absolute devotion to human rights, Carter continued to worry primarily about communism. In a June 1978 discussion with the presidents of Panama, Mexico, Costa Rica, Colombia, and Venezuela, the talk was about human rights, but also "about how to constrain Cuban and other communist intrusion in the internal affairs of Caribbean and Latin American countries, and how to encourage freedom and democracy in Nicaragua and minimize bloodshed there."[26] This meant discovering a way to turn Somoza into a humanitarian democrat or else finding an alternative untainted by communist support. Such an objective, wrote one American commentator, was virtually unattainable, because "the minimal institutions of a democratic political order do not come easily into being in a country ruled for more than forty years by one family, the sword, the dollar, and every imaginable form of graft and venality."[27]

Somoza, in any event, would not and could not introduce democracy and remain in power. In January 1979, he refused a proposal for elections to be supervised by the Organization of American States (OAS) and thereby ended a long American effort at mediation. The Sandinistas, it should be noted, also rejected mediation as "treason." The people of Nicaragua, said Sandinista leader Daniel Ortega, have too much awareness of history ever to put their faith in the United States.[28] With the failure of mediation, the United States took some slightly stronger action— terminating military aid, continuing only those economic-aid projects "aimed at the basic needs of the poor," withdrawing Peace Corps volunteers, and reducing the number of officials in the Managua embassy.[29]

The Sandinistas opened a major military offensive in June. During the fighting, an American journalist was murdered by one of Somoza's soldiers. He was ordered to lie on his face on the ground, then was shot in the back of the head. The scene was seen on television by millions of Americans who previously had only the vaguest awareness of what was happening in Nicaragua.[30]

Now that it was clear that Somoza would soon be forced out, the United States launched a high-level effort to find an alternative to the Sandinistas. Secretary of State Vance warned the OAS foreign ministers assembled in Washington on June 21, 1979, of "mounting evidence of involvement by Cuba and others in the internal problems of Nicaragua. This involvement may transform these internal problems into international and ideological issues, making it increasingly difficult to arrive at a peaceful solution." Then Vance presented the American plan:

Formation of an interim government of national reconciliation acceptable to all major elements of the society;

The dispatch by this meeting of a special delegation to Nicaragua;

A cease-fire;

An OAS peacekeeping presence to help establish a climate of peace and security and to assist the interim government in establishing its authority and beginning the task of reconstruction; and

A major international relief and reconstruction effort.[31]

The OAS peacekeeping force was the crux. Not a single other American nation supported it, and the Vance plan died the moment it was presented. Neither the Administration nor the United States Congress was prepared to send a purely American "peacekeeping" force to do the job, not while memories of Vietnam still lingered.

Somoza resigned on July 19 and fled the country (eventually ending up in Paraguay, where he was assassinated in September 1980, unmourned and unnoticed). The Sandinistas took Managua, and the National Guard surrendered. The United States then decided to work with the new junta, controlled by the Sandinistas but including some non-radical opponents of Somoza. Diplomatic relations were established on July 24 and the United States sent emergency food and medical aid. For the remaining eighteen months of the Administration, while Washington was preoccupied with events in Iran and Afghanistan, Nicaragua received little attention. American policy was, in President Carter's words, "to maintain our ties with Nicaragua, to keep it from turning to Cuba and the Soviet Union."[32] The Sandinistas had their own agenda. Pleasing the United States was not on the list. They followed a Cuban model of politics, accepted Cuban advisers, alienated many Nicaraguans who had once cooperated with them, and helped set the stage for the limited covert war which the United States would initiate in the Reagan Administration.[33]

The Carter Administration, by trying to find a middle way between Somoza and the Sandinistas, incurred the criticism of both sides in Nicaragua and of the right and the left in the United States. To the dismay of American liberals, Nicaraguan policy was dominated by Cold War considerations more than by the protection of human rights. After the Sandinista victory, the Carter Administration accepted what it was unable to prevent and extended economic aid. And yet, to critics on the right in the United States, the episode was another defeat, another consequence of weakness and an ill-advised human-rights policy. Jeane Kirkpatrick, for example, accused the Carter Administration of bringing down both the Shah of Iran and Somoza, staunch anti-communists and friends of the United States. She wrote that "the American effort to impose liberalization and democratization on a government confronted with violent internal opposition not only failed but actually assisted the coming to power of new regimes in which ordinary people enjoy fewer freedoms and less personal security than under the previous autocracy—regimes, moreover, hostile to American interests and policies."[34]

DEATH IN EL SALVADOR

The small, densely populated country of El Salvador, on the Pacific coast of Central America, had never attracted attention from the United States comparable to Nicaragua. Since 1932, El Salvador had been governed by an alliance of reactionary landowners and the military—an alliance which mouthed the rhetoric of anti-communism while denying democracy and using force to crush dissent.[35]

Here was a textbook case for the application of foreign policy based on human rights. Any hope that El Salvador might return to democracy was dashed in February 1977 with the fraudulent election of General Carlos Humberto Romero as president. In the same month, government troops fired on a crowd of demonstrators, killing an undetermined number. As in the case of Nicaragua, Congress prodded the Carter Administration by questioning the wisdom of sending military aid to such a regime. The Administration did respond by blocking an Inter-American Bank loan to El Salvador. Meanwhile, the El Salvador government, offended by American criticism, refused military aid before it could be denied. In August, Patricia Derian, Assistant Secretary of State for Human Rights, investigated the situation firsthand. But at the same time Terence Todman, Assistant Secretary for Inter-American Affairs, signaled to Romero and others like him that the United States understood the "cruel dilemma between a government's responsibility to combat terrorism, anarchy and violence, and its obligation to avoid applying any means which violate human rights." As a gesture to American concern, President Romero suspended martial law and the United States restored economic aid.[36]

But two months later Romero enacted legislation making criticism of the government a crime; in effect, suspending all civil rights. At the same time, right-wing terrorist groups—the feared "death squads"—became more active. In October 1979, there was a brief moment of rejoicing for American diplomats. Some younger, seemingly more liberal officers overthrew General Romero and established a junta with moderate civilians among the membership. Deputy Secretary of State Warren Christopher proclaimed: "El Salvador has a new government pledged to open the political system, to pursue urgently needed economic reforms, and to respect human rights."[37]

The junta proved powerless to end the killings. Its land-reform program, encouraged by the United States, was blocked by the far right. The death squads continued unchecked and through their brutality may have created more implacable revolutionaries than they killed. Then, on March 24, 1980, the Archbishop of El Salvador, Oscar Arnulfo Romero, was murdered while celebrating mass in his cathedral. Death was the price he paid for daring to speak out against the government and the right. He was one of an estimated nine thousand to die in political violence during 1980 at the hands of both the right and the left. [38]

By 1980, El Salvador had become the most difficult issue in U.S. relations with Latin America. But in the year of Afghanistan, the captivity of the hostages in Iran, and President Carter's battle for reelection, that said little about El Salvador's priority in foreign policy as a whole. The President, the Secretary of State, and the National Security Adviser had no time for El Salvador. (Neither Vance nor Brzezinski deal with El Salvador in their memoirs.) The United States muddled along—extending aid with each sign of hope and restricting it in response to new atrocities. Within the State Department, the human-rights advocates struggled, and seemed to be losing, with those who put first emphasis on suppressing terrorism. One idea considered by the latter group was to provide training for the Salvadoran army in "clean counterinsurgency," in preference to the dirty, uncontrolled terror of the right-wing death squads. [39]

The murder in December 1980 of four American Catholic missionaries, three nuns and a lay woman worker, by Salvadoran soldiers demanded high-level attention. President Carter suspended military aid once again and sent a special mission headed by William D. Rogers, former Under Secretary of State in the Ford Administration, to investigate and report. The junta promised it would spare no effort to find the murderers and bring them to justice. But, on returning to Washington after a three-day visit, the Rogers mission told President Carter that they had heard "hand grenades and automatic rifles going off all during the night as people were killed. They don't have anybody in the jails; they're all dead. It's their accepted way of enforcing the so-called law."[40] In January 1981, two American advisers to the ill-fated land-reform program and a Salvadoran official were murdered by a death squad while they drank coffee in a San Salvador hotel—and the Carter Administration resumed sending military aid to the government. After that, the situation was in the hands of the Reagan Administration.

GROWLING AT GRENADA

Nearly two thousand miles to the east of El Salvador, on the Atlantic frontier of the Caribbean sea, lies the small island nation of Grenada. There, on March 13, 1979, the government of a corrupt and idiosyncratic leader was overthrown by a popular leftist leader who turned to Castro's Cuba for help. Although the country was too small to command much awareness from senior American officials, the new government became the target of growling displeasure from Washington. The episode illustrated the Carter Administration's difficulty in Central America and the Caribbean in refraining from intervention and at the same time blocking Cuban influence. The episode also gained obvious after-the-fact importance as background to the Reagan Administration's military takeover of the island in 1983.

From 1951 until 1979, the dominant political figure in the British colony and (after 1974) independent nation of Grenada was Sir Eric Gairy, a corrupt dictator with a bizarre obsession with unidentified flying objects, a subject which he believed should be taken seriously by the United Nations. Gairy, who admired the strong-arm regime of General Augusto Pinochet in Chile, used intimidation and death to keep the opposition under control. But in 1979, while he was out of the country, he was ousted by Maurice Bishop, the eloquent and popular leader of the New Jewell Movement, a left-wing group. Grenadans at a rally chanted: "Freedom come, Gairy go, Gairy gone with UFO."[41]

Grenada fell within the diplomatic responsibility of the American ambassador to a group of eastern Caribbean countries, with an embassy in Barbados. In 1979, the ambassador was the staunchly anti-communist Frank Ortiz. Ortiz, while assiduously collecting intelligence concerning secret Cuban arms shipments to Grenada, visited Grenada on April 10. He found the Bishop regime fearful of an invasion led by Gairy. The tone and content of Ortiz's comments to Bishop are in dispute. Critics said he told Bishop that Grenada could receive no significant aid from the United States unless it renounced ties with Cuba. Ortiz claimed that he spoke primarily about various aid projects while simply observing, as instructed, that Grenada's relationship to the United States would be "complicated if it developed close ties with Cuba."

Bishop, however, heard a threat. "We have always striven to have and develop the closest and friendliest relations with the United States," he said in a speech three days after meeting Ortiz. "But no one must misunderstand our friendliness as an excuse for rudeness and meddling in our affairs, and no one, no matter how mighty and powerful they are, will be permitted to dictate to the government and people of Grenada whom we can have friendly relations with and what kind of relations we must have with other countries. We are not in anybody's back yard."

Bishop—while carrying out improvements in health, education, welfare, and agriculture—did postpone elections, suppress dissent, jail some opponents, and celebrate his admiration for Castro. Cuban military advisers came to the island with shipments of arms. Cuban construction workers began to build a new airport. In Washington, hard- and soft-liners contended—and the hard-liners won. The State Department carried out a campaign to isolate Grenada diplomatically and took every opportunity to condemn Bishop's apparent journey into the communist camp. The National Security Council staff considered the possibility of imposing a blockade.[42]

One of the soft-liners within the Administration, Richard E. Feinberg, wrote subsequently that the way the United States handled the Bishop regime was a classic example of how to create enemies. It would have been better, he said in 1983, to have ignored Bishop; but "Bishop's importance was inflated and he gained some justification" for his military buildup.[43] Did the Carter Administration's hostility actually push Bishop toward Cuba? Ambassador Ortiz in 1984 said no. "It is a great pity that Bishop brought confrontation and totalitarianism to one of the most accommodating, gentle, and democratic regions of this hemisphere. But . . . a Marxist–Leninist like Bishop is not 'driven' into the Communist camp; that is where he started out to go."[44]

TROUBLE WITH THE ABCS

United States relations with the three largest and most powerful nations of South America—Argentina, Brazil, and Chile—have throughout history been significantly different from relations with the small, weak countries of Central America and the Caribbean. The ABC powers have maintained close ties with Europe and have often been resistant to pressure from Washington. Resentment reached one of its several historical peaks during the Carter Administration when the military governments in all three countries reacted bitterly to criticism of human-rights violations and, in the case of Brazil, to an attempt to prevent a contract with West Germany for the construction of nuclear-power plants. But the three countries were not without an ally in Washington. Brzezinski saw the human-rights policy as biased against the right-wing regimes and warned the President in 1978 that we were "running the risk of having bad relations simultaneously with Brazil, Chile, and Argentina."[45]

The violations of human rights perpetrated in the 1970s by the ruling military junta of Argentina were by far the worst in the Western Hemisphere. There were no political freedoms or civil rights. An estimated fifteen thousand people suspected of criticizing the regime had simply disappeared—murdered by the military without a trace, with no information ever provided to the grieving families.

If the Carter Administration had failed to condemn the Argentine government and withhold aid, its human-rights policy would have had no meaning at all. Secretary Vance did, in fact, move quickly. He announced in February that the Administration, as a gesture of disapproval, would cut foreign aid from the $32 million set by the Ford Administration to $15 million. In Buenos Aires, the Argentine Foreign Minister called in the U.S. ambassador and denounced this interference in his country's internal affairs. Meanwhile, the human-rights advocates in Congress wanted the Administration to go further and cut off all military aid. The State Department and General George Brown, chairman of the Joint Chiefs of Staff, argued that long-term U.S. interests called for keeping the ties and influence which would result from a small aid program. Congress said no. President Carter acquiesced and in November signed legislation cutting off all military aid because of violations of human rights. The Administration also halted the commercial sale of arms, blocked loans to Argentina through the Inter-American Development Bank, and held up an Export-Import Bank credit for the purchase of generator turbines.[46]

But the severe sanctions had a greater impact on American companies doing business in Argentina than on the human-rights record of the junta, which showed no significant improvement. "You have no idea of the pressure," said one State Department official. The President noted the complaints and, perceptibly, the hard line began to ease. Also, the Argentine junta seemed to respond a little. In March 1978, President Jorge Rafael Videla promised that civilian government would be restored in 1979 (the promise was not kept), and in April he released Jacobo Timerman, an outspoken human-rights activist, from prison—where he had endured prolonged torture. In November 1978, President Carter ordered the Export-Import Bank to release the credit for the electric generators.[47]

The Soviet invasion of Afghanistan introduced a new element. President Carter was anxious that Argentina not increase its grain sales to the Soviet Union to compensate for the American embargo. The Argentine military reportedly made cooperation conditional on a suspension of American criticism over human rights. In Washington, Assistant Secretary of State Derian was so annoyed over what she saw as a retreat from principle that she threatened to resign.[48] But Argentina went ahead with grain sales, the ban on military aid remained in force, and Derian did not resign.

On balance, the application of human-rights principles in U.S. relations with Argentina was a compromise, but one weighted on the side of sticks rather than carrots. The American record was not pure, but it was good. The junta continued to feel the breath of American displeasure and it did release some prisoners, permit a visit by the Inter-American Commission on Human Rights, and reduce somewhat the number of new "disappearances"—although it did not provide any information on the fate of those who were already gone.

The largest country in Latin America—in population, geographical extent, and economic resources—is Brazil, the most developed nation of the Third World and the most important of those which Brzezinski was fond of calling "the new influentials." To Brzezinski's dismay, the Carter Administration's relations with Brazil began very badly. During his campaign, Jimmy Carter had criticized Brazil sharply, while also sticking a barb into Henry Kissinger: "When Kissinger says . . . that Brazil is the sort of government that is most compatible with ours—well, that's the kind of thing we want to change. Brazil is not a democratic government; it's a military dictatorship. In many instances, it's highly repressive to political prisoners."[49] When the State Department early in 1977 publicly reported human-rights violations in Brazil, the government of President Ernesto Geisel ostentatiously canceled a twenty-five-year-old military-assistance agreement with the United States and refused any aid—before it could be denied.[50]

Human rights, however, were not the most serious problem.

In June 1975, Brazil signed a contract with West German suppliers which would not only increase its nuclear-generating capacity but would also give it the ability to reprocess exhausted uranium and thereby gain weapons-grade material. The fact that Brazil had refused to sign the 1967 treaty of Tlatelolco banning nuclear weapons from Latin America added to American apprehension over the West German deal. The Ford Administration had tried unsuccessfully to have the deal modified. President Carter attacked the issue immediately. He instructed Vice President Mondale to protest to Chancellor Helmut Schmidt of West Germany during a trip in the first week of the Administration. The Brazilians were outraged—not only at the interference but at the way the United States went to Bonn, behind Rio's back.[51]

In the next four years, the Administration struggled to undo the damage—without retreating entirely from its principles. Rosalynn Carter visited Rio in June 1977,[52] Secretary Vance in November 1977, and the President himself in March 1978. The United States stopped protesting the nuclear deal with Germany, and nothing strident was said about human rights. Instead, the United States began to praise Brazil for its movement toward a more open political system. That progress continued through 1979 and was commended by the Department of State in its annual human-rights report, released in February 1980. Relations were far better than in 1977—but not good enough to persuade Brazil to join the grain embargo against the Soviet Union after the invasion of Afghanistan.

Relations with the repressive military regime of General Augusto Pinochet of Chile were simpler. During his election campaign, Carter had frequently attacked as immoral the involvement of the Nixon Administration in the 1973 overthrow of the duly elected Salvador Allende and the installation of the junta headed by Pinochet. Although the worst of Pinochet's excesses were over by 1977, the State Department kept up a drumbeat of criticism and cut back on aid. Relations went from bad to worse when Chile refused to deliver for trial in the United States three Chileans accused of the murder in Washington of Orlando Letelier, an opponent of the Pinochet regime living in exile. Brzezinski regretted the poor relations with Chile, but in that he was alone.

MEXICO: BORDER PROBLEMS AND THE SHAH

For Mexico and the United States, and for Canada and the United States, there is in their relationship no clear dividing line between domestic and foreign issues. Furthermore, since the issues are largely bilateral and without substantial ramifications for international relations as a whole, Presidents, Secretaries of State, and National Security Advisers have traditionally paid them little heed. Jimmy Carter during his campaign criticized his Republican predecessors for neglecting Mexico and promised to be different. He considered it a happy coincidence that Mexico's new president, Jose López Portillo, was inaugurated only a week before his own term began. He sent Rosalynn Carter to attend López Portillo's ceremony and in the following month the Mexican president was the first to pay a state visit to the Carter White House. Carter went to Mexico City in February 1979 and López Portillo came to Washington in September 1979 for a second time.

The major subject of continuing discussion between the two presidents and by several boards and commissions at the "working level" was the movement of undocumented Mexican workers across the border and their treatment in the United States. President Carter recognized that the Mexican workers, while they were viewed by many Americans as unfair and illegal competition, were frequently cheated and denied basic rights in the United States. He wrote to all state governors and issued a memorandum to the executive branch asking or demanding that the human rights of Mexican workers in the United States be fully respected. "No one in our country should be vulnerable to mistreatment or exploitation because he or she is afraid to secure protection of the law."[53]

The two countries reached agreement on the sale of Mexican natural gas, on control of illegal narcotics, and on water pollution.

The overall record would have been good, except for one incident. The Shah of Iran, in his exile wanderings during 1979, came to rest in Mexico. From there he was admitted to the United States in October 1979 for medical treatment, an event which precipitated the seizure of the hostages in Teheran and President Carter's greatest problem. But when the Shah was sufficiently recovered to leave the United States the Mexicans, without any warning, said he could not return. "López Portillo is not a man of his word," Carter noted bitterly in his diary. The fact that Mexico had no diplomatic personnel in Iran and no need for Iranian oil made the refusal all the harder for Carter to understand or forgive.[54]

During his final year in office, President Carter had no time to attend to Latin American issues because of the demands of the hostage situation and the Soviet invasion of Afghanistan. These large, far-distant crises produced the very neglect of Latin America which Carter had once deplored in his predecessors. He had to his credit one great achievement—the settlement of the Panama question. The negative consequences of failing on that issue could well have been catastrophic for Carter and his successors. But the positive consequences for Latin American relations generally and for Carter's own political future never developed. The Panama triumph did not make other countries more willing to respect human rights, did not bring about normalization of relations with Cuba, or prevent turmoil and violence in Nicaragua and El Salvador. Carter did try to put United States relations with Latin America on a new and positive course. He tried as hard as any previous President. His failure stemmed less from his misunderstanding of Latin American problems—for he was sensitive and informed far above the Presidential average—than from problems originating outside the hemisphere and from divisions within his own Administration and country. Sadly for him, he was attacked both for trying to adhere to his ideals and for sacrificing national interest to those ideals.

6

Majority Rule and the Cold War in Africa

The Carter Administration devoted more attention to improving the relations of the United States with the black nations of Africa than had any of its predecessors. The President and his advisers sincerely believed it was right in principle and was also in the nation's interest to commit the United States wholeheartedly to racial justice and majority rule. Their initial instincts were to treat African issues on African terms, not as elements to be manipulated in a global conflict with the Soviet Union. Sometimes they succeeded—for example, in supporting self-determination based on majority rule for Zimbabwe (Rhodesia until 1980). Sometimes they compromised, as with continued non-recognition and muted hostility toward the leftist MPLA regime in Angola. Sometimes they did not condemn injustice as sharply as many critics of white supremacy wished, specifically in regard to South Africa's policy of apartheid and that country's continued illegal control of Namibia. And sometimes they allowed Cold War considerations to dominate, as in support for Somalia against Ethiopia on the eastern Horn of the continent. In no part of the world was the interplay of morality, reason, and power more continuous or fascinating.

Moral ideals, the domestic political advantage of the Carter Administration, and broad American national interest in 1977 all seemed congruent in calling for a new activism, for a deliberate

effort to depart from the accommodationist approach of the Nixon–
Ford Administrations toward white regimes. Africa seemed an
ideal arena for demonstrating a commitment to human rights,
for what wrong was worse than suppression of one race by another?
American conservative ideologues could defend authoritarian regimes like the Shah's in Iran and could attack Carter for allegedly
undermining them. But even the most rigid conservative could
not defend racial oppression—at least, not in public.

Domestic American politics pointed the Administration in the
same direction. Carter might not have gained the Democratic
nomination and almost certainly would have lost the election had
he not had strong support from black voters. By forcefully en-
dorsing and working for majority rule in Africa, Carter could
reward and retain that support. By denouncing apartheid, Carter
also helped establish his credentials among liberal church and
academic groups who, after Vietnam, had adopted racial justice
in South Africa as a major issue.[1]

President Carter's appointment of Andrew Young as United
States ambassador to the United Nations, the first black to hold
such a high diplomatic position, was a signal both to Africans
and to a domestic constituency. Young immediately became a
vociferous and uninhibited spokesman who won acclaim among
black African leaders and caused consternation among African
whites and some conservative Americans because he belittled the
Soviet threat in Africa.[2] Young's main thesis was that the continuation of repressive white regimes was the Soviet Union's greatest asset in Africa. End those regimes, he said, and there would
no longer be a need for Africans to seek Soviet weaponry or Cuban
advisers and troops. Young also put great emphasis on American
economic self-interest in developing the supposedly huge African
market. Those who had dreamed of a China market at the turn
of the twentieth century would have recognized the economic
gospel according to the Reverend Young.[3] Secretary of State Vance
put little emphasis on economic interests but did agree with Young's
unwillingness to imagine the Soviet bear at work in every local

crisis. "A negative, reactive American policy that seeks only to oppose Soviet or Cuban involvement in Africa would be both dangerous and futile," Vance said in a major speech before the NAACP. "Our best course is to help resolve the problems which create opportunities for external aggression."[4]

National Security Adviser Brzezinski, in contrast, related African issues, as he related all issues, to conflict with the Soviet Union. But early in 1977 he saw no cause for deep alarm. He advised Carter that the United States should press the Soviets to end their activities in Africa, "but do so outside of Africa through diplomatic leverage, trade denial, etc., but not through direct involvement on the continent." In his memoirs he recalled his secondary role in pursuit of majority rule and his concern "that we did not ignore the Soviet–Cuban military presence in Africa to the point that the conservative whites in South Africa would be fearful of accepting any compromise solution. Moreover, I feared that indifference to the Soviet–Cuban role would eventually maximize U.S. domestic opposition to a policy more sympathetic to majority rule."[5]

An additional factor loomed behind American policy toward Africa: oil. During the Carter Administration, almost forty percent of American imports of crude petroleum came from Africa and half of that came from Nigeria, a country which had almost overnight become the world's sixth largest oil exporter and the second most important exporter to the United States. Furthermore, Nigerian oil was especially important because of its low-sulphur, low-polluting qualities. Thus it was no accident, as they say, that President Carter's only visit to a black African nation (the first by any American President) was to Nigeria—in April 1978. Given the centrality of the energy crisis in President Carter's overall view of American security, a little flattery of His Excellency Lieutenant General Olusegun Obasanjo, head of the federal military government and commander in chief of the armed forces of the Federal Republic of Nigeria, seemed in order. The Nigerian government was a vociferous critic of apartheid and of any country which seemed to condone South Africa's behavior. This fact provided an additional reason for the United States to maintain a credible posture on racial justice. In this instance, oil made brothers of morality and self-interest.

THE LEGACY OF KISSINGER'S AFRICAN POLICY

Until the middle of the twentieth century, the United States had no African policy distinct from policies toward the white colonial powers, including the white government of South Africa, which controlled the continent. But in the late 1950s, and with increasing speed, the British, French, and Belgians began to grant independence to their former colonies in black Africa. Within a half-dozen years, virtually all of central Africa, from Nigeria in the west, through the Congo (Zaire) in the heart of the continent, to Kenya on the Indian Ocean, had gained independence. By the early 1970s, there were three large areas not yet independent, where blacks did not govern in their own countries. All lay south of the Zambesi River. They were the Portuguese colonies of Mozambique (on the Indian Ocean) and Angola (on the Atlantic); Rhodesia, where a white minority population refused to relinquish power; and the rigidly white-ruled Republic of South Africa including its illegitimate colony of South-West Africa (Namibia).

Every American Administration since the beginning of the independence movement had given lip service to the ideal of supporting majority rule and insulating Africa from the competition of the Cold War. On the rhetorical level, it is possible to find isolated quotations from every Administration since Eisenhower which would demonstrate that nothing new was being said during the Carter years. But every Administration had also watched and sought to counter the moves of the Soviet Union on the continent. The relative balance between supporting African nationalist movements and acting primarily in terms of blocking Soviet influence had oscillated from one Administration to another. The Eisenhower Administration was deeply involved in the chaotic situation in the Congo after the departure of the Belgians. It used covert and overt methods to support factions deemed amenable to American influence, while undermining those which seemed too friendly to the Soviet Union. In 1960, the CIA assisted in the overthrow of the leftist Congolese leader Patrice Lumumba (the contribution of the CIA to Lumumba's assassination the following year is less certain). The Kennedy Administration attempted, with limited success, to restrain covert intervention and be more sensitive to the new African nations on their own terms. The Kennedy State Department was the first to have an Assistant Secretary of State for African Affairs: the liberal former governor of Michigan, G. Mennan Williams.[6] During the Johnson Administration, with Washington preoccupied with the Vietnam war, there was little change.

The Nixon years began with a retreat from relatively liberal policies toward qualified support for the white regimes in the southern zone, on the assumption that the whites in Rhodesia, the Portuguese colonies, and South Africa had the power and will to remain indefinitely and that the United States had to work with the whites, not against them, in preventing violence. The basic policy document, National Security Study Memorandum 39, prepared in 1969 at the direction of National Security Adviser Henry Kissinger, suggested that through non-confrontational dialogue the United States could persuade white regimes to embark on evolutionary reforms and thereby prevent the intrusion of Soviet and Chinese influence.[7]

The assumptions of NSSM-39 collapsed dramatically during 1975–76. The immediate cause was the revolution of April 1974 in Portugal, which overthrew the repressive regime that had continued the policies of dictator Antonio Salazar (in power from 1922 until his death in 1968). Neither the new government nor the officers and men of the Portuguese Army had any stomach for continuing the wars against the black population of the colonial territories—wars fought with American weapons and the tacit support of the Nixon Administration. The Portuguese conceded defeat and departed, leaving the United States no white regime to support, and destroying a basic assumption of NSSM-39.

Mozambique was granted independence in June 1975. It emerged as a one-party leftist state and was accorded diplomatic recognition and modest aid by the United States. Angola also gained independence, in November 1975, although its long war for independence changed into civil conflict involving three factions. The strongest was the MPLA (Popular Movement for the Liberation of Angola), led by Agostinho Neto and supported by the Soviet Union. The rival FNLA (National Front for the Liberation of Angola) was tied to pro-Western President Mobutu of neighboring Zaire (formerly the Belgian Congo) and was headed by Holden Roberto. The third group was UNITA (National Union for the Total Independence of Angola), a faction which split from FNLA and was headed by Jonas Savimbi. The fact that MPLA was supported by the Soviet Union converted the civil war, in the eyes of Henry Kissinger, into a crucial test of the ability of the United States to put limits to Soviet expansionism. Against the advice of many within the Administration, Kissinger ordered secret aid, through the CIA, for FNLA and later for UNITA.[8] Simultaneously, the MPLA asked for and was sent military advisers and combat soldiers from Cuba. Kissinger's secret involvement soon became public knowledge, stirred powerful opposition among senators and congressmen determined to keep the United States out of another Vietnam war, and led to the passage in January 1976 of the Clark Amendment (sponsored by Senator Dick Clark, Democrat of Iowa), barring the expenditure of funds for the conflict in Angola without explicit congressional approval. The assertive post-Vietnam Congress thus curbed the Administration in Africa, much as it had already done on the larger question of renewed combat in Vietnam.

The departure of the Portuguese from Angola and Mozambique led to intensified guerrilla warfare in neighboring Rhodesia, where a heavily armed minority of white settlers had long been fighting to retain control of the country against the more than ninety percent of the population who were black. The Rhodesian situation had developed in the following manner. In the late 1950s and early 1960s, the British government was successful in moving its African colonies to majority rule and independence—all but Rhodesia. When the British government insisted on independence with majority rule for Rhodesia in 1965, the white settlers, led by Ian Smith, proclaimed independence from the British crown. This was a travesty of the idea of freedom. The act was carried out in order to maintain white domination. Most Americans agreed with the position of the British government that Rhodesia was in a state of rebellion and that the Ian Smith regime had no legitimacy. The United Nations Security Council voted an embargo on imports from Rhodesia. The United States supported the resolution (it could have cast a veto) and complied with the embargo—until 1971, when Congress passed an amendment sponsored by Senator Harry F. Byrd, Democrat of Virginia, prohibiting the President from barring the importation of strategic minerals from a non-communist country. The purpose was to allow the purchase of Rhodesian chrome by the United States. By thus defying the UN sanctions, the Nixon Administration gave tacit moral encouragement to Ian Smith in the war against the blacks.[9]

But the collapse of the Portuguese empire caused Secretary of State Kissinger to reassess American policy toward Rhodesia. He concluded that the Smith white-supremacist regime could not prevail and, further, that it was in the interest of the white South African government to encourage majority rule in Rhodesia lest it, too, be engulfed in a racial firestorm. During 1976, his last year in office, Kissinger visited Africa for the first time and spoke in a new and uncharacteristic way. "We know from our own experience that the goal of racial justice is both compelling and achievable," he said in a much publicized address in Lusaka, Zambia, in April. "Our support for this principle in southern

Africa is not simply a matter of foreign policy but an imperative of our moral heritage." He then affirmed American insistence on majority rule before Rhodesia could be independent, and he condemned apartheid and demanded that South Africa commit itself to a definite schedule for the self-determination of Namibia.[10] Jimmy Carter or Andrew Young could not have said it better.

RHODESIA BECOMES ZIMBABWE

Although members of the Carter Administration were understandably prone to claim that all good things began with them, in the matter of Rhodesia they continued a change which Kissinger, as Secretary of State for President Gerald Ford, had begun. The first step was to align the United States with the rest of the United Nations by persuading Congress to repeal the Byrd amendment which mandated the importation of Rhodesian chrome. Secretary Vance testified personally before the African affairs subcommittee of the Senate Foreign Relations Committee on February 10, 1977. He said the Byrd amendment was a "violation of our own often proclaimed devotion to international law." Its repeal would symbolize a return to international law, would tell Africa that we were sincere in our commitment to racial justice, and would contribute to a settlement of the Rhodesian issue by persuading Ian Smith that he could not count on the support of the United States.[11] In March, the Congress repealed the amendment by a vote of 66–26 in the Senate and 250–146 in the House. It was a signal victory for the Administration.

Ian Smith countered with a proposed "internal solution" involving a new government to include Bishop Abel Muzorewa, a black. Secretary Vance agreed with British Foreign Secretary David Owen that the "internal solution" was a sham designed to leave power in white hands. President Carter, however, was interested in exploring the possibility. He was impressed by Muzorewa's apparent popularity with the American Congress and by the fact that he was untainted by communist backing—unlike the most forceful of the black leaders at war with Smith, Robert Mugabe. Brzezinski, fretting that Vance was tying the United States too closely to the British, was also attracted to the "internal solution." Carter even toyed with the idea of American involvement in a secret deal with Muzorewa or Joshua Nkomo, another talented leader, in order to exclude Mugabe.

Richard Moose, the newly appointed Assistant Secretary for African Affairs, and Anthony Lake, the head of the State Department's Policy Planning Staff, said an attempt at a secret deal was a prescription for disaster on every count—it would leave Smith in control, would not end the fighting, and would severely damage American relations with the black African states. Vance, agreeing, persuaded Carter that the idea was a bad one. The United States stood firm for a solution based on true majority rule, encouraging the British to take the initiative, working to keep the confidence of the black African "front-line" governments (Angola, Botswana, Mozambique, Tanzania, and Zambia), and striving to get the government of South Africa to encourage Smith toward a settlement.[12]

At times, it looked as if the United States would backslide. Senator Jesse Helms and twenty-six of his colleagues, most of whom had voted against the repeal of the Byrd amendment, invited Ian Smith to visit the United States in October 1978, although sanctions against Rhodesia included a ban on travel to the United States. Brzezinski reportedly recommended that the United States grant permission—and it was done. Smith arrived to lobby for an end to the trade embargo and to declaim ominously about the Soviet support behind the guerrilla opposition. The war itself was intensifying—with deaths occurring at the rate of a thousand a month by early 1979. In the spring of 1979, Smith contrived an election in Rhodesia which returned Muzorewa as Prime Minister. The United States did not recognize the legitimacy of the election, but Brzezinski persuaded Carter to receive Muzorewa at Camp David in July. This was a move, said Brzezinski later, to placate Senator Helms.[13] After the Rhodesian elections, Congress passed resolutions lifting the sanctions—unless the President formally declared it was not in the national interest. The President made the necessary declaration and the sanctions remained.

The autumn of 1979 saw both a desperate British effort to arrange a settlement and a triumph of pro-Ian Smith forces in the United States. Andrew Young was no longer in the government, having been dismissed in July because of a blunder in meeting with a representative of the Palestinian Liberation Organization. Secretary Vance's influence on all questions was declining. The Iranian hostage crisis, beginning on November 4, would monopolize the President's time and diminish his ability to act creatively on many issues. The British effort was successful. After three months of talks at Lancaster House in London, involving Muzorewa, Nkomo, and Mugabe, agreement was reached on the temporary restoration of British rule over the Rhodesian colony, free elections, and the establishment of independence for Zimbabwe, as the new country would be called, on the basis of majority rule. In April 1980, Robert Mugabe became Prime Minister and proceeded to govern with far more moderation than had been predicted by those who had feared him as a communist-backed extremist. The United States lifted its sanctions the moment the Lancaster House agreements were reached and extended economic aid when Zimbabwe became independent. In August 1980, President Carter received Prime Minister Mugabe in the White House. Former Ambassador Andrew Young was, fittingly, invited to attend the ceremonies. In that summer of the hostage crisis and the Soviet invasion of Afghanistan, it was a rare occasion for optimism.

BATTLING APARTHEID

Apartheid is the system of law and custom whereby the white minority of South Africa holds the black majority in a position of inferiority only a few steps removed from slavery. Although rooted in centuries of white conquest, the system in its modern form came into being after the Second World War. In the early years of the Cold War, the United States welcomed South Africa's proclaimed anti-communism and was not bothered by apartheid. Secretary of State Dean Acheson, for example, argued that the United States "should not intervene for what are called moral reasons in the internal affairs of another country. Moral reasons for interfering are merely a cover for self-indulgent hypocrisy."[14] Thus, the United States abstained in 1952 on the first resolution introduced in the United Nations condemning apartheid. Although not accepting the South African idea for a South Atlantic Treaty Organization paralleling NATO, the United States in those years formed a close military relationship with South Africa, used Cape Town as a stopping place for American warships, eagerly sought South African minerals as vital to the defense of the free world, established satellite tracking stations (with white personnel), entered into agreements on the production of nuclear energy, exchanged information between the CIA and the South African security police, and generally touted the country as a stable and profitable place for American investment. The Cold War was in the saddle in the 1950s and the steed of power would not be turned aside by the "internal" issue of apartheid.[15]

The year 1960 was a turning point because of the near-simultaneous rise of the civil-rights movement in the United States, the election of John F. Kennedy, the independence of black African nations, and the Sharpeville massacre, in which South African police fired on a crowd of demonstrators and killed nearly a hundred and wounded far more. Many of those shot were women and children, hit in the back while trying to flee. Sharpeville demonstrated the brutality of apartheid, which none could ignore. The rhetoric of the American government changed. American spokesmen became more outspoken in criticizing conditions in South Africa, and the United States joined in a voluntary United Nations embargo on arms shipments to the country.

In the Nixon–Ford–Kissinger years, the rhetoric became less condemnatory, although by 1976 the criticism was increasing again. One reason was the uprising in June 1976 in Soweto, an all-black area on the outskirts of Johannesburg in which 1.5 million people were forced to live in segregated and humiliating conditions. The South African government suppressed the uprising and intensified its repression, but the event sent tremors through the country and the world.

This was the situation when Jimmy Carter became President and Andrew Young his spokesman for African policy. The Administration opened with an unprecedented tattoo of condemnation. Two days after his inauguration, President Carter said bluntly: "I believe very strongly in majority rule, which means relinquishing the control of the government by the white minorities in the countries affected."[16] In May 1977, Vice President Mondale met South African Prime Minister John Vorster in Vienna and delivered such a sharp attack, threatening a deterioration in relations with the United States if South Africa did not abandon its obnoxious practices, that Vorster complained that the United States was attempting to intervene in South Africa's internal affairs—which, of course, it was.[17] The United States also criticized the South African policy of shunting some of the black population into allegedly independent "homelands" in parched areas of little value. "We do not recognize the Transkei, and we will not recognize Bophutswana if its independence is proclaimed in December" (it was), said Secretary Vance.[18] Meanwhile, Andrew Young traveled to Africa, was quoted almost daily in criticism of racism in general and South Africa in particular, and attended a conference of black nations in Maputo, Mozambique, held in support of the independence and liberation of the people of Namibia and Zimbabwe.

Prime Minister Vorster responded with even harsher repression. He jailed black leaders, suppressed publications, banned organizations, and put some white supporters of justice for blacks under house arrest. One black leader, the articulate and charismatic Steve Biko, died in prison under circumstances that indicate he was murdered by his captors. In an alarming related move, the Prime Minister denied he had ever given his word that South Africa would refrain from producing or testing nuclear weapons. President Carter said Vorster was lying.[19] Vorster's party also won a sweeping electoral victory in 1977 by—to quote an Australian observer—"in effect running against Jimmy Carter."[20]

The United States did not back off. It supported an unequivocal UN Security Council resolution attacking the "racist regime" in South Africa and imposing a mandatory arms embargo on the grounds that the acquisition of arms by that country constituted "a threat to the maintenance of international peace and security."[21] The United States, in fact, went beyond the UN embargo and cut off the export of police as well as military equipment, barred some South African military and police officers from visiting the United States, and urged American companies doing business in South Africa to abide by a code of fair labor practices opposed to apartheid.[22]

STALEMATE OVER NAMIBIA

In the late nineteenth century, Germany occupied a vast desert region in the southwest corner of Africa, adjacent to British-controlled South Africa. During the First World War, troops from the Dominion of South Africa conquered German South-West Africa. After the war, the South African government received a League of Nations mandate over the region. This was tantamount to annexation, subject only to required periodic reports to the Mandates Commission of the League and vague commitments not to exploit the natives. After the Second World War, the United Nations Trusteeship Council was established as heir to the extinct Mandates Commission. The government of South Africa, however, refused to accept that it was responsible to the

United Nations. The United States, agreeing that the South African position was illegal, supported one resolution after another calling on South Africa to accept its obligations under the UN and set South-West Africa, or Namibia, as the African population called it, on the road to independence.

South African intransigence both produced and was intensified by the rise of an armed liberation movement headed by the South-West African People's Organization (SWAPO). After the departure of the Portuguese from Angola, along Namibia's northern border, the SWAPO forces found there a refuge and a base for operations. The circumstances were parallel to those in the war for liberation in Rhodesia. In 1976, the South African government arranged a "settlement" by which, by excluding SWAPO, it could continue in control. The United States joined Britain, France, Germany, and Canada—the so-called contact group— in trying to persuade South Africa to be truly responsive to the UN call. The effort failed.

At this point, the Carter Administration took office. Vice President Mondale lectured Prime Minister Vorster in Vienna, and Andrew Young at the Maputo conference said the United States saw the liberation of Namibia as certain. "We are here to discuss measures that can hasten the inevitable day of freedom. We all know that among these measures will be continuing military efforts by the liberation forces. They will insist on continuing their struggle as long as fundamental political rights are denied the majority."[23]

Secretary Vance took up the main burden of working through the "contact group" to persuade South Africa to agree to free, supervised elections. He was not beguiled by any of Prime Minister Vorster's proposed internal solutions, although President Carter seemed tempted, as he was in the parallel situation involving Ian Smith and Bishop Muzorewa in Rhodesia. In that case, the President had been suspicious of Robert Mugabe's alleged communist ties. In Namibia, he found the SWAPO people rigid and unyielding. Vance, however, had the President's support and undertook long, tedious negotiations year after year. At one moment the goal would seem in sight, only to disappear, as South Africa used one excuse or another to obfuscate, obstruct, and delay. For Vance, however, the effort was itself the message. "Without the Namibia negotiating process—together with the Zimbabwe settlement—the United States would have no workable strategy for improving its relations with black Africa and blocking the spread of Soviet and Cuban influence in southern Africa."[24]

THE ANGOLA CONNECTION

At first glance, the newly independent country of Angola, immediately to the north of Namibia, offered the Carter Administration an excellent opportunity to demonstrate creative new policies markedly different from those followed by Henry Kissinger during the Ford Administration. Instead of being "inordinately" obsessed with communism, the Administration could have extended diplomatic recognition to the MPLA regime, effectively opposed South Africa's military incursions into Angola in alleged pursuit of SWAPO insurgents, and built on close economic ties already established between the Angolan government and the Gulf Oil Company, an American firm. This would have contrasted with Kissinger's effort to use the CIA and covert support to defeat the MPLA and involve the United States in another potential Vietnam, an effort blocked by the Clark amendment of 1976, with which President Carter declared himself in agreement.

President Carter and Secretary Vance both believed in establishing diplomatic relations with Angola. The Angolans said they were ready—both before and after the death of their first president, Agostinho Neto, after surgery in Moscow in 1979. The obstacle throughout the four years of the Administration was the presence of approximately twenty thousand Cuban troops in the country. Andrew Young and Secretary Vance, accepting that the MPLA regime was legitimate and unlikely to be toppled, saw the Cubans as Angola's defense against an armed opposition supported by

South Africa and against the direct threat of South Africa. They believed withdrawal could be negotiated as part of a settlement of the conflict in Namibia. Vance, however, did not go as far as Young in saying the Cubans brought "a certain stability and order."

Brzezinski, like Kissinger before him, saw the Cubans as Soviet proxies bent on serving Moscow's objectives. The Brzezinski position was simple and politically appealing. It prevailed. There could be no normalization of relations with Angola as long as the Cuban troops remained in Angola—regardless of the State Department's preferences to the contrary. For example, Assistant Secretary Moose in a major statement in September 1980 reiterated the policy of non-recognition and then gave four reasons why the policy was foolish. The American absence from Angola gave the Soviets and Cubans an opportunity to extend their influence, prevented the United States from working toward a peaceful solution of the remnants of civil war in the country, impeded the expansion of American trade and business opportunities, and made it impossible to "offer consular services to Americans in Angola, including those who are in prison."[25]

Angola's relations with neighboring Zaire complicated the situation considerably. President Mobutu of Zaire had for years been unable to subdue completely a rebel movement in the province of Katanga (subsequently renamed Shaba), where the country's substantial mineral wealth was located. At the same time, Mobutu had supported raids by the FNLA based in Zaire against the MPLA regime in Angola. Turnabout was fair play, and in April 1977 and again in May 1978 forces in rebellion against Mobutu invaded Shaba province from bases in Angola. The American response is best described as low-profile intervention. On the first occasion, President Carter at a press conference invoked the memory of Vietnam: "We have an aversion to military involvement in foreign countries. We are suffering, or benefiting, from the experience that we had in Vietnam. It would not be possible for the American people to support an invasion force of the United States into the Shaba region of Zaire."[26] Instead, the United States encouraged the French, Egyptian, and Moroccan governments to aid President Mobutu in turning back the incursion. Throughout, the Administration stressed the African, as opposed to the East vs. West, nature of the conflict.

The 1978 invasion was more powerful. It resulted in heavy loss of life and also endangered many Europeans in Shaba. This time, the United States provided transport aircraft to support a French and Belgian rescue effort and placed airborne units on alert. President Carter, perhaps taking his cue from Brzezinski, blamed the governments of both Angola and Cuba for the attack and complained, in words reminiscent of Henry Kissinger, of congressional restrictions on his ability "to act promptly and decisively to help countries whose security is threatened by external forces."[27] Soviet Foreign Minister Gromyko happened to be visiting the White House at the time and he received a tongue-lashing from Carter on Russia's alleged misdeeds in Africa—a charge immediately denied by *Pravda*.[28] The weight of evidence indicates that neither the first nor the second Shaba invasion was encouraged by Cuba or the Soviet Union. The reason for the different American response on the second occasion stemmed from the generally hardening attitude in Washington toward the Soviet Union, not from different circumstances in Africa.[29]

The second Shaba crisis ended quickly. President Neto soon concluded an agreement with President Mobutu whereby each promised to restrain insurgents operating from one country against the other. Thereafter, it was quiet on the Angolan–Zaire border.

Liberals in Congress were not happy about the extent of American aid to Zaire. Mobutu was an unsavory military dictator who had mismanaged the country while amassing an enormous personal fortune. His human-rights record was bad—nevertheless, the Carter Administration maintained the flow of economic and military aid and repeatedly praised Mobutu as a true friend of the United States. The policy was a triumph of practical self-interest over idealism. Zaire's mineral resources in copper, cobalt, and uranium were too extensive and the country's size and location too significant to take the risk of applying such pressure for reform that Mobutu's position would be endangered. Who knew what chaos might follow his ouster? Mobutu repaid the United States with diplomatic gestures which cost nothing and won more praise from Washington: a call on Iran to release the American hostages, condemnation of the Soviet Union for invading Afghanistan, participation in the boycott of the Moscow Olympics.[30]

THE RELUCTANT BOYCOTT OF IDI AMIN

The difficulty of reconciling the multiple values of non-intervention in the internal affairs of other countries, self-determination, support for human rights, opposition to violent solutions of political conflicts, and restraint in the sale of arms is well illustrated by the Carter Administration's difficulties in dealing with Congress in regard to the murderous regime of President Idi Amin Dada in Uganda.

There was no bloodier tyrant in Africa than Idi Amin. In his eight years of megalomaniacal and genocidal rule, he murdered tens of thousands of the country's citizens, killing for sport, it seemed, as well as for political advantage. The United States closed the American Embassy in Kampala in 1973, cut off all military and economic aid, voted against loans to Uganda through international development banks, and banned the export of weapons or other material which could aid in the suppression of human rights. But Congress did not consider these sanctions sufficient. One congressman in particular, Donald J. Pease (Democrat of Ohio), urged that the United States end all trade with Uganda and thereby exclude the country's one valuable export: coffee. Pease was candid in saying that he hoped a trade embargo would assist in Amin's overthrow, not merely pressure him into being less brutal.

Although the proposed trade embargo seemed to the congressmen who supported it an appropriate and practical application of human-rights considerations to foreign policy, the Carter Administration was opposed. We must apply pressure designed to make the government of Uganda end its violations of human rights, said the Department of State. Punitive measures which limited the American ability "to influence the situation in a positive direction" were inappropriate. Furthermore, "the Administration does not believe it is appropriate for the United States to attempt to bring about the overthrow of foreign governments, and does not endorse measures designed to this end."[31]

Congress was not convinced. The Administration's procedural qualms seemed out of place in the presence of a genocidal monster like Idi Amin. Legislation to embargo all trade with Uganda passed easily. President Carter did not veto, but signed the law on October 10, 1978. In January 1979, neighboring Tanzanian forces, supporting Ugandans wishing to liberate their country from Amin, began an invasion. Amin received support from his one friend, Colonel Muammar Qadhaafi of Libya, but it was not enough. Kampala was captured by the liberating forces in April, and Amin fled to Libya. Congress repealed the embargo and the Administration extended aid to the new regime. Many Africans were reported to believe that the American embargo helped bring down Amin. If so, from the Administration's point of view, the help was most reluctant.[32]

AIDING THE MOROCCAN MONARCH

In the case of the Administration's conflict with Congress over special military aid to Morocco, different principles were in conflict. This time, the Administration won. The problem involved a fierce little war between Morocco and the Polisario guerrillas in a disputed region of the western Sahara. Polisario stood for Popular Front for the Liberation of Saguia el Hamra and Rio de Oro. The region was once the colony of Spanish Sahara—until Spain withdrew in 1975, leaving the territory to Morocco and

Mauritania (which subsequently abandoned its claim to a portion of the region). The people living in the region did not want to be subjects of Morocco. Their legal case was strengthened by a decision of the World Court at The Hague that the will of the inhabitants should determine the sovereignty of the area. They began to fight. King Hassan fought back, using weapons supplied by the United States under an agreement dating back to 1960.

Hassan prided himself on being a good friend of the United States. He permitted American naval and air bases in his country. He was consistently anti-communist, had sent forces to Zaire during the 1977 invasion of Shaba by rebels based in Angola, and he supported the United States on most international issues. He had the President's mother, Lillian Carter, as a guest in his palace and in November 1978 paid a state visit to the White House. He told the President he was a great admirer of Abraham Lincoln, and Carter took him upstairs to see the Lincoln bedroom.[33]

In 1979, Hassan said he needed more weapons from the United States. The State Department had qualms; Brzezinski had none. Our record of supporting friends around the world is none too good, he said, in an obvious reference to the Shah of Iran. Carter decided on October 22, 1979, on an aid package ultimately worth $235 million and featuring helicopter gunships, armed reconnaissance planes, and F-5E jet fighters.[34] The next day, the Shah came to New York for medical treatment, and within days the hostages had been seized. In December 1979, the Soviet Union invaded Afghanistan. The Administration used these events as additional arguments to persuade Congress to approve the deal. "With Southwest Asia in turmoil we need to nurture our relations as never before with all Islamic and non-aligned states, but we particularly need to stand up for and support our avowed friends and supporters," said Assistant Secretary of State Harold Saunders, who broke away from his almost continuous involvement in the hostage crisis in order to testify.[35] As a concession to Congress, the Administration agreed that the sale would be conditional on negotiations between Morocco and the Polisario. Congress agreed, but since negotiations did not take place, no arms were delivered.

CONFRONTATION AT THE HORN

The northeast corner of the continent of Africa, known as the Horn, borders on the Red and Arabian Seas. Ethiopia and Somalia, the two principal countries of the region, are drought-stricken and without significant natural resources. But their strategic location on the flank of the Middle East, and their enmity to each other, invited a confrontation of the United States and the Soviet Union in a struggle for dominance. The question for the Carter Administration was whether to avoid entanglement in the Ethiopian–Somali conflict or to manipulate the situation for a larger global purpose, because the Soviet Union was already doing precisely that.

Nowhere else in Africa was the divergence between Secretary Vance and National Security Adviser Brzezinski more sharply illustrated. Vance preferred relative non-entanglement, in the belief that Soviet influence in the region would diminish in the face of nationalistic feelings, as it had in Egypt. If the United States took hostile measures against Ethiopia because that country was receiving Soviet support against an attack from Somalia, the influence of the Soviet Union would be enhanced, not removed. Furthermore, by complaining stridently about Soviet behavior and demanding the total withdrawal of the Soviet and Cuban presence in Ethiopia, the United States might jeopardize the satisfactory conclusion of the strategic-arms limitation talks, a goal that Vance wanted to pursue without linkage to anything else.

Brzezinski could not have disagreed with Vance more. He believed the Soviets, and their Cuban proxies, were present in the Horn in order to challenge the United States and specifically in order to put the Middle East in a strategic vise. The Soviets already had a client in South Yemen, at the bottom of the Arabian peninsula. The merits or demerits of the local conflict between Ethiopia and Somalia were of secondary importance, Brzezinski believed, and fear of a confrontation lest the chances of a SALT treaty be harmed was cowardly. The vital interests of the United States were involved and the nation must act accordingly. Brzezinski agreed wholeheartedly with the sentiments of the president of the Sudan, in a note to President Carter, that "the Soviet Union is pursuing a sinister grand strategy in Africa leading to some definite goals. We are truly alarmed at the extent of Soviet influence . . . We expect and hope that the United States . . . would respond favorably to requests of help from those countries ready and eager to defend themselves against the Soviet threat."[36]

After the overthrow and death of the aged Emperor Haile Selassie in 1974, a Marxist group gained control of the Ethiopian government and began a brutal civil war, using weapons which had been supplied by the United States, against the people of the province of Eritrea. Ethiopia in December 1976 signed an agreement to receive arms from the Soviet Union. The Carter Administration at the beginning of 1977 terminated military-assistance grants to Ethiopia in public protest against the government's violation of the human rights of the Eritreans, while holding open the possibility of continuing to supply weapons on credit. Congressional liberals wanted a complete end of military aid. The State Department frankly admitted a dilemma. The continuation of some aid might prevent Ethiopia from turning totally to the Soviet Union for weapons and by balancing Somali military power "would contribute to even stability . . . [but] it is a very difficult decision for us to make because we would be reluctant to abandon Ethiopia to total Soviet domination. On the other hand, we do not like to see our weapons used in this fashion."[37]

Ethiopia's hostile neighbor, Somalia, at that time had a military relationship with the Soviet Union—established in 1969 when President Muhammad Siad Barre came to power. The Soviets supplied weapons and had the use of a naval base at the port of Berbera. But now President Siad was preparing an invasion of the Ethiopian province of Ogaden, and the Soviets disapproved. Siad asked the United States for military aid, claiming his country was threatened by Ethiopia. The United States said it was agreeable in principle to helping Somalia acquire defensive arms, not arms to attack a neighbor. But in July 1977 Somalia invaded the Ogaden and in November abrogated the treaty of friendship with the Soviet Union, closing access to Berbera and expelling Soviet advisers. The Soviets responded with an effective airlift of weapons to Ethiopia, accompanied by approximately twenty thousand Cuban combat troops.[38]

The Ethiopians, so assisted, drove back the Somali invasion force in January and February 1978. The American position remained unchanged: Somalia could receive defensive arms only after it ended its aggression. Brzezinski protested. He suggested sending an American naval force to the region and providing air cover for the Somali troops should they be driven farther back; and he said publicly that Soviet behavior would affect the SALT negotiations. President Carter tried to support Vance and Brzezinski. He said the United States would not supply weapons, or permit third countries to supply American weapons, until Somalia ended its invasion of the Ogaden. But he simultaneously endorsed the Brzezinski idea that the United States insist that Cuban and Soviet troops withdraw from Ethiopia. He then said, in words which must have made Vance cringe, that a Soviet failure to accept that principle "would make it more difficult to ratify a SALT agreement or comprehensive test-ban agreement if concluded and therefore, the two are linked because of actions by the Soviets. We didn't initiate the linkage."[39] Vance prevailed for a while longer on the question of military aid. He had assurances from Ethiopia, the U.S.S.R., and Cuba that they did not intend to cross into Somalia—and they did not. With his forces in retreat, President Siad in March gave the United States a pledge of nonaggression, but he soon went back on his word and therefore did not receive the aid he sought.

Brzezinski's victory and the granting of Siad's request came in

1979—thanks to the Iranian revolution. The United States, concerned about its deteriorating strategic position, asked Oman, Kenya, and Somalia to permit American naval vessels access to their ports. The Soviet invasion of Afghanistan and the declaration of the Carter doctrine that the United States was prepared to use military force against "an attempt by any outside force to gain control of the Persian Gulf region" added urgency to this request. An agreement with Somalia was concluded in August 1980. The United States had the right of access to port and air facilities, and Somalia received the military aid it had long been seeking. Cuban troops and Soviet advisers remained in Ethiopia.

The great Horn of Africa reversal of alliances was complete. The primary focus of the Carter Administration's African policy, which looked first to support racial justice and majority rule in southern Africa, had shifted geographically to Africa's frontier with the Middle East and philosophically to fighting a Cold War with the Soviet Union.

7

Searching for Peace in the Middle East

Every Administration, from that of President Harry S. Truman onward, has pursued the same goals for the United States in the Middle East: independence and security for Israel, access to oil, and containment of Soviet influence. The Carter Administration pursued those goals with more vigor than any of its predecessors and achieved one major success: the conclusion of a formal peace agreement between Egypt and Israel. But the Carter Administration was no more successful than its predecessors in solving four underlying dilemmas which have plagued American policy in this region since the Second World War.

The first dilemma was how to protect the independence and security of the State of Israel while maintaining friendly relations with the Arab states. The latter was necessary in order to ensure unimpeded access by the non-communist world to the oil of the region. This led to a second dilemma: how to assure Israel that the American commitment to her survival was absolute, while persuading her to moderate the more aggressive aspects of her own search for security. A third related dilemma was how to find a humane solution to the problem of Palestinian refugees from Israel and territories conquered by Israel, while refusing to give aid or comfort to Israel's apparently irreconcilable enemies; i.e., the Palestinians as an organized political force. A fourth dilemma was how to build sufficient military strength among selected Arab states so that they could resist Soviet influence, without making them so strong that they would threaten the security of Israel.

From the establishment of the State of Israel in 1948 until the Suez crisis of 1956, it was American policy to work with Great Britain and France to limit the volume of arms available to Middle Eastern nations and hold conflict at the lowest possible level of violence. The Suez crisis undermined British and French power, enhanced that of the Soviet Union, and stimulated the ambitions and hatred for Israel of Egypt's President Gamal Nasser. After 1956, the United States pursued a unilateral policy. In the aftermath of Suez, President Dwight D. Eisenhower proclaimed and Congress endorsed the doctrine that keeping the region out of Soviet control was a vital American interest; therefore, the United States would be prepared to intervene militarily to protect any nation in the region threatened by communist aggression. In 1980, President Carter would say almost the same thing.

Throughout the years after 1948, Israel's military prowess simultaneously evoked congratulations and unease from Americans. This was especially the case with Israel's spectacular victory over Egypt, Jordan, and Syria in the Six-Day War of June 1967. The war had profound consequences. Israel's short-term military security was increased through the occupation of territory seized from her foes. But the return of these territories—the Sinai to Egypt, the Golan Heights to Syria, half of the city of Jerusalem and the west bank of the Jordan valley to Jordan or perhaps a new Palestinian entity—became a concrete and emotional goal for the Arabs and a standing invitation to renewed war.[1]

The problem was addressed in November 1967 in resolution 242 of the United Nations Security Council, a seminal document of modern Middle Eastern diplomacy. The key provisions of resolution 242 were a call for the "withdrawal of Israeli armed forces from territories occupied in the recent conflict"; and "acknowledgement of the sovereignty, territorial integrity and political independence of every State in the area and their right to live in peace within secure and recognized boundaries free from threats or acts of force." The withdrawal clause contained two significant ambiguities. It spoke of the withdrawal of "Israeli armed forces," but was silent on whether other types of Israeli presence, such as settlements, could remain in the occupied territories. And it spoke of withdrawal from "territories," not from "the territories"—thus leaving an opening for the Israeli interpretation that withdrawal from some of the territories would be sufficient. The resolution also called for freedom of navigation through international waterways in the region; i.e., the Suez Canal and the Gulf of Aqaba, leading from the Red Sea to the Israeli port of Elat.

On the intractable problem of the Palestinians, UN resolution 242 was almost mute, except for a pious call for "a just settlement of the refugee problem." The resolution called for the right of every state to be recognized and to live in peace. That was an implicit call on Palestinians to recognize Israel. But what rights did the Palestinians have, should they accept resolution 242? Did they have a reciprocal right to be recognized and to live in peace? Not necessarily, since they were not a state. The issue was so explosive that it could not be confronted directly in a resolution which had any chance of passing. But, by avoiding the issue, resolution 242 became permanently inadequate as a basis for comprehensive peace in the Middle East.[2]

Although resolution 242 passed the Security Council unanimously, there was no immediate progress toward its implementation. In October 1973, Egypt, determined to redress the humiliation of 1967 and regain the Sinai, attacked Israel in what became known as the Yom Kippur War. This time the losses were heavy on both sides. The United States rushed military aid to Israel to make up for her losses, went on a worldwide alert when it appeared that the Soviet Union might intervene on Egypt's side, and ultimately backed a ceasefire. Secretary of State Henry Kissinger then engaged in prolonged "shuttle diplomacy" designed to produce the disengagement of opposing armed forces and lay the foundation for further "step-by-step" progress. Kissinger achieved modest success in 1974–75 with agreements on disengagement zones in the Sinai and the Golan Heights and the emplacement of both United Nations and American peacekeeping forces.

Kissinger's activity prevented war from breaking out again, but did not produce much progress toward a fundamental settlement. Israel still occupied most of the territory seized in 1967. The problem of the Palestinian refugees was as intractable as ever. And the imposition of an oil embargo by the Arab states after the Yom Kippur War had introduced a new and ominous element for all oil-importing countries. Such was the situation when Jimmy Carter became President in January 1977.

GENEVA DEADEND

President Carter, Secretary Vance, and the Middle East specialists in the Department of State quickly decided that the time was ripe for a more active role in achieving a comprehensive settlement in order to prevent yet another disastrous war. The risks to the President of being criticized by the Arabs, the Israelis, or both were real—but far less serious than the risks of doing nothing. The Administration's first intention was to bring Egypt, Israel, and other nations back to the Geneva conference, a gathering co-sponsored by the United States and the Soviet Union which had some limited usefulness after the Yom Kippur War.

Three weeks after the inauguration, Vance departed on his first overseas trip—to the Middle East. He visited Israel, Egypt, Jordan, Saudi Arabia, Syria, and Lebanon and won a fragile consensus in support of reconvening the Geneva conference. He also invited the government leaders to visit President Carter in Washington. The first leader to come was Prime Minister Yitzhak Rabin of Israel, in March. His conversations with Carter went badly, but not as badly as his political life in Israel, where he was forced to resign because of a minor breach of ethics involving an illegal bank account. Elections in May returned the rightist Likud coalition, and Menachem Begin—noted for lifelong intransigence in support of extreme Israeli ambitions—became Prime Minister. As Carter would soon discover, Begin was a formidable and exasperating negotiator.

"Then, on April 4, 1977," Carter wrote in his memoirs, "a shining light burst on the Middle East for me. I had my first meetings with President Anwar Sadat of Egypt, a man who would change history and whom I would come to admire more than any other leader."[3] Carter was not merely indulging in his usual hyperbole. His relationship with Sadat was closer than that of any American President and a foreign leader, except for the bonds between Franklin Roosevelt and Winston Churchill. Sadat's eloquence in describing Egyptian goals in terms of mankind's universal longing for peace and his deep religious commitment won over the President. Carter, in turn, convinced Sadat that he would take large political risks at home in order to find a just peace for the Middle East.

Other Arab leaders trooped through Carter's office in April and May. Carter found them frank in private discussion but afraid in public to appear at all accommodating to Israel. Carter's first glimpse of Menachem Begin came from watching the new Israeli Prime Minister interviewed on television. "It was frightening to watch his adamant position on issues that must be resolved," the President wrote in his diary.[4] In July, Begin made his visit to Washington and Carter found the conversation less grating than he had feared. But Begin dissipated the good feeling by announcing, immediately on his return to Israel, that some of the Israeli settlements on the West Bank would be permanent. This, said Carter in a news conference, was both illegal and a serious obstacle to peace. Israeli Foreign Minister Moshe Dayan, a more moderate man than Begin, discussed the issue with Carter in September and saw "cold hostility in his blue eyes." Carter struck Dayan as accusatory, and Vice President Mondale seemed even worse.[5]

Another problem was how to include Palestinians in a comprehensive negotiation. Carter's official position, which never changed, was that the Palestinians should be represented—but not until they renounced "their commitment . . . that Israel should be destroyed" and accepted Israel's right to exist as a nation in permanent peace. Neither Begin nor the Arab leaders had a solution that the other side would accept. Soviet Foreign Minister Andrei Gromyko told Carter: "If we can just establish a miniature state for the Palestinians as big as a pencil eraser, this will lead to a resolution of the PLO problem for the Geneva Conference."[6] But a Palestinian state of any size was unacceptable to Israel. Indeed, the idea of Palestinian participation in negotiations even after the Palestinians had recognized Israel's right to exist was anathema to Begin and to many American supporters of Israel.

Meanwhile, Secretary Vance made another trip to the Middle East and conferred again with Gromyko. On October 1, 1977, the United States and the Soviet Union formally issued a call for the Geneva Conference to convene, not later than December. That was both the high point of Soviet–American cooperation on the Middle East during the Carter years and the end of the line, because in November Anwar Sadat seized the initiative.

THE ROAD TO CAMP DAVID

Sadat knew that without pressure on Israel by the United States there was slight chance of a settlement. Winning and holding President Carter's sympathy and support was, therefore, his first priority. He had gone along with the idea of convening the Geneva Conference because that approach was favored by the United States. At the same time, he had been in touch with the Israeli government through secret talks held in Morocco between his deputy prime minister and Moshe Dayan.[7] But by November 1977 it was clear to Sadat and to everyone else that the procedural question of a Palestinian role at Geneva was not likely to be solved. Accordingly, he proposed his dramatic visit to Jerusalem. President Carter was excited by the idea and helped secure an invitation to Sadat from Prime Minister Begin to address the Israeli Knesset (parliament). On the morning before Sadat's arrival in Israel, President Carter in Washington attended a special church service and prayed publicly for peace, "and then the congregation adjourned so we could return to our homes in time to watch the arrival ceremonies on television."[8]

Sadat used television for diplomatic purposes more masterfully than any statesman of his time. His emotional address, broadcast live in the United States and coinciding with Thanksgiving week, invoked the one God worshipped by Jews, Christians, and Moslems; recalled the common grief of Jew and Arab over sons lost in war; and spoke of peace as something for which all humanity yearned. He brought tears of hope to the eyes of millions of people, changed the American public image of Egypt, and altered permanently the diplomatic landscape.

The other Arab states condemned Sadat as a traitor and eventually broke diplomatic relations with Egypt. The extremist leader of Libya, Colonel Muammar Qadhaafi, even called for Sadat's assassination. The Soviet Union sided with the Arab opponents and thereby excluded itself from the negotiations, which henceforth involved only Egypt, Israel, and the United States.

At the turn of the year 1977–78, Carter took a foreign trip—stopping in Poland, Iran, Saudi Arabia, Egypt, India, and France. King Hussein of Jordan joined him in Teheran for discussions with the Shah. Hussein and the Shah agreed to support Sadat's initiative as well as the specific goals of Israeli withdrawal from most (but not necessarily all) of the occupied territories and some form of undefined self-determination, short of independence, for Palestinians in the Gaza Strip and the West Bank. In Saudi Arabia, Carter found the leaders supportive of Sadat in private but unwilling to say so publicly. He noted, however, that "they were adamant in their commitment to an independent Palestinian state."[9]

The euphoria of the Sadat visit to Jerusalem dissipated by early 1978. Against the advice of both Vance and Brzezinski (who rarely agreed on anything), Carter decided to take an even more assertive personal role. He invited Sadat and Begin to come consecutively to Washington and found them growing hostile and suspicious of each other's good faith. Sadat said Begin placed his determination to annex the West Bank ahead of peace. Begin said Sadat's trip to Jerusalem was a mere gesture behind which he was pursuing his goals of complete withdrawal by Israel from the occupied territories and the establishment of an independent Palestinian state. Carter tried, unconvincingly, to persuade both leaders that they misunderstood the other. But there was no misunderstanding.

Carter decided that the United States should move even more forcefully, develop the main features of a settlement, and then get the two sides to accept. He saw Begin as the principal obstacle and his mood fluctuated between mild optimism and near-despair. One particularly bad moment came in March 1978 when Israel invaded Lebanon in retaliation for a Palestinian Liberation Organization (PLO) terrorist attack which took the lives of thirty-five Israeli civilians. In the retaliation, the lives of more than a thousand non-combatants were lost.[10] Carter ordered the United States to take the lead in the United Nations Security Council in condemning the invasion, demanding Israel's withdrawal, and establishing a UN peacekeeping force. These goals were accomplished with the passage of resolution 425 on March 19, 1978.[11] The United States also complained that Israel had violated a pledge, going back to a mutual-defense-assistance agreement of 1952, to use American weapons only for legitimate self-defense.[12] In the attack on Lebanon, American weapons were used, especially the notoriously lethal anti-personnel cluster bombs.

Begin came twice to the United States that spring, but Carter began to feel the situation might be hopeless. After the second visit, the President wrote in his diary: "I told him that peace in the Middle East was in his hands, that he had a unique opportunity either to bring it into being or kill it . . . My guess is that he will not take the necessary steps."[13] At the end of July, Carter decided "it would be best, win or lose, to go all out." He invited

Sadat and Begin to join him at Camp David, the Presidential retreat in the Maryland mountains north of Washington, in September. The three leaders would isolate themselves from the press and stay as long as necessary to work out an agreement. Sadat and Begin agreed, and the Camp David meetings began on September 5, 1978.

THE CAMP DAVID ACCORDS

Not since Woodrow Wilson attended the Paris Peace Conference of 1919 had an American President thrown himself so deeply and personally into diplomatic negotiations. Franklin D. Roosevelt during the conferences of the Second World War was, in contrast, a mere waterbug dancing on the surface. Carter studied thousands of pages of documents, familiarized himself with every kilometer of disputed territory, learned the names and populations of scores of villages—and during each of the thirteen days added to the record with his own voluminous notes. During his Presidency, the Middle East took more of his time than any other issue. The fact that he devoted thirty percent of his memoirs to the Middle East, and eighty-five pages to Camp David alone, is an accurate measure of his involvement.

Originally, Carter thought the Camp David meeting would last three days. It lasted thirteen, during which Carter excluded all other business. With Vance, Brzezinski, and various American experts on the Middle East to assist him, he shuttled endlessly the few yards between the Egyptian and Israeli cabins on the Camp David grounds, struggling over the nuances of every word, trying to get Begin to keep his eyes on the ultimate objective and not quibble over technicalities, pleading with Sadat not to leave in discouragement.

There were two clusters of problems. The first was difficult and the second almost impossible—and they were linked. The first was how to remove the bilateral obstacles between Egypt and Israel which stood in the way of a peace treaty. The Israeli government had agreed in principle to a withdrawal from the Sinai back to the 1967 border. But the pace of the withdrawal, the question of continued access to Sinai oil, and limitations on Egypt's future military forces in the region all had to be settled. Less difficult issues involved the precise definition of Israel's right of secure access to the port of Elat through the narrow Strait of Tiran and the Gulf of Aqaba, unhampered passage through the Suez Canal, and the stationing of UN peacekeeping forces.

The impossible problem involved what Israel was willing to do by way of withdrawal from the West Bank and Gaza and, above all, what kind of self-determination could be attained for the Palestinians. Sadat insisted that there could be no peace between Israel and Egypt unless Israel agreed to move toward a solution of those questions. The Egyptian president's preference was for an independent Palestinian state, but since that was totally unacceptable to Israel, he was willing to compromise on some sort of self-determination.

The Americans took an important procedural step in proposing that the Camp David meetings produce two documents: guidelines for the bilateral Egyptian–Israeli peace treaty, and guidelines for the comprehensive settlement involving the other occupied territories and the Palestinians. Begin fought tenaciously and successfully for the most elastic possible language on the second document—and won.

The resulting "Framework for Peace in the Middle East" called for Egypt, Israel, and Jordan to negotiate a transitional self-governing authority to replace the existing Israeli military government in the West Bank and Gaza. This authority would last for not more than five years, during which further negotiations would determine the final status of the territories, recognizing both the "legitimate security concerns of the parties involved" and "the legitimate rights of the Palestinian people and their just requirements." Finally, Israel's other neighbors—Lebanon and Syria—were invited to negotiate a peace according to the same general principles.[14] The "framework" was hardly self-executing, because there was scarcely a phrase in it not vulnerable to stalemate. What were the "legitimate security concerns" of Israel, of Jordan, of the Palestinians? What were Palestinian "legitimate rights"? Since most Palestinians and the Arab states, other than Egypt, said those rights began with independence, and since Israel insisted that a Palestinian state and Israeli security were incompatible, there was little chance that the "framework" would achieve its objectives.

The signing of the two documents that constituted the Camp David accords was, however, a glorious moment for President Carter. With Sadat and Begin present, he declared to a joint session of Congress: "Today we are privileged to see the chance for one of the sometimes rare, bright moments in human history . . . We have a chance for peace, because these two brave leaders found within themselves the willingness to work together."[15]

The old pattern had not been broken. Euphoria gave way again to despair as Begin and Sadat were unable to conclude the bilateral peace treaty within the three-month period. Carter, now confronting the chaos of the Iranian revolution and working toward the conclusion of the SALT II agreement with the Soviet Union, was tempted to withdraw from the game. But once more he made a dramatic gesture—inviting himself on a moment's notice in March 1979 to visit Jerusalem and Cairo. There, in one further intense burst of negotiation, he helped the two sides hammer out the text of a treaty while simultaneously easing the process by offering both countries substantial new military assistance and promising Israel that the United States would supply oil if oil from the Sinai was for any reason cut off. The peace treaty was signed amid much pomp and ceremony in Washington on March 26, 1979.

There was no further progress in the remaining two years of the Carter Administration. Two special envoys, Robert Strauss and Sol Linowitz, wrestled with the problem of Palestinian autonomy. King Hussein of Jordan was uncooperative, caught between Israel's unwillingness to relinquish real control over the

West Bank and the PLO's adamant hatred of Israel. Prime Minister Begin kept increasing the Israeli presence in the West Bank by opening new settlements. And President Carter, looking ahead to reelection, faced sharp charges from some American Jews that he was no friend of Israel. The Administration suffered in the summer of 1979 when UN Ambassador Andrew Young met with the UN observer for the PLO—in seeming violation of an American pledge to Israel never to recognize or negotiate with the PLO until that organization acknowledged Israel's right to exist in peace. Young resigned under pressure—i.e., was fired—and was replaced by Donald McHenry. In March 1980, on the eve of the New York Democratic primary, there was a further embarrassment when the United States voted in favor of a resolution condemning Israel's presence in eastern Jerusalem. The vote was not intended and was the result, as Carter said, of a "failure to communicate."[16]

There was also a furor over accusations from unnamed senators that Hamilton Jordan, the President's chief of staff, and Jody Powell, his press secretary, had made "anti-Semitic remarks."[17] But most politically damaging of all was the unseemly and unethical involvement of the President's younger brother, Billy, as an agent for the government of Libya. "There are a lot more Arabs than there are Jews," said Billy when questioned about this.[18]

ARMS FOR THE ARABS

American military assistance to the Arab states was first used as an instrument of policy during the Second World War. Initially, arms were tendered as a way of establishing American influence alongside or superior to the British. As British power diminished and almost vanished after the Suez debacle of 1956, American military aid became a means of supporting anti-Soviet regimes, of saying that the United States was "evenhanded" in the Arab–Israeli dispute, and of protecting access to oil. The policy was marked by considerable success—and some failures. Iraq was a member of the anti-Soviet Baghdad pact in the 1950s, but then moved sharply to the left and became a Soviet client. Lebanon was so riven by internal factional conflict, and by the problem of Palestinian refugees using its territory for attacks against Israel, that no amount of American aid could have produced peace and stability. Syria's war with Israel and its support of the Palestinians created deep animosity toward the United States. Jordan's King Hussein, on the other hand, was able to walk a line between radical anti-Israel and anti-American elements and full support for the United States. American military aid helped make that possible.

The two great successes were Egypt, already discussed, and Saudi Arabia. The modern state of Saudi Arabia came into existence in 1932 when King Ibn Saud consolidated his control over several tribal factions on the Arabian peninsula. Ibn Saud lived and ruled until 1953, and after that, the country continued to be controlled by his extended royal family. In 1932 there was no known oil in the country, but the next year the Standard Oil Company of California secured a concession to explore—and found oil in 1938. By the 1950s, Saudi Arabia had become the most important oil producer in the Middle East. American oil interests and the American government worked well with the Saudi government. The small Saudi Army was supplied and trained by the United States, and during the 1950s and early 1960s the United States maintained an air base at Dhahran on the Persian Gulf.

After the Yom Kippur War of 1973, Saudi Arabia led the oil embargo against the industrial nations and was a decisive voice in OPEC's (Organization of Petroleum Exporting Countries) quadrupling of oil prices almost overnight. But after the embargo was lifted in 1974 the Saudis advertised their moderation in sustaining oil production at a level and at prices which would not strangle the industrial world. At the same time, Saudi Arabia acquired enormous financial power, thanks to billions of dollars of oil revenue—far beyond the country's capacity to spend on even the most extravagant development projects.

The Nixon, Ford, and Carter Administrations shared a single perception: the United States and the Saudi royal family needed each other. Saudi Arabia needed military assistance against potential internal revolt or a combination of internal revolt and a foreign-based invasion—for example, one originating in the neighboring Soviet-backed People's Democratic Republic of Yemen (South Yemen). And the United States and its allies needed Saudi oil. The problem which the Carter Administration inherited was how to keep Saudi Arabia happy without damaging relations with Israel, or, more precisely, without incurring the politically expensive wrath of Israel's supporters in the United States.

During his 1976 campaign, candidate Carter discovered that talking tough about the Arabs usually was good for applause—especially before Jewish groups. For example, he said in September 1976 that he was opposed to heavy arms sales to Saudi Arabia. He would not accept the argument that such sales were necessary to prevent oil from being cut off. The moment the Arabs embargoed oil during his Presidency, he added: "We will instantly prohibit the sale of anything to those countries who embargo us—no weapons, no nothing."[19]

President Carter later adopted a different tone. He quickly discovered that Saudi hostility would not only jeopardize access to oil but would also prevent a settlement between Egypt and Israel. Therefore, he invited Saudi leaders to the United States and visited the kingdom himself in early 1978—finding the Saudis reasonable and accommodating, at least in private discussions. The Saudis, however, made it clear that the test of American friendship would be approval of the sale of sixty F-15 jet fighter planes. Carter said he would oblige. The sale then became a test of the Administration's political power in the United States.

The F-15 was the most advanced and expensive jet fighter in the American arsenal. It had a top speed of 2,000 mph and could climb seven miles in a minute after takeoff. With advanced radar and missiles, it could seek out and destroy other aircraft within a fifty-mile radius. It had a range of nine hundred miles as a fighter; slightly less when carrying bombs. The Administration knew that a proposed sale to Saudi Arabia alone had no chance of approval by Congress; therefore, a package was worked out and announced in February 1978: the sixty F-15s for Saudi Arabia; fifteen F-15s and seventy-five less formidable F-16s for Israel; and fifty of the older F-5s for Egypt.

The package did not silence criticism. Prime Minister Begin asked that the sales to Israel be considered first and separately. No, said the Administration.[20] Senator Jacob Javits (R–NY) said it was ominous that the President was making assistance to Israel conditional on supplying comparable weapons to the Arabs. "There is a psychological meaning to this package that goes beyond the military," said an influential Jewish lobbyist. "This," he added, "suggests to people that the United States has made a decisive turn against its special relationship with Israel."[21] The Administration and the Saudis both replied that the planes were intended for defense against Saudi Arabia's radical enemies. Secretary of Defense Brown told the Senate Foreign Relations Committee in May 1978 that Iraq to the north was a Soviet client with over four hundred combat aircraft; the People's Republic of Yemen to the south had already used its planes for incursions against Saudi Arabia; and "the Soviet Union has delivered over $1 billion in military hardware to Ethiopia in a single year . . . These circumstances are of considerable concern to the United States; to Saudi Arabia they are a clear and present danger."[22]

Brown also denied that the planes could threaten Israel. To underline the point, the Administration secured an agreement that the planes would not be based close to the Israeli border and would not be equipped with bomb racks or special fuel tanks permitting extended range. Brown also pointed out that the first of the planes would not be ready for delivery until 1981.

The Administration won. On May 15, 1978, the Senate accepted the sale by a 54–44 vote. Since arms sales could be blocked only by both houses of Congress, the House of Representatives was not brought into the vote. The fall of the Shah in January 1979 and the Soviet invasion of Afghanistan in December confirmed the wisdom of the F-15 sale, from the Administration's perspective. Although oil prices doubled again in the spring of 1979, due in large part to events in Iran, Saudi Arabia continued to be a moderating voice within OPEC. After the fall of the Shah, a visit by Defense Secretary Brown to Saudi Arabia touched off rumors that the United States wanted to have bases and station troops in Saudi Arabia. The President denied it, but days later, during the crisis over North and South Yemen, the United States offered to send Saudi Arabia a squadron of F-15s and two AWACS planes (airborne warning and control system) manned by American Air Force personnel. Saudi Arabia accepted the AWACS, but not the F-15s. The AWACS remained only a short time, and were withdrawn after the outbreak of the war between Iraq and Iran in September 1980. As the Carter Administration came to an end, the President was contemplating providing the Saudis with the bomb racks and fuel tanks, which would enhance the performance of the F-15s they were purchasing.

THE TWO YEMENS

The south coast of the Arabian peninsula is occupied by three small countries. Oil-rich Oman to the east looks across the Gulf of Oman to Iran. Oman was ruled during the Carter years and before by a moderate pro-Western regime. In 1980, Oman granted the United States access to the island of Masirah for a naval base.

To the west are North and South Yemen.[23] The Yemen Arab Republic (North Yemen) overlooks the entrance to the Red Sea. North Yemen since 1975 had been receiving American arms paid for by and transported through Saudi Arabia, but had also received some aid from the Soviet Union.

In between North Yemen and Oman lies the People's Republic

of Yemen (South Yemen). The principal city of South Yemen is Aden, until 1967 an important British naval base. After the British withdrawal from what was then the Aden Protectorate, a Marxist faction gained control of the new country and welcomed Soviet military aid. In return, the Soviet Navy, just beginning to acquire the ability to operate far from home waters, gained access to the facilities at Aden. Despite a small population—estimated at just under two million—South Yemen engaged in propaganda attacks and military skirmishing against both North Yemen and Saudi Arabia. When the Soviets and the Cubans began their heavy support of Ethiopia in the dispute with Somalia, Brzezinski immediately saw a strategic connection. He wrote in his journal in December 1977 that "if Ethiopia and South Yemen become Soviet associates, not only will access to Suez be threatened, and this involves the oil pipeline from Saudi Arabia and Iran, but there will be a serious and direct political threat to Saudi Arabia."[24] In early 1979, just after the fall of the Shah removed Iran as an element of pro-Western military security, and while President Carter was engaged in his final effort to bring Egypt and Israel to sign their peace treaty, the endemic crisis between the two Yemens appeared to escalate suddenly. The North Yemenis, eager to get aid directly from the United States rather than through Saudi Arabia, sent exaggerated reports of an invasion from South Yemen.

Washington took the bait. American intelligence reports indicated that there were between thirteen hundred and seventeen hundred Soviet and Cuban advisers and troops, and possibly also some Ethiopians, assisting South Yemen. The Saudi government put its forces on alert. And the Carter Administration rushed a large amount of weapons to North Yemen on an emergency basis not requiring congressional approval. The $390 million package included twelve F-5s, heavy artillery, a considerable quantity of anti-tank weapons, and a contingent of American advisers. President Carter also ordered the aircraft carrier *USS Constellation*, with a supporting task force, detached from the Seventh Fleet in the Pacific and sent to the Arabian Sea, "to demonstrate our concern for the security of the Arabian Peninsula."[25] These ships became the nucleus of the force that would operate in the same area during the crises over the hostages in Iran and the Soviet invasion of Afghanistan.

While the United States was rushing weapons to North Yemen, a group of Arab states, led by Iraq, Syria, and Jordan, arranged a ceasefire and brought the two Yemens into constructive conversations. The crisis was over. The presidents of the two Yemens even discussed the possibility of unification. The most ironic touch was North Yemen's conclusion, shortly afterwards, of an agreement with the Soviet Union to receive twice the amount of arms supplied by the United States. As a careful scholar of Soviet policy has concluded, the Soviets had not instigated the skirmishing between the two Yemens. The United States was responding, not to reality, but to imaginary possibilities based on the assumption of a sinister Soviet grand design.[26] The determination of the Carter Administration to prove that the United States was not powerless dictated the response. As one American intelligence official remarked, "If Yemen had not happened at that particular time, it would have been invented."[27]

THE CYPRUS PROBLEM AND RAPPROCHEMENT WITH TURKEY

One of the oldest and truest clichés of geopolitics is that the Middle East is the bridge connecting Europe, Asia, and Africa. The Carter Administration's concern over Soviet activity in Ethiopia and South Yemen illustrated the African dimension. Its policy toward Turkey and Turkey's long-standing quarrel with Greece over the island of Cyprus made the European connection.

Greece and Turkey were among the first recipients of American protection at the outset of the Cold War. President Harry S. Truman's famous doctrine of March 1947, declaring that the

United States would "support free peoples who are resisting attempted subjugation by armed minorities or outside pressure," was specifically addressed to the right-wing Greek government's effort to put down a guerrilla insurgency and Turkey's efforts to stand up to Soviet demands for a special defense relationship which might make Turkey little more than a satellite. The American protective umbrella was reinforced in 1951 when Greece and Turkey became members of NATO. Heavy American military aid flowed to both countries, and a particularly close relationship developed with Turkey. Some of the first-generation American nuclear missiles were deployed in Turkey, aimed across the border into the Soviet Union. Although these missiles became obsolete and were removed after the Cuban crisis of 1962, nuclear warheads continued to be stored in Turkey. The United States also established elaborate radar and electronic surveillance facilities in Turkey with which to monitor Soviet weapons testing and troop movements.

But Greece and Turkey, although partners in NATO, were ancestral enemies. In the 1960s, that enmity twice led to the brink of war. The issue was Cyprus. The British had controlled this large island forty miles off the Turkish coast (and one hundred miles from Lebanon) since the nineteenth century, until it was granted independence in 1960 under the presidency of the Greek Cypriot Archbishop Makarios. The archbishop's goal was to maintain Cyprus as an independent nation, non-aligned in the Cold War, with mutual respect at home between the Greek majority and the Turkish minority (about eighteen percent of the population of 600,000). The principal obstacle to Makarios's goal was the passionate and violent commitment of many Greeks to union, enosis, with Greece. The advocates of enosis also had the habit of killing Turkish Cypriots. The Turkish government, in turn, felt protective of the Turks on Cyprus and welcomed every opportunity to assert itself against Greek extremists. In 1964 and 1967, the United States intervened politically to avert invasions by Turkey—on the second occasion, Cyrus Vance was President Lyndon Johnson's emissary in a particularly hectic round of shuttle diplomacy.

During the Nixon–Kissinger years, the United States supported the brutal military government of Greece (which had seized power in 1967) and silently condoned that government's objective of ousting Makarios and annexing Cyprus. The climax of the Greek military government's program and the downfall of that government took place simultaneously in the summer of 1974. Makarios was overthrown, barely escaping with his life, and the agents of the military rulers in Athens launched attacks on the Turkish settlements on Cyprus. Turkey responded with a full-scale invasion. The military dictators in Athens lost their nerve and resigned. Amid great rejoicing, democracy was restored in Greece—with Constantine Caramanlis as Prime Minister. The new government, however, withdrew Greece's military participation in NATO.

The United States supported an effort to work out a diplomatic settlement at Geneva among the Turks, Greeks, and Cypriots. But the effort collapsed. The Turks resumed military operations and de facto annexed the northern part of the island. The Turks were using American weapons in clear violation of American laws, which required that recipients use military aid only for legitimate purposes of self- or collective defense. Liberal congressmen and senators—busy in the wake of Vietnam with efforts to force the executive branch to heed the dictates of law and morality—demanded that the United States cut off all military aid to Turkey. Secretary of State Kissinger deplored the proposed embargo, both as unwarranted congressional interference in the President's conduct of foreign policy and as a blow to NATO and American security. Twice, President Ford vetoed embargo legislation, but a powerful and assertive Congress prevailed. The embargo went into effect in February 1975. Turkey retaliated by closing down the American radar sites.[28]

The incoming Carter Administration confronted a shambles.

Turkish troops were still on Cyprus. Turkey and Greece had both ceased to be viable members of NATO, and both were at odds with the United States. Carter during his campaign blamed Kissinger for this outcome. While avoiding direct endorsement of the congressional arms embargo, he deplored Kissinger's "tilting away from Greece and Cyprus" and said that morality and long-term American interests demanded that Turkey agree to a peaceful solution of the Cyprus issue as a condition to improved relations with the United States.[29]

Vance considered the Cyprus problem serious and "time urgent"—almost on a par with the Arab–Israeli dispute.[30] He urged that the United States undertake a major initiative. Carter agreed and after his inauguration sent Clark Clifford—eminent Washington insider, an important national security adviser to Truman, and Secretary of Defense at the end of the Johnson Administration—on a special mission to Greece, Turkey, and Cyprus. Also, President Carter talked with Turkish Prime Minister Suleyman Demirel in London in May 1977, and Vance went to Greece and Turkey in January 1978. The result of this high-level flurry of attention was to persuade the contending parties that talking was more useful than fighting—although Turkish forces remained on Cyprus, and there was no significant progress toward a settlement.

By 1978, the Carter Administration had decided its overriding objective should be the repeal of the legislation placing an embargo on arms shipments to Turkey. Although the embargo was justified when applied in 1975, said President Carter, it had simply failed. "It has not resulted in any progress being made in . . . restoring the human rights of the Greek Cypriots, who have indeed suffered and who suffer today. It's driven a wedge between Turkey and the rest of the NATO countries, between Greece and NATO, between us and Turkey. And I hope that the Congress will act expeditiously" to repeal it.[31] Congress complied, but conditioned repeal on Turkey's "good-faith" commitment to a peaceful settlement in Cyprus. The key vote in the Senate, 57–42, in

July 1978, showed that Carter on this issue had strong Republican support (27–10) but had lost among senators of his own party (30–32). Many liberals were dismayed by the President's abandonment of moral principle in favor of expediency.

The wisdom of repeal seemed amply confirmed by the fall of the Shah of Iran and the loss of American intelligence-collection facilities in that country, and even more by the Soviet invasion of Afghanistan. With the resumption of military aid, the Turkish facilities were reactivated. Turkey's economic problems were addressed by her NATO partners, with West Germany offering the most assistance; and the Greek government agreed to discuss the reintegration of her forces into NATO. In September 1980, the Turkish military overthrew the civilian government. The United States responded calmly—noting with approval the military's declared intention of restoring democracy, and promising that military and economic aid would continue. The place of Greece and Turkey as linchpins of American security in both Europe and the Middle East seemed secure.

President Carter had reason to be satisfied with his Administration's achievements in the Middle East (excluding Iran, of course). The Camp David accords and the subsequent peace treaty between Egypt and Israel constituted the centerpiece and were a tribute to Carter's personal tenacity and capacity for hard work. There had been no progress on the Palestinian question and no agreement between Israel and her other neighbors, but as long as Egypt and Israel were at peace, other armed conflicts—for example, Israel against the Palestinians in Lebanon—were not likely to escalate.

By maintaining a solid relationship with Saudi Arabia and repairing the torn fabric of U.S.–Turkish–Greek relations, the Administration strengthened its military strategic position in the region. Much of the overall success was due to the skill and motivation of foreign leaders, especially Sadat of Egypt. But it also rested on general agreement within the Administration and between the Administration and Congress. Vance and Brzezinski had some small tactical disagreements, but they saw eye to eye on fundamental questions—in contrast to their disagreements over the primacy to be accorded a SALT agreement, over relations with China, and over Africa. Some congressmen thought the Administration was insufficiently committed to Israel or too ready to forget Turkey's military action in Cyprus, but they never came close to blocking basic policy as the Senate did with SALT II and almost did with the Panama treaties.

_8_

Iran, the Shah, and the Hostages

Three times between 1949 and 1979, major revolutions on the Asian landmass derailed American foreign policy and within the United States contributed to the discrediting and loss of power of American Presidents. The victory of the Chinese communists over the American-supported Nationalist regime of Chiang Kai-shek damaged the Truman Presidency and helped the Republicans to victory in 1952. The victory of the Vietnamese communists over the United States and its client government in South Vietnam led Lyndon Johnson to virtual abdication in 1968 and was an indirect cause of Richard Nixon's resignation in 1974 in the face of impending impeachment. Well might Jimmy Carter have prayed in 1977 to be protected from similar domestic consequences of a revolution in a distant country, a revolution beyond the power of the United States to stop or control and yet an event from which it would prove impossible to escape.

But this was not to be. The Islamic uprising in Iran against the Shah—an authoritarian ruler whose power had been synonymous with American presence in the country for a quarter century—and the seizure a year later of the American Embassy in Teheran and the holding of hostages led to Jimmy Carter's political downfall and overshadowed everything else that he had achieved or tried to do. In contrast to the problems with China and Vietnam, the situation in Iran was an almost completely unanticipated catastrophe. Carter scarcely mentioned Iran during his campaign. Cyrus Vance in his tour-of-the-horizon memorandum of October 1976 wrote only of the national interest in maintaining friendly and cooperative relations; he foresaw no problems.[1] The general public was unaware of Iran. Television, on which most Americans depend for their news, ignored the country. In the six years from 1972 through 1977, the three networks had devoted an average of only five minutes per year to material on Iran.[2] During the 444 days of the American hostages' captivity, television seemed to have time for nothing else.

That is not to say that Iran was ignored by diplomatic and national-security specialists. They viewed Iran as an essential part of the American security system—a reliable military ally and keeper of the peace in the Persian Gulf region, a secure source of petroleum when less friendly nations curtailed or embargoed exports, and a valuable customer for American exports. In 1977, the Iranian–American relationship seemed to be one of the shining success stories of American foreign policy since the Second World War.

"AN ISLAND OF STABILITY"

The interest of the United States in Iran (the modern name for Persia) began during the Second World War. While the Soviet Union and Great Britain temporarily occupied the country in order to block German influence, American diplomats and President Franklin D. Roosevelt came to believe that the United States was Iran's unselfish protector against imperialist encroachment. After the war, the British withdrew their troops but retained their exclusive control of Iran's oil production through the Anglo–Iranian Oil Company. The Soviets, in violation of a wartime pledge, kept troops in northern Iran into 1946 and supported an anti-Teheran separatist movement in the province of Azerbaijan. President Harry S. Truman demanded that the Soviets withdraw. When they did, he believed the United States had triumphed as

Iran's savior and that talking tough to the Soviets worked.[3] Six years later, the Truman Administration persuaded the British not to use military force to turn back Iran's nationalization of the oil industry, lest Iran be pushed into the arms of the Soviet Union. With the United States acting as mediator, Iran won a degree of control over its own oil. Seven international oil companies (five of which were American) replaced the Anglo–Iranian company in the marketing of the oil.[4]

Mohammed Mossadegh, the intensely patriotic Iranian politician who had engineered the nationalization of the oil industry, decided in 1953 to oust the young Shah, Mohammed Reza Pahlavi, and turn Iran into a republic. The United States, perceiving this as a move which would enhance Soviet influence and possibly convert Iran into a communist satellite, used the Central Intelligence Agency to arrange a countercoup whereby the Shah, supported by right-wing officers in the Army, consolidated his power and removed Mossadegh.[5] The United States thereupon became Iran's principal supplier of technical, economic, and military aid. By the 1970s, Iran's military forces, armed and trained by the United States, were the most powerful in the Middle East. Their importance, from the American point of view, was enhanced by Britain's decision to withdraw its military presence east of Suez. In 1973–74, the Shah earned American gratitude by refusing to join the Arab embargo on oil shipments to the United States, inflicted because of American support for Israel during the Yom Kippur War. But Iran and the Shah received full benefit from the soaring oil prices, which were a consequence of the war and the embargo. With apparently limitless billions of dollars to spend on military equipment, the Shah placed orders, mostly in the United States, with the abandon of an alcoholic using a credit card in a liquor store. The Nixon Administration encouraged the Shah in this course. His purchases helped the American balance-of-payment problem, brought profit to the American defense industry, and seemed to make a staunch friend and opponent of the Soviet Union even stronger. The Shah in turn developed ever grander concepts of Iran's military role as the major power of the Middle East, perhaps even as a world power.[6] He also indulged a penchant for lecturing the United States on its lack of social discipline and firm political purpose.[7]

By 1976, there were over twenty-five thousand Americans working and seventy thousand living in Iran, most of them connected in some way to the buildup of the Shah's military forces. These Americans resided primarily in the wealthy northern part of the capital, Teheran. Their Iranian associates were the military and other favorites of the Shah—wealthy, Westernized politicians and businessmen. Very few Americans could speak Farsi, the language of Iran. Hardly any had even the slightest knowledge of Iranian society outside the Shah's opulent circle. They had no contact with the rural poor, the overcrowded urban slums of Teheran, the discontented traditional merchants who were not benefiting from the Shah's high-technology modernization, or with the pent-up anger of the fundamentalist Islamic clergy, who believed that the Shah was desecrating the religious principles of the country.[8]

During his Presidential campaign in 1976, Carter had criticized the high level of American arms sales to Iran. But as President he soon found himself arguing with Congress and against his own principles. The issue involved seven AWACS (airborne warning and control system) aircraft desired by the Shah, which required congressional approval before they could be sold. These large jet planes were packed with very advanced and secret electronic surveillance and communication devices, the pride of American technological achievement. When cruising high above the earth, AWACS planes could track movement on the ground or in the air over thousands of square miles. They would give any force a tremendous military advantage, both defensive and offensive, over forces not similarly equipped. The Shah, who had been denied nothing short of nuclear weapons by the Nixon–Ford Administrations, wanted these new toys, and the American military considered their sale a good idea. But Congress raised the possibility that the AWACS planes and their secret devices might fall into Soviet hands. Faced with certain disapproval of the sale, the Carter Administration withdrew the request in the summer of 1977 in order to present it in amended form. The Shah was furious and threatened to cancel the order for the planes. "I don't care whether he buys them from us or not," President Carter wrote in his diary.[9]

That was not entirely true. Perceived strategic necessity quickly prevailed over personal pique. The United States and its European and Asian allies needed Iranian oil. American radar and listening stations in Iran close to the border with the Soviet Union were important for observing Russian missile tests. The outbreak of fighting between Ethiopia and Somalia suggested that Iranian military power might be necessary in the strategic Horn of Africa. There was no alternative to pressing ahead with the AWACS deal. The Administration finally won approval of the sale in the fall of 1977, but only after months of delay and the insertion of safeguard provisions which reflected on the reliability of the Shah's regime. The episode was a major embarrassment both to relations between the United States and the Shah and to Carter's image as an idealist pledged to restrain the sale of arms.

The Administration decided that the Shah needed some hand-holding and reassurance. He and the Empress were invited to make a state visit to Washington in November 1977. An additional reason for the invitation was President Carter's desire to win the Shah's support for Anwar Sadat's peace mission to Israel, which would take place at the end of the month. Some Iranian students in the United States seized the opportunity to publicize their dislike of the Shah's rule. While President and Mrs. Carter received the Shah and the Empress on the White House lawn, shouting demonstrators assembled outside the grounds. The police sprayed the crowd with tear gas, and the gas drifted over the Carters and their guests, causing considerable discomfort.

Afterwards, President Carter spoke privately to the Shah about

American uneasiness over political repression and reports of widespread violations of human rights in Iran, through the operations of the feared SAVAK (security police). Rosalynn Carter concluded this was "probably the first time an American official had ever addressed the issue with him."[10] She was probably right. The Shah, who had occupied the throne for nearly four decades, did not take well to being lectured by an upstart American politician. He replied that harsh methods would be necessary as long as the communist menace remained. He dismissed those demonstrating outside the White House fence as mere hirelings of communists and said that those who complained were "just a tiny minority, and have no support among the vast majority of Iranian people."[11] When the Shah had gone, President Carter told Hamilton Jordan that he felt reassured about conditions in Iran; the United States was "fortunate to have this strong leader as an ally."[12]

The Shah invited President Carter and Mrs. Carter to return the state visit, and since the President was already scheduled for foreign travel over New Year's to eight countries in Europe and Asia, Iran was added to the itinerary. Seldom in American diplomatic history had flattery been carried to such excess as it was on that occasion. The Carters were entertained at a lavish banquet in Niyavaran Palace. The journalist Pierre Salinger, who was present, was bemused by the spectacle. "The Iranians, richly dressed, seemed like the modern equivalent of the bewigged French men and women who had filled the halls of the Palais de Versailles in the days of Louis XIV, an illusion reinforced by the dozens of liveried waiters who passed among us, offering Dom Perignon champagne."[13]

At the appropriate moment, Carter rose to toast his host. He began by noting that some people had asked why a visit so close upon the Shah's trip to Washington. The reason, he said, was that when he asked Mrs. Carter with whom she would like to spend New Year's Eve, she replied: "Above all others, I think, with the Shah and Empress Farah." What President Carter then said would afterwards be thrown back in his face many times, and deservedly so, for seldom have more wrong assumptions been crammed into so few words.

> Iran, because of the great leadership of the Shah, is an island of stability in one of the more troubled areas of the world.
>
> This is a great tribute to you, Your Majesty, and to your leadership and to the respect and the admiration and love which your people give you . . .
>
> As I drove through the beautiful streets of Tehran today with the Shah, we saw literally thousands of Iranian citizens, standing beside the street with a friendly attitude, expressing their welcome to me. And I also saw hundreds, perhaps even thousands of American citizens who stood there welcoming their President to a nation which has taken them to heart and made them feel at home . . .
>
> We have no other nation on Earth who is closer to us in planning for our mutual security . . . And there is no leader with whom I have a deeper sense of personal gratitude and personal friendship.[14]

For the next six months, Americans saw no intimations of trouble, despite sporadic rioting led by Islamic fundamentalists opposed to the Shah's programs. Ambassador William Sullivan, picked for his post because of experience in coordinating diplomatic and military programs during the Vietnam war and because of his success in dealing as ambassador with the dictatorial Ferdinand Marcos of the Philippines, was concerned that Iran was being stuffed with more military equipment than it could assimilate.[15] But when David Newsom, Under Secretary of State for Political Affairs, visited Teheran in July, he heard the Shah expatiate on his desire to leave to his son a legacy of a modern as well as a technologically advanced state. Newsom was impressed. The Shah seemed "genuine."[16] In July, the Shah asked the United States to sell seventy additional jet fighter planes to Iran.

ALL HELL BREAKS LOOSE

In August and September 1978, all hell broke loose in Iran. Terrorists (whose identity and affiliation have not been established) set fire to a movie theater in the oil-refinery city of Abadan, and 377 people died. Rioting throughout the country intensified and hundreds were killed when the Shah's forces faced the mobs. Demonstrations were banned and martial law declared. There were more demonstrations—and more deaths. The worst occurred on September 8, "Black Friday," when troops fired on demonstrators in Jaleh Square, Teheran, and killed more than two hundred (some estimates put the number of dead as high as two thousand). President Carter, then in the midst of the Camp David meetings, became aware for the first time of the enormity of the problem. He telephoned words of support and sympathy to the Shah.

On October 4, 1978, the Ayatollah Ruhollah Khomeini, leader of the Shah's fundamentalist enemies, was expelled from Iraq (where he had been living in exile for fifteen years and whence he had been dispatching inflammatory cassette-recorded sermons against the Shah to be played in the mosques of the faithful). He went to Paris and became an instant television celebrity, sitting in his white robes, dark eyes above a flowing beard, thundering his denunciations of the Shah and of the greater Satan, the United States.

The next three months brought the end of the Shah's rule. The American role in the debacle has been minutely explored by dozens of participants and other commentators and has been subject to endless recriminations.[17] The Carter Administration was very slow to realize the seriousness of the situation. It was hampered by a lack of understanding of Iranian history and society, and especially of the political character of the Islamic clergy. It acted in a confused way in the face of a very confusing situation. There were conflicting voices in Washington, and no coordination. Above all, there was no agreement on how far to back the Shah in using force to suppress the revolution or on when to accept the inevitability of the collapse of his government and begin to disentangle American prestige from a political corpse. Those in the State Department, led by the head of the Iranian desk, Henry Precht, who believed the Shah's days were numbered felt frustrated by an inability to get their views accepted. They saw National Security Adviser Brzezinski as their principal bureaucratic enemy and reacted toward him with animosity of "nearly pathological proportions."[18] But even if American officials had possessed the ability to see into the future, had understood the Islamic clergy, had spoken with one voice and coordinated their efforts, and had decided precisely how to back the Shah—even if all these things had been the case, would the outcome have been fundamentally different? The answer is almost certainly no. When the Carter Administration took office in 1977, too much had occurred over too many years. The Shah could not have retained his throne, except temporarily, through the use of force on a massive scale. The United States could not have escaped identification with the Shah no matter what American officials said and did after 1977. Those who boil over with accusations and who believe in the might-have-been approach to history must go back to at least 1953, when the Shah first became an authoritarian ruler supported by the armed forces and the United States, if they want to argue plausibly that Iran was "lost" because of American error. President Carter inherited an impossible situation—and he and his advisers made the worst of it.

THE IRON FIST OR LIBERALIZATION

An unpopular regime faced with revolt can either reform itself and seek to become popular or use whatever means are necessary to crush the revolt—or a combination of both. Timing is crucial. Beyond a certain point, reform and apology for the past will naught avail and may indeed intensify the revolt by indicating the regime's lack of confidence. Brute force, on the other hand, makes peaceful accommodation impossible, increases popular hatred of the regime, offends humanitarian values, and makes the inevitable end all the more terrible. Both the Shah and the unhappy American observers realized these things in the fall of 1978 and could not decide which way to go.

The Shah made several gestures toward reform. He renewed a promise that there would be parliamentary elections in 1979, he freed fifteen hundred political prisoners on his fifty-ninth birthday (October 25), and he ordered the dismissal of nearly two thousand SAVAK officials because of their excesses. Americans applauded these measures, and some, especially those who saw violations of human rights as the basic cause of Iran's instability, hoped he would go further.

National Security Adviser Brzezinski, on the other hand, believed that the revolution had reached a stage where only the application of firm, unwavering, and confident force could hold the regime in power. Brzezinski was fond of citing historian Crane Brinton's *The Anatomy of Revolution* to the effect that no regime with the confidence to use adequate force had ever been dislodged by a revolution. He believed that this tautological wisdom provided the answer to Iran: the iron fist.

Brzezinski tried to encourage the Shah in this direction by sending messages through Ardeshir Zahedi, the Iranian ambassador in Washington and son of the general who in 1953 played a key role in the Shah's and the CIA's victory over Mohammed Mossadegh. But Brzezinski's views were strongly challenged within the Department of State. Assistant Secretary Patricia Derian, responsible for keeping human-rights considerations to the fore, saw Iran as a test case. She consistently argued in favor of pressing the Shah to institute reforms. Ambassador Sullivan in Teheran, though not a human-rights idealist, doubted that the Shah retained sufficient support to use force effectively. Sullivan was also struck by a change in the Shah's character—from straight-backed self-confidence to depressed indecision and delusions that the CIA was out to get him.[19] The Shah's still-secret illness with cancer, and the related medication, may have been a cause. The Shah in his self-pitying memoirs not surprisingly concluded, after it was over, that Brzezinski had been right. He dismissed the State Department's call for liberalization as a Herculean fantasy and praised Brzezinski for having "his priorities straight. He called me in early November to urge that I establish law and order first, and only then continue our democratization process."[20]

Ambassador Sullivan decided in early November that the United States ought to open communications with the Ayatollah Khomeini and be prepared to carry on business with a new government, should the Shah fall, as seemed likely. He sent a long cable—entitled "Thinking the Unthinkable"—making such a recommendation.[21] The cable caused "consternation" in Washington and made President Carter confront for the first time the fact that the Shah might not survive. But Sullivan never received a response. Instead, he was increasingly distrusted by Carter and Brzezinski as an ambassador disloyal to the Administration's policies. The State Department did, however, eventually instruct its most senior Farsi-speaking officer, Theodore Eliot, to visit Khomeini in Paris to convey American support for an orderly transition and to discuss mutual interest in avoiding Soviet intervention. But the Eliot mission was cancelled out of fear of its impact on the Shah.[22]

At the end of November, Secretary of the Treasury Michael Blumenthal visited Iran and was appalled at the conditions he found. Blumenthal suggested that George Ball, Under Secretary of State in the Kennedy and Johnson Administrations, be invited as an outside wise man to look at the Iranian mess and make recommendations. In the 1960s, Ball had earned a reputation as a lone high-level dissenter against American involvement in the Vietnam war, and more recently had garnered praise and vilification for warning that the United States was tying its Middle East policy too closely and uncritically to Israel. He was a good friend of Secretary Vance's—and Vance welcomed his appointment.

Ball's first step was to decline all suggestions that he visit Iran.

"I had learned from our Vietnam experience how dangerous it can be when travel is substituted for thought," he wrote later. Although Ball was given office space at the National Security Council in the White House, he quickly concluded that Brzezinski was part of the problem. When Brzezinski told Ball not to leak information to the State Department, Ball decided to rely primarily on the department for information and perspective. Ball's report, submitted to President Carter on December 11, 1978, reflected Ambassador Sullivan's and the department's view that the Shah was about to collapse. Ball suggested that the United States arrange for the appointment of a "Council of Notables," older Iranian political figures not tainted by previous subservience to the Shah. The council would preside over a transition and give legitimacy to a new government, with the Shah remaining on the throne but with diminished power. If the idea ever had any merit (which is doubtful, given the lack of talent among those who might form such a council), its time was long past.

Carter and Brzezinski rejected the recommendation. They still hoped the Shah could survive. Brzezinski thought that if the Shah did fall, the alternative should be a military government which would sustain Iran's strategic ties to the United States. President Carter told Ball that he was sending Brzezinski to Iran. Ball replied by calling this, "with all due respect, the worst idea I have heard." Brzezinski's presence would only exacerbate anti-American feeling in the country. Brzezinski did not go.

Secretary Vance was in Florida when Ball submitted his report, but he read a copy and telephoned his praise. Ball took the opportunity to warn Vance that the situation in the National Security Council was "shockingly unhealthy." Brzezinski was "doing everything possible to exclude the State Department from participation in, or even knowledge of, our developing relations with Iran."[23]

There was nothing but bad news for the Shah throughout December. Hundreds more were killed during demonstrations. Strikes virtually closed down the economy and put an end to oil

exports. The State Department began urging American depen-
dents to leave the country. On the last day of the year, the Shah
named Shahpour Bakhtiar, a onetime associate of Mossadegh's,
to be Prime Minister. Bakhtiar had no significant following and
no power or influence. Exactly one year after President Carter's
fulsome toast to the Shah's strength and leadership, the end was
at hand.

THE RETURN OF THE
AYATOLLAH KHOMEINI

The year 1979 opened with President Carter on his way to the
French Caribbean island of Guadeloupe for a summit meeting
with French President Valéry Giscard d'Estaing, British Prime
Minister James Callaghan, and German Chancellor Helmut
Schmidt. The moment the President arrived, he received a tele-
phone call from Vice President Mondale on the latest bad news
from Iran. At dinner that evening, Mrs. Carter listened to the
European leaders discuss the Shah. She later noted in her diary:

> Schmidt: We all knew how weak he was, but I'm surprised
> that he's going under before the Saudis.
>
> Callaghan: Everybody is of the same opinion . . . very weak.
> Nobody has been willing to tell the shah the truth. We haven't
> told him the truth about the disintegrating situation in ten
> years.
>
> Schmidt: There was absolutely no dissent around him. The
> only one ever to disagree with him was his wife.

It was a fine display of wisdom after the event, as Mrs. Carter
noted.[24] The Shah afterwards concluded that his ouster was planned
and agreed upon at Guadeloupe. He said the meeting might be
considered the "Yalta of the Mideast"—except that the benefi-
ciary, the Soviet Union, was not present.[25] The Shah was, of

course, wrong. Nothing was planned for him at Gaudeloupe, because his end had already been accepted as a fait accompli.

Although President Carter did not send Brzezinski to Iran, he did contemplate a mission by Secretary of Energy (and onetime Secretary of Defense) James Schlesinger, and then decided on General Robert Huyser, deputy to the NATO commander, General Alexander Haig. General Huyser arrived in Teheran on January 3, 1979. The precise purpose of his mission was unclear to everyone. Officially, Huyser was to encourage the military to remain loyal to the Bakhtiar government upon the departure of the Shah. At the same time, he embodied Brzezinski's hope that somehow the United States could rally the military to put down the revolution. His task was to demonstrate that Ambassador Sullivan was wrong in saying that the armed forces were incapable of such action because the enlisted men would not wage war against their brothers and were more likely than not to join the revolution.

As the Shah prepared to leave Iran, President Carter invited him to come to the United States and arrangements were made for him to stay at the lavish Walter Annenberg estate in Beverly Hills, California, made available through the good offices of Henry Kissinger and Nelson Rockefeller. On January 16, the Shah left, but for Egypt, not the United States. Ambassador Sullivan believed the Shah expected the events of 1953 to repeat themselves, with the military regaining control and thus opening the way for his triumphant return to the throne. The Shah never returned, but the Ayatollah Khomeini did—from Paris on February 1, 1979.

In the next twelve days, Iranian military forces ceased opposing the revolution. Twenty-six American military advisers were trapped, under fire, in the military headquarters and saved thanks to the intervention of two of the Ayatollah Khomeini's closest aides. Prime Minister Bakhtiar disappeared (he surfaced eventually in Paris). There remained no group or person to challenge Khomeini. In Washington, Brzezinski to the last retained his dream of a military coup. When Ambassador Sullivan, in the midst of chaos, was queried by telephone from Washington about the feasibility of a coup, he made an indelicate suggestion to Under Secretary Newsom as to what Brzezinski could do with the idea.

"That is not very helpful," said Newsom.

"Do you want me to translate it into Polish?" said Sullivan.[26]

THE FORLORN HOPE OF ACCOMMODATION

With Khomeini's followers now in charge (insofar as anyone was in charge), the Iranian military guard which had been protecting the American Embassy compound was withdrawn. Ambassador Sullivan ordered all the remaining personnel to prepare to meet an attack. There were fewer than one hundred Americans attached to the embassy, where once there had been thousands. On the morning of February 14, the ambassador had just fulfilled an instruction from Washington to dispatch a formal note announcing that the United States would maintain diplomatic relations with the new government. Suddenly "a murderous barrage of automatic-weapon fire opened up on the embassy from all sides."[27] Soon, dozens of guerrillas came over the gates. Most of the Americans retreated to the vault area on the second floor of the main embassy building, where they began destroying codes and documents. Armed Iranians rushed into the building, and to Sullivan's surprise, they comprised both attackers and rescuers acting under the direction of Ibrahim Yazdi, Khomeini's newly appointed Foreign Minister. The rescuers prevailed, and there was no loss of American life. Yazdi explained that the attackers represented irresponsible elements of the revolution, and Khomeini himself sent an emissary to Sullivan to apologize. Thus ended the first attack on the American Embassy. It lasted but a few hours and left the Americans with the belief that the Ayatollah's government had the desire and the power to prevent anything which would rupture relations.

After the attack on the embassy, Carter agreed to rescind the invitation to the Shah to come to the United States. He acted on the basis of predictions from the embassy in Teheran, conveyed and supported by Secretary Vance, that Americans would be seized and lives endangered if the Shah came to the United States. Brzezinski deplored the decision. "It is unlikely we can build a relationship with Iran until things there have sorted themselves out," he told President Carter. "But it would be a sign of weakness not to allow the Shah to come to the United States to live. If we turned our backs on the fallen Shah, it would be a signal to the world that the U.S. is a fair-weather friend."[28] On this occasion, however, the President sided with Vance rather than with Brzezinski.

The Shah, then in Morocco, was told the bad news in March. He went instead to the Bahamas and then to Mexico—brooding, writing his memoirs, and losing his battle against cancer. David and Nelson Rockefeller, Henry Kissinger, and their associates led a campaign to persuade President Carter to change his mind and admit the Shah. But Carter stood firm, because he continued to fear that the Shah's presence in the United States might lead to Americans in Iran being taken hostage.[29] Those Americans were now a small band of embassy officials and staff, business people trying to disentangle the wreckage of broken contracts, and journalists.[30]

In March, Ambassador Sullivan returned to the United States on vacation, but with the knowledge that the White House wanted his resignation. Although he was offered another post, he resigned in bitterness from the Foreign Service after a thirty-five-year career. The possibility of appointing another ambassador was discussed with the Khomeini government, but no appointment was made, because of Teheran's objection to the Javits resolution in the Senate in May 1979 expressing abhorrence at the regime's mass executions of its opponents without proper trial.[31]

In June 1979, the Department of State sent Bruce Laingen to Teheran to take command of the embassy as chargé d'affaires.

Throughout the summer and early fall, there were small signs of improved relations. Laingen gradually extended his contacts with Iranian officials. The embassy resumed offering consular services—in order to provide documents for the large number of Iranian students who still wished to come to the United States. In October, Secretary Vance and several other high officials met with Iranian Foreign Minister Yazdi, who was in New York for the UN General Assembly meetings. Yazdi was not in a conciliatory mood as he defended the revolution and condemned the American relationship to the Shah. The Americans replied gently that the United States had no intention of intervening in Iran's internal affairs. Under Secretary Newsom, who participated in the conversations, came away modestly confident. He told Robert Shaplen (who was writing a profile for *The New Yorker*) that Iranian suspicion of the United States was understandable but that common interests would soon lead to cooperation—"not on the scale of before but sufficient to demonstrate that Iran has not been 'lost' to us and to the West."[32]

Common interests, of course, meant a mutual desire to contain the expansion of the Soviet Union. Moscow had belatedly given verbal support for the revolution and condemned the United States for its ties with the Shah; but in the autumn of 1979 the Soviet Union was obviously behind the suppression of Islamic dissent by the communist government of Afghanistan, Iran's neighbor to the east. Iran's Islamic leaders abhorred communism and shared their country's long-standing historical fear of Russia. In order to pursue these common interests, Henry Precht of the Department of State visited Iran to discuss the status of old contracts for the sale of military equipment, and especially to explore ways in which Iran could receive spare parts for the American equipment it already had. But the Vance–Yazdi talks and the Precht visit were moments of false light before descent into darkness.

The descent began when President Carter agreed that the Shah could come to New York from Mexico for medical treatment for his illness, now at a life-threatening stage. Chargé Laingen in Teheran was asked to sound out Foreign Minister Yazdi on the consequences of this move. Yazdi was not happy. But he gave Laingen the impression that the government could probably protect the embassy against a takeover, as it had done in February. On October 23, the Shah arrived in New York. For several days, the situation in Teheran remained relatively quiet. The government even succeeded in getting a large scheduled demonstration moved away from the vicinity of the embassy compound.[33]

But on November 1 another provocative incident occurred. Brzezinski went to Algiers for the celebration of the anniversary of Algerian independence. Iranian Prime Minister Mehdi Bazargan and Foreign Minister Yazdi also attended. Brzezinski talked with them briefly, and the next day photographs of the three together appeared in Teheran newspapers, inflaming fears among the more radical and anti-American elements of the revolution that the United States, "the great Satan," was about to perpetrate some new evil.[34]

Three days later, a mob of chanting students broke down the gates to the compound and seized the embassy within. The fatal crisis of the Carter Administration had begun.

THE POWER OF IMPOTENCE

It was 3 a.m. in Washington and 10:30 a.m. in Iran, Sunday morning, November 4, 1979, when the Operations Center in the Department of State received a telephone call from the Teheran embassy that a huge mob of youths had invaded the twenty-three acre embassy compound and was breaking into the buildings. Two hours later, seventy-six Americans had been captured. Chargé Laingen and two others, who happened to be at the Foreign Ministry on routine business, remained there. Six Americans escaped unseen and were granted secret asylum in the Canadian Embassy.[35]

The first hope of the Americans was that the events of February

14 would be repeated. Foreign Minister Yazdi had rescued the embassy once. Why not again? But now Yazdi and Prime Minister Mehdi Bazargan were powerless. Two days later, they resigned, and the Americans in Washington knew that the Ayatollah Khomeini had no intention of rescuing the hostages, that indeed he applauded their seizure. The capturing mob saw themselves and were seen by the fervent revolutionaries as heroic symbols of the triumph over the "Great Satan."

From the moment the hostages were seized until they were released minutes after Ronald Reagan took the oath as President 444 days later, the crisis absorbed more concentrated effort by American officials and had more extensive coverage on television and in the press than any other event since World War II, including the Vietnam war. Other issues were, perforce, neglected as the Administration tried every conceivable device to free the hostages unharmed while upholding American honor. The first objective was achieved. But since "honor" is more a question of subjective self-regard than of objective reality, the verdict on the second objective depended on the values of those rendering judgment. Unfortunately for Jimmy Carter, the verdict of the majority of voters in 1980 was negative. Robert Strauss, a shrewd appraiser of American politics and Carter's special trade representative, sensed within the first two weeks what was happening. "Poor bastard," he said of Carter, "he used up all his luck in getting here. We've had our share of victories and defeats, but we've not had a single piece of good luck in the past three years."[36]

Policy with regard to the hostage problem was more coordinated than policy regarding the predicament of the Shah had been; nevertheless, there was a fundamental conflict of values within the Administration. On one side was Secretary Vance's and the Department of State's preference for patient exploration of every avenue for a negotiated settlement, regardless of the number of setbacks or the months expended. And if negotiation was impossible, simply waiting for Iran to grow tired of the whole business was preferable to anything which would endanger lives. On the other side was Brzezinksi's insistence from the very beginning that the honor and foreign-policy interests of the nation were more important than the lives of the hostages. "At some point that greater responsibility could become more important than the safety of our diplomats," he told the President.[37]

In the first weeks, the State Department asked every friendly government, and some not so friendly, to use influence with Iran to secure the release of the hostages; brought the question to the International Court of Justice (World Court) and won a remarkably quick decision that Iran was acting illegally and must return the hostages and pay compensation; prepared the presentation of the American grievance for the UN Security Council; and worked to soothe and support the families of the hostages. The President sent former Attorney General Ramsey Clark, noted for his liberal sympathy for the Iranian revolution and his distaste for the Shah, to Iran in a conciliatory attempt at negotiation, but Khomeini's people would not receive him. Clark got no further than Turkey. Clark may have been responsible, however, for planting the suggestion that the Iranians release some of the hostages who were part of the support staff rather than policy officials in the embassy. On November 18, the Iranians did free thirteen lower-level members of the embassy staff, all of whom were black or women.

The President also prohibited the importation of Iranian oil (before Iran could impose an embargo) and froze Iran's substantial financial assets in American banks and under American banking control overseas—in anticipation of Iranian removal of those funds. No one at the time anticipated how complicated the eventual disposition of those funds would become in the ultimate negotiations for the release of the hostages.

Brzezinski took charge of considering the use of armed force. There proved to be two types of difficulty in the way of using force—the tactical and the political-psychological. Tactically, there seemed no way that the hostages, held by fanatical captives in the heart of a huge city five hundred miles from the nearest potential American launching point, could be rescued by an

American strike force. The instant such a force approached, assuming it could get as far as Teheran, the hostages would likely be killed. The political-psychological problem was even more difficult. The United States had the capacity, of course, to inflict military damage on oil refineries, military bases, or any targets it chose. It could bomb anywhere, mine harbors, even seize and hold an island or two in the Persian Gulf. All of these things were considered. But such attacks would strengthen, not punish, the revolution, and would be received with devout excitement as confirmation of the evil nature of the United States. Precisely because Khomeini's regime was so hysterically unstable, so impotent by ordinary Western standards of government, it was almost impervious to pressure. The kind of attack which would inflict enormous pain on an organized, operating government would have no effect—except to increase morale and help consolidate the revolution. Had the Khomeini regime commanded a stable, organized society dependent on international trade and finance and on the efficient functioning of public services, it would have been more vulnerable to coercion. The powerless, with little to lose, have a special power.

Nevertheless, planning and training for military action continued. Naval Captain Gary Sick of the National Security Council staff was the coordinator. Plans were based, Sick has since written, on five implicit guidelines. [38]

First, the United States should apply the arithmetic of calculated violence, making the cost of holding the hostages greater than the benefits. A difficulty here was trying to understand how Khomeini calculated costs and benefits.

Second, peaceful means for extricating the hostages should be exhausted before violence was applied. But who would define the meaning of "exhausted"—Brzezinski, the State Department, political advisers concerned about the President's loss of public support, the President himself?

Third, the United States would retaliate immediately if the

hostages were put on trial or physically harmed. The President issued such a warning and it appeared to be effective in preventing the trials which the Iranians kept threatening to hold. Captain Sick concluded that "the military option provided the United States at least a limited veto over certain potential excesses of Iranian behavior."

Fourth, the United States would make no threats it was unwilling or unable to carry out. In preparation, the United States added the carrier *Kitty Hawk* and supporting naval vessels to those already in the Arabian sea.

Fifth, no military action would be launched which was not reversible; i.e., which could not be called off at any time.

This was fine in theory, but the history of military operations teaches that violence, like sex, carries a momentum of its own which often takes charge of the will of those engaging in it. The President's intuition was correct. "The problem with all of the military options," he said, "is that we could use them and feel good for a few hours—until we found out they had killed our people. And once we start killing people in Iran, where will it end?"[39] The refusal of any Iranians in positions of authority to speak with American officials added to the Administration's frustration. Iranian conditions for the release of the captives were not precise, but they included return of the Shah for trial in Iran, the delivery of his supposedly enormous wealth stolen from the country, and abject apology from the United States. Although President Carter had been reluctant to allow the Shah into the United States for medical treatment, it was inconceivable that the Shah would be delivered to the Ayatollah. The President had no way of determining the extent of the Shah's assets in the United States or of legally turning them over. And an abject apology for having supported the Shah in the past was out of the question. UN Ambassador Donald McHenry, however, was instructed to say in a speech on December 4 that the United States was not "deaf to the passionate voices that speak of injustice, that cry out against past wrongs," and that the United States would support the convening of an appropriate forum to consider grievances—after the hostages were freed.[40]

Meanwhile, the Shah recovered sufficiently from surgery to leave the United States. Mexico, where he had been staying prior to his trip to New York, would not readmit him. Hamilton Jordan, the President's chief of staff, then arranged an invitation from General Torrijos of Panama for the Shah to stay on Contadora Island. After pausing in Texas, the Shah went to Panama in mid-December. He remained there until March, when, in fear that Panama might accede to Iranian demands for his extradition, he flew to Egypt.

The Soviet invasion of Afghanistan at the end of December 1979 had both a positive and a negative impact on the hostage situation. Iran condemned this military attack on a brother Islamic state and thus put itself and the United States in accord on one issue. But the Soviet action also increased the overall danger of violence in the region and doubled the strain on already over-worked American officials.

The new year brought two promising developments. Iran and the United States did agree, through the good offices of United Nations Secretary General Kurt Waldheim, on the visit to Iran of a UN commission. The United States, however, believed Iran had agreed to release the hostages as a precondition for the commission's publication of commentary on Iran's grievances. Iran was unwilling. The commission spent a few days in Iran and then left. The first development had proved a dead end.

The other development began with a secret overture to White House chief of staff Jordan, through Panama, from two French law partners working for the Iranian government: Christian Bourguet and Argentine-born Hector Villalon. Jordan and Assistant Secretary of State Harold Saunders met often with Bourguet and Villalon, usually in Europe and always in secret. The lawyers demonstrated that they truly did represent Iranian Foreign Minister Sadegh Ghotzbadeh and Abolhassan Bani-Sadr, a favorite of the Ayatollah Khomeini who was elected president on January 25. These two non-clerical Iranian leaders believed that it no longer served Iran's interests to hold the hostages. But, as relative moderates, they were vulnerable to attack from extremists. Thus, contacts with the United States had to be kept absolutely secret. The first crucial step, which would prove Bani-Sadr's and Ghotzbadeh's capacity to conclude an agreement, involved the transfer of the hostages from the custody of the youths in the embassy compound to the government itself. But this did not happen. Bani-Sadr is "gutless," said President Carter on April 3.[41] The secret channel also had come to a dead end. Four days later, Khomeini announced that the hostage question would be decided by the new parliament. That might not be for months.

THE RESCUE ATTEMPT

The hostages had now been held for more than five months—with nightly television coverage and a mounting refrain throughout the United States that the country was being humiliated and that the President was a weak, dithering incompetent. In public, President Carter sent several signals that his patience was running out and that Iran might soon face sharp punishment, even of a military nature. In private, he agreed to a daring attempt to rescue the hostages.

This operation is one of the best-known events of recent history. The details need not be repeated here. The military planners and the team which had been training for months were confident they stood a reasonable chance of success. The very implausibility of moving hundreds of miles undetected and descending on the compound with such surprise that the captors would be paralyzed was the scheme's greatest recommendation. The Iranians simply are not prepared, it was argued, to deal with what, by any rational standard, is impossible. The annals of military history, after all, were filled with impossible triumphs: Wolf's capture of Quebec in 1759, the Japanese at Pearl Harbor, MacArthur at Inchon, the

Israelis going into Entebbe, Uganda, to free the passengers on a hijacked airliner.

The decision to proceed was deliberately made when Secretary Vance was out of Washington, for his opposition was known to the inner circle. He believed the operation's chance of success was almost nil and that a more likely outcome would be the death of many and perhaps all of the hostages, the rescuers, and many Iranians. The chances of repairing relations with Iran would be grievously injured. The United States would be condemned throughout the Islamic world and would lose the confidence of allies. When Vance returned to Washington, the President allowed him to present his case. But the decision stood. Vance told the President he would announce his resignation when the rescue attempt was over—whether or not it succeeded.[42]

The attempt involved the flight of eight helicopters to a remote desert site where they would be refueled by cargo planes before moving several hundred miles farther to another secret base closer to Teheran. The rescue team would then transfer to trucks, descend on the embassy, and overcome the captors. Hostages and rescuers would then be lifted off by the helicopters to a nearby airport, and all would fly out of Iran. The operation failed in the first stage when three helicopters encountered mechanical difficulties, caused largely by clouds of atmospheric dust for which the pilots had not been prepared. The commander of the team, Colonel Charles Beckwith, recommended that the mission be terminated. President Carter agreed. During the evacuation, an American plane and a helicopter collided and eight men died in the resulting fire. After the rest were safely out of Iran, President Carter reported to the nation and the world what had happened.

On April 27, Vance announced his resignation because of his disagreement with the rescue attempt. That issue, however, was only the most prominent of many on which Vance's advice had not been followed. Although sufficient in itself for a resignation, it was also the proverbial last straw. A resignation of a Secretary of State on a clear matter of policy was a rare act in American history. Only William Jennings Bryan in the Administration of Woodrow Wilson had done a similar thing (he resigned because he believed Wilson's policy toward Germany's use of submarines would lead to war).

President Carter accepted Vance's resignation, not very graciously, and named Senator Edmund S. Muskie of Maine as the new Secretary of State. Vance's colleagues in the State Department applauded his integrity and lamented his departure. Assistant Secretary Saunders, the man who had worked most closely with him throughout the crisis, later wrote: "Vance's resignation came as a blow to the State Department for many reasons. Basic were his decency as a human being . . . and the depth and soundness of his judgment on how people and nations should deal with each other. Equally important was the conviction of his colleagues . . . that he stood firmly for the resolution of conflict through determined negotiation and other peaceful efforts rather than by impetuous use of force."[43]

MOVEMENT AT LAST

After the rescue attempt, the plight of the hostages lost its dominant position in the American press. Television and the press turned to other things, and President Carter came out of his comparative isolation in the White House to begin his campaign for reelection.

In July, the Iranians released one hostage because he was seriously ill; the Majlis (parliament) elected a speaker and was ready to conduct business; and the Shah died in Egypt. On September 4, Iraq launched an attack on Iran, beginning a war that would continue for years. On September 9, the Iranians indicated secretly through the German ambassador in Teheran that they were ready for serious conversations—to be held in Bonn, West Germany. To confirm that their emissary would be speaking for the Ayatollah Khomeini, the Iranians indicated that the Ayatollah would announce new conditions on the hostages in a speech. He did so, declaring on September 12 that the hostages would be released if the United States pledged not to intervene in Iran's internal affairs, released all of Iran's frozen assets, cancelled all claims by Americans against Iran, and returned the wealth of the Shah. Significantly and deliberately absent was the old demand that the United States make an apology. Deputy Secretary of State Warren Christopher went to Bonn and met the emissary—who now revealed himself to be Sadegh Tabatabai, a relative by marriage of Khomeini.

The Iranians refused to have any public communication with the United States, but they did agree to the government of Algeria as intermediary, to convey messages back and forth. The Algerians were willing and in the months ahead performed with tireless, extraordinary competence—for which the Americans were deeply appreciative. The formal negotiations in Algiers began on November 2, two days before Ronald Reagan's lopsided victory over Jimmy Carter in the Presidential election. But the Carter Administration would still be responsible for American foreign policy until noon on January 20, 1981. The diplomats pressed ahead. An American pledge not to intervene in internal Iranian affairs was no problem. But the late Shah's wealth was not accessible to the American government, and the problem of unfreezing the assets was an almost indescribable labyrinth of disagreement over how many dollars were involved, fluctuations in the value of currencies, the status of loans, the payment of interest on frozen accounts, the banking laws of other countries where some of the funds were located, and hundreds of interlocking claims.

Lawyers, diplomats, and financial experts worked for weeks, subsisting on coffee and little sleep, in an effort to present a proposal acceptable to Iran and legally and politically feasible for the United States. Since no President can bar Americans from pressing claims against Iran—for example, for confiscated property, unpaid bills, broken contracts—Iran had to accept binding arbitration for the settlement of claims. After seeming to demand as much as $24 billion for the release of the hostages, Iran abandoned the condition that $10 billion of the Shah's alleged assets be turned over, and adjusted the balance toward reality. But not until January 18 did the two sides agree on the amount of $7.955 billion, which would be collected in the Bank of England, to be turned over to Iran upon release of the hostages.

Jimmy Carter stayed up all of his final night in office, hoping to hear that the hostages had been released while he was still President. It was not to be. Not until a few minutes after Ronald Reagan became President did the American team in Algiers send this telegram to Washington:

1. Formal notification of departure of hostages given to Deputy Secretary Christopher in Algiers January 20, 1981 at 1845 local.

2. In atypical State Department fashion, your most dutiful, respectful and deferential negotiating team ends its mission with an unequivocal—Hooray!!![44]

9

Confronting the Soviets: From Vienna to Afghanistan

In June 1979, President Carter announced that the United States would develop the MX missile. He then flew to Vienna for his only meeting with Soviet President Leonid Brezhnev and the signing ceremonies for the SALT II treaty. The occasion was originally intended to be a joyous culmination of a successful negotiation and the beginning of a new, safer, more cooperative era in Soviet–American relations. Instead, it was a mere instant of good feeling, evanescent as a soap bubble, the slightest of pauses in a deteriorating relationship.

Carter and his advisers had reached agreement with the Soviet Union, but, despite two years of discussion, they had not built support for the treaty with the public or with the Senate, whose vote would decide whether the agreement would be ratified. Instead, Senate support was probably thinner in June 1979 than it had been two years before at the time of the narrow confirmation of Paul Warnke as chief negotiator. Henry M. Jackson was the single most influential senator on matters of defense; without him, the President was unlikely to win the Senate. Three days before

Carter went to Vienna, Jackson declared war on the treaty and on the Administration. In a speech before the Coalition for a Democratic Majority, a neo-conservative group related to the Committee on the Present Danger, he said:

> To enter a treaty which favors the Soviets as this one does on the ground that we will be in a worse position without it, is appeasement in its purest form . . . Against overwhelming evidence of a continuing Soviet strategic and conventional military buildup, there has been a flow of official administration explanations, extenuations, excuses. It is all ominously reminiscent of Great Britain in the 1930s, when one government pronouncement after another was issued to assure the British public that Hitler's Germany would never achieve military equality—let alone superiority. The failure to face reality today, like the failure to do so then, that is the mark of appeasement. [1]

Brezhnev, seventy-three and in power since the fall of Nikita Khrushchev in 1964, was in poor health. Sometimes he seemed alert and intellectually in command. At other times, he was reported to be almost senile. For example, a participant in a 1977 meeting between Brezhnev and UN Secretary General Kurt Waldheim described the Soviet president as having "a glazed look to his eyes that suggested he was under heavy medication . . . [He] wore a pacemaker, a hearing aid, and the look of a man on whom age was playing increasingly cruel tricks . . . His delivery was without inflection, like that of a robot."[2] Soviet Ambassador Anatoly Dobrynin advised Brzezinski on the eve of the summit that "Carter knows so much more . . . that Brezhnev will be on the defensive and embarrassed if Carter presses him . . . Stick to one or two major issues, and don't embarrass the old man."[3]

Carter turned for special advice to Averell Harriman, who as businessman and diplomat had known the Soviets since the 1920s. Harriman, himself eighty-eight, also emphasized Brezhnev's age but said he is "emotional, but much more vigorous than you might have been led to expect." Harriman said that Brezhnev's "deepest commitment was to keep war away from his own people" and that "the entire Soviet leadership supports detente."[4] Harriman's assessment appealed to Carter's own emotional belief that personal contact with Brezhnev would make a difference.

The meetings, stretching over four days, seemed pleasant confirmation of Harriman's predictions. On the first day, Brezhnev placed his hand on Carter's shoulder and said, "If we do not succeed, God will not forgive us." And then, to quote Carter's description, as the two men "walked down a few steps to leave the building, Brezhnev kept his hand on my arm or shoulder to steady himself. This simple and apparently natural gesture bridged the gap between us more effectively than any official talk."[5]

The talk itself covered many topics, mostly introduced by Carter: the human-rights issue, Iran and the Middle East, Africa, Southeast Asia. Brezhnev was most voluble and insistent in warning the United States against threatening the Soviet Union through the new relationship with the People's Republic of China. Each leader described what he considered the provocative behavior of the other country, while claiming nothing but a desire for peace and concord on his own side. The exchanges were frank, with Brezhnev usually speaking from a text supplied from a file kept at hand by an aide. There was none of the browbeating characteristic of the last summit meeting in Vienna—that between Khrushchev and Kennedy in 1961.[6]

The most discussed subject was the future of arms control. Carter took a yellow pad and printed in his own hand a list of twelve suggestions for SALT III. To the dismay of Harold Brown and Hamilton Jordan, the President gave the sheet to Brezhnev. No harm or good came of that overture, although the list was interesting testimony to Carter's undiminished hopes that real progress might yet be achieved. For example, he suggested a freeze on all production of warheads and launchers, a total ban on tests, designated "safe havens" where submarines would be immune from anti-submarine tracking, five percent annual reductions in strategic weapons, and annual summit meetings.[7] On the morning of June 18, Carter and Brezhnev signed the SALT II agreements. Somewhat to Carter's surprise, they embraced "in the Soviet fashion" and parted. Carter flew back to Washington and that night addressed Congress and the nation.

THE LOSING FIGHT FOR THE TREATY

The embrace between Jimmy Carter and Leonid Brezhnev was the last friendly gesture in Soviet–American relations during the Carter Administration and for years to come. President Carter and his advisers calculated that they could win the required two-thirds vote of approval for the treaty from the Senate only by demonstrating that the United States was balancing the treaty with a significant strengthening of American nuclear forces and with a generally assertive policy toward the Soviet Union. They also believed that a stronger military posture was essential on its own merits. For Secretary of State Vance, the task was to persuade the Senate of the value of the treaty in itself, regardless of other aspects of Soviet behavior. To National Security Adviser Zbigniew Brzezinski, criticism of the treaty was welcome because it forced the Administration to put more emphasis on military strength. Although Brzezinski favored ratification, the outcome from his point of view was almost irrelevant as long as the United States became militarily stronger.

The Senate Foreign Relations and Armed Services Committees began hearing testimony for and against the treaty in July and continued through the fall. The hearings dealt not only with the specifics of the treaty but with every aspect of American strategic defense, with the intentions and capabilities of the Soviet Union, and ultimately with fundamental assumptions about the nature of force and threats of force in foreign policy in a nuclear age. The Administration was able to answer specific criticisms to its satisfaction, but the deeper issues of the nature of the Soviet Union and the role of war were not and could not have been resolved. As Frank Church, chairman of the Foreign Relations Committee, said at the outset, "we recognize the insanity of nuclear war, but that recognition delivers no easy answer to the question of how best to manage the relations between the Soviet Union and the United States in order to minimize the danger."[8] The most prominent specific criticisms dealt with verification, the encoding of Soviet test data, the failure of the United States to make the Soviets reduce the number of heavy missiles, the issue of whether the Soviet intermediate-range bomber called the Backfire should be counted as a strategic weapon, "fractionation" (or how many warheads can dance on the end of a missile), and the vulnerability of American land-based intercontinental missiles.

Administration witnesses reflected the harder attitude toward the Soviet Union by spending an enormous amount of time describing the military measures, such as MX, which would be undertaken simultaneously with approval of the treaty. Vance began his testimony by deliberately disassociating himself from an attitude identified with much-abused and departed Warnke: "I reject the notion that unilateral restraint in weapons programs is the way to enhance our security . . . I also state to you my strongly held view that the United States must not permit the Soviet Union to attain nuclear superiority."[9]

The opposition repeated the arguments they had been advancing for two years. Their ranks now included Lieutenant General Edward Rowny, who had resigned in June from the SALT delegation (where he had represented the Joint Chiefs of Staff) and the Army, in order to be able to criticize the treaty in public. The fact that he had been part of the negotiating team added credibility to his charge that the United States had been so pathetically eager for an agreement that it made concession after concession to the Soviets. Fred Iklé, director of the Arms Control and Disarmament Agency in the Ford Administration, put it succinctly: "We have been had, Mr. Chairman. We have been had by the SALT process. Hence, what we must now do is to redirect the process fundamentally, not, as the Carter Administration argues, continue it."[10]

None of the fifteen members of the Foreign Relations Committee were exuberant supporters of the treaty. All believed it could be improved, or at least that conditions and understandings surrounding its ratification could be stated emphatically. There was a difference, however, between those who wanted amendments to the text of the treaty itself—something strongly opposed by the Administration because that would require going back to the Soviets for renegotiation—and those who were content with amendments to the Senate resolution of approval, statements which might require some acknowledgment by the Soviets but which would not require reopening negotiations. The Administration said it would accept the second type of amendment.

On November 9 the committee voted 9–6 in favor of the treaty, but with a long list of explanatory and admonitory comments reflecting suspicion of the Soviet Union and urging the United States to repair its defenses. Two Republicans—Charles Percy and Jacob Javits—voted with seven Democrats in favor. But two Democrats—John Glenn and Richard Stone—voted with four Republicans in opposition. In the Armed Services Committee, the treaty fared less well. In December, that committee issued a harsh report, reflecting the views of Senator Jackson, that the treaty "is not in the national security interests of the United States." The vote on the report was ten in favor, with "seven present but not voting."[11]

THE ALLEGED COMBAT BRIGADE IN CUBA

While the Carter Administration embarked on an intensive lobbying and public-relations campaign in favor of SALT II during the summer of 1979, opponents of the treaty searched the horizon for evidence of Soviet aggressive intent and general untrustworthiness. Brzezinski searched also, not because he wanted the treaty defeated, but because he wanted to convert Carter into a "Truman-like" President, ready to confront the Soviet Union in every corner of the globe.

Cuba was a likely place to look. The most dangerous of all Soviet–American confrontations had followed the Soviet emplacement of intermediate-range nuclear missiles in Cuba in 1962. In the settlement of that crisis, the United States pledged not to invade Cuba and the Soviets agreed to withdraw their missiles and refrain in the future from stationing offensive weapons on the island. But several thousand Soviet ground troops remained to train their Cuban counterparts. Cuba had become a Soviet protectorate and the Monroe Doctrine was dead—something which stuck like a bone in America's throat.[12]

There had never been a shortage of alarming tales emanating from anti-Castro exiles about sinister Soviet activity in Cuba and from time to time the United States had questioned the presence of naval vessels or fighter planes. In April 1979, Brzezinski asked the CIA to keep a closer eye on the Russians in Cuba. In July, Richard Stone, a conservative senator from Florida, got wind that something was happening, and publicly asked the President if the Soviets were violating their agreement not to place offensive weapons in Cuba. Secretary Vance wrote Stone that "there is no evidence of any substantial increase of Soviet military presence over the past several years." But the United States would continue to monitor the situation closely. President Carter in Vienna had told President Brezhnev that any buildup "would adversely affect our relationship."[13]

In August, American intelligence picked up fragmentary information that the Soviets might in fact be operating a "combat brigade" with its own command center, as distinct from a training unit. The interpretation of the evidence was biased in a "worst-case" direction, reflecting pressure from Brzezinski and the natural desire of the CIA not to be caught napping. "This is an extremely serious development which could adversely affect SALT," Brzezinski told the President. Just before Labor Day, Senator

Frank Church, chairman of the Senate Foreign Relations Committee, received a confidential briefing on the subject and then went public with what he had been told—a move designed to improve his personal political position against right-wing attack in Idaho. If the brigade is not removed, he said, SALT cannot possibly be approved by the Senate.[14]

The uproar over the "combat brigade" lasted more than a month, damaged SALT's chances, and gave the Administration the opportunity to bungle spectacularly. Vance told a press conference on September 5 that the unit had probably been in Cuba for many years, but that the matter was very serious. He then delivered this unwise sentence: "Let me say very simply that I will not be satisfied with maintenance of the status quo."[15] That sounded like an ultimatum. But the Soviets said there was nothing they could do because the issue was phony; there had been no significant change in the character of Soviet forces in Cuba since 1962.

The Administration was in a corner. But Brzezinski saw an opportunity to consolidate his ascendancy over Vance and the State Department while turning the President toward a harder line. In a memorandum entitled "Acquiescence vs. Assertiveness," he stated: "I think that the increasingly pervasive perception here and abroad is that in U.S.–Soviet relations, the Soviets are increasingly assertive and the U.S. more acquiescent. State's handling of the Soviet brigade negotiations is a case in point. I recommend that in the future we will have to work for greater White House control." The President wrote "Good" on the margin of the memorandum. Brzezinski urged Carter not to "pretend through some cosmetic formula that he had solved the problem . . . We need more defense, more intelligence, limited steps on the PRC, and a tough line on Soviet adventurism."[16] Carter responded on October 1 with an address to the nation. The message was muddled and contradictory. The President reported that the Soviets had assured the United States that the unit was a "training center, that it does nothing more than training and can do nothing more."

But, in response, the United States would set up a full-time Caribbean military task force with headquarters in Key West, expand military maneuvers in the region, and increase economic aid to friendly nations. We were improving our "rapid deployment forces" and had "reinforced our naval presence in the Indian Ocean." And yet "I have concluded that the brigade issue is certainly no reason to return to the cold war."[17] A week later, Secretary of Defense Brown was asked how the status quo had been changed. By our own military movements, he answered.[18]

The affair was a fiasco. The issue had not served, as Brzezinski had hoped it would, to dramatize a new tough line against the Soviet Union. But a more suitable occasion was not far off: the Soviet invasion of Afghanistan.

CRUISE AND PERSHING II MISSILES FOR EUROPE

The Adminstration's effort to win Senate approval for the SALT II agreements was accompanied by decisions to develop and deploy new nuclear missiles: the intercontinental MX in the United States, and intermediate-range land-based theater weapons in Europe. Part of the pressure for new weapons came from European and American military planners who wanted to replace aging and relatively limited systems with the more accurate and modern devices made possible by new technology.

In the late 1970s, American strategic planners began to doubt that manned bombers could any longer penetrate improved Soviet defenses. An alternative was the cruise missile—the small, pilotless craft which, thanks to new radar navigation, could literally skim over housetops, wiggle and waggle to evade interception, and land on a target more than a thousand miles away with pinpoint accuracy. Western European defense ministries were strongly attracted to the device. The second new weapon was a replacement for the old American Pershing I intermediate missile, a single warhead device with a range of about four hundred miles, not enough to strike targets in the Soviet Union from Western Europe. A modernized version, the Pershing II, had a very accurate warhead and double the range. It could reach the Soviet Union. European defense officials also liked the Pershing II.[19]

Some participants in the European and American decisions to deploy cruise and Pershing II missiles believed that the momentum for modernization would have carried the day, regardless of Soviet behavior. But the Russians were also involved in the same game, and their prior decisions provided the public with political justification for the cruise and Pershings. The new Soviet weapon was the SS-20—a mobile, solid-fueled, three-warhead weapon of great accuracy and enough range to reach all of Europe. The SS-20s were designed to replace old, inaccurate, single-warhead, and liquid-fueled (hence slow to prepare for firing and unreliable) SS-4s and SS-5s. The first SS-20s were deployed in 1977.[20]

Initially, officials in the Carter Administration were not overly concerned about the SS-20s. They believed that the first need for European defense was to strengthen conventional forces. But German Chancellor Helmut Schmidt feared that the American preoccupation with the bilateral pursuit of a strategic-arms agreement with the Soviet Union and the new, menacing SS-20s meant that the United States, in a crisis, might leave Europe to protect itself.

Schmidt voiced his fear publicly in what became perhaps the most quoted speech on nuclear issues of the decade. Speaking on October 28, 1977, before the International Institute for Strategic Studies in London, he said:

> SALT codifies the nuclear strategic balance between the Soviet Union and the United States. To put it another way: SALT neutralizes their strategic nuclear capabilities. In Europe this magnifies the significance of the disparities between East and West in nuclear tactical and conventional weapons . . . Strategic arms limitation confined to the United States and the Soviet Union will inevitably impair the security of the West

European members of the Alliance . . . if we do not succeed in removing the disparities of military power in Europe parallel to the SALT negotiations.[21]

Carter's decision not to proceed with the development of the neutron bomb infuriated Schmidt and increased the pressure for the United States to endorse new weapons. In February 1978, a special NATO High Level Group chaired by David McGiffert of the United States endorsed in principle the need for more modern weapons. In August 1979, with the SALT treaty before the Senate, Brzezinski chaired a National Security Council committee meeting which decided on the numbers: 108 Pershing IIs and 464 cruise missiles. In October, the NATO High Level Group approved the numbers, and in the same month Soviet President Leonid Brezhnev warned that their deployment could jeopardize arms control. The answer to Brezhnev came in the "two-track" decision of the NATO foreign and defense ministers at a special meeting in Brussels on December 12. The 572 missiles would be deployed (first track), but if arms-control negotiations on theater nuclear weapons (second track) led to agreement on reducing both Soviet and Western theater nuclear weapons, the deployment might be canceled before 1983, when the first weapons would be in place.[22]

While Secretaries Vance and Brown were at the NATO meeting in Brussels, Brzezinski back in Washington was noting intelligence reports pointing to potential Soviet military action in Afghanistan.

AFGHANISTAN BACKGROUND

The dry, mountainous, landlocked nation of Afghanistan is shaped like a triangle, with its shortest side in the west forming a four-hundred-mile border with Iran. The northern side borders the Soviet Union for eight hundred miles, and the southern side lies along Pakistan for an equal distance. The apex to the east touches the People's Republic of China. The population, estimated at 15 million in 1980, is ninety percent Moslem.

In the nineteenth and early twentieth centuries, the British fought a series of small wars to keep the kingdom of Afghanistan out of Russian control. Britain's purpose was the defense of India. In 1947, the Indian sub-continent was partitioned into independent Pakistan and India. British military forces withdrew. Afghanistan for a quarter century succeeded in maintaining a non-aligned position in the Cold War, receiving a small amount of aid from the United States and more from the Soviet Union. It served as a buffer between Russia and pro-Western Pakistan.

In 1973, Muhammad Daoud, a veteran politician who had served as prime minister under the king from 1953 to 1963, led a coup which overthrew the monarchy and established a republic, with himself as president. During the next five years, Daoud aligned Afghanistan with Pakistan and Iran, and by implication against the Soviet Union. In March 1978, the American ambassador to Afghanistan, Adolph Dubs, reported that "President Daoud remains very much in control and faces no significant opposition."[23] One month later, Daoud was overthrown in a coup led by Marxist army officers. Nur Muhammad Taraki became president of the newly proclaimed Democratic Republic of Afghanistan. The American government's reaction was almost placid. "We are aware of the fact that the Secretary General of the Communist Party has now emerged as the President of Afghanistan. We are in touch with other governments on this subject. We deplore the bloodshed that took place in the course of the coup."[24] Secretary of State Vance decided the United States should maintain diplomatic relations with the new regime, and the United States persuaded the Shah of Iran to do the same. Taraki assured the United States that he was not under Soviet domination and asked for aid. Vance sent Under Secretary of State David Newsom to Kabul to investigate.

Newsom came back with a negative report on the new regime's character and intentions but recommended that limited aid be continued as a means of retaining some small leverage.[25] The decision was consistent with the Carter Administration's attempt at that stage to avoid an inordinate obsession with communism per se. It also reflected a belief in the State Department that no strategic threat was present in Afghanistan's move to the political left, as long as Iran remained strong and stable. The desire to conclude the SALT II agreements with the Soviet Union also inhibited any tendency to point accusing fingers. In retrospect, it's clear that 1978 was the decisive year when Afghanistan was incorporated into the Soviet security sphere. The invasion of 1979 did not reflect a radical shift in policy but simply a brutal effort to keep what the Soviets already had.[26]

In February 1979, American Ambassador Dubs was kidnapped in Kabul by unidentified gunmen and killed during a supposed rescue attempt by the police. The American government believed that the Soviet Union had connived in the killing or had deliberately failed to take measures to save Dubs's life. Kabul and Moscow denied this. Newsom now recommended that the United States cut its aid program and delay appointing a new ambassador. "We shouldn't do anything abruptly. There are some advantages in keeping a presence there as long as possible. Let's let them make the next move," he said.[27]

The Department of State's rather relaxed view of the situation in Afghanistan was challenged by National Security Adviser Brzezinski, Secretary of Defense Harold Brown, and Vice President Walter Mondale. Throughout the spring and summer of 1979, Brzezinski urged that strong warnings be sent to the Soviet Union about their "creeping intervention." He stressed grave strategic possibilities, recalling traditional Russian expansion toward the Indian Ocean and Moscow's suggestion to Berlin, during the period of the Nazi–Soviet non-aggression pact, that the Soviet Union be granted control of South Asia. Brzezinski also "pushed a decision through . . . to be more sympathetic to those Afghans who were determined to preserve their country's independence"— a euphemism for clandestine aid to insurgents, who were growing in strength throughout the country. He recalled in his memoirs that "Mondale was especially helpful in this, giving a forceful pep talk, mercilessly squelching the rather timid opposition of David Newsom, who was representing the State Department."[28]

The Taraki regime had two serious problems: an immediate threat from rival communist politicians, and an inability to subdue guerrilla insurgency in the countryside. The insurgents were motivated primarily by Islamic fundamentalism akin to that which swept the Ayatollah Khomeini to power in Iran. They resented the efforts of the communists in Kabul to impose a social system subversive of their religious convictions. In September 1979, President Taraki lost his life to the first threat, when another communist regime, headed by Prime Minister Hafizullah Amin, seized power. Amin, however, was no more successful in overcoming the insurgency than his predecessor.

The State Department still played down the gravity of the situation. Secretary Vance advised against supporting an anticommunist coup, and the department's press spokesman denied any knowledge of American aid for the insurgents.[29] "We have repeatedly impressed on the Soviet government the dangers of more direct involvement in the fighting in Afghanistan," said Assistant Secretary of State Harold Saunders before a congressional committee. "We will continue to monitor developments in this area closely."[30] But, as Vance subsequently admitted, the monitoring was inadequate. Although the department noted a visit of Soviet General Ivan G. Pavlovsky to Kabul in October, not enough importance was attached to the event. Brzezinski, however, continued to urge that the situation in Afghanistan be given more serious attention.

The seizure of the hostages in Teheran on November 4, 1979, left even less time to analyze and react to other events. Brzezinski enlisted Defense Secretary Brown and CIA director Stansfield Turner in his campaign for heavier American involvement and belittled the State Department's fear that Soviet–American relations would be damaged if the United States appeared to be meddling in Afghan internal affairs. The National Security Council staff prepared contingency plans for an American response to a Soviet invasion of Afghanistan, and Brzezinski consulted the Saudis and the Egyptians. In December, information reached Washington that a Soviet military move of major proportions was imminent. The press reported the same. *Pravda* denounced these reports on December 23 as "pure fabrication" and went on to accuse the CIA of supporting the insurgents.[31]

During the last week of December 1979, Soviet troops poured into Afghanistan, allegedly at the invitation of Prime Minister Amin. But that hapless politician was immediately murdered, and a new government headed by Babrak Karmal installed. A long, violent counterinsurgency war had begun.

Given the closed nature of Soviet decision-making, we cannot know what leaders in the Kremlin were thinking. It is possible that they believed they were reacting defensively to a local situation that threatened their security—the mushrooming power of the insurgency and the ineffectiveness of the Amin government—and had scarcely thought about the larger consequences.[32] They may simply have been doing what they saw as necessary to maintain a pro-Soviet communist regime against an Islamic challenge, doing, in short, what the United States had decided not to do in Iran when the Shah first began to demonstrate his inability to suppress that revolution. Or Moscow may have been applying a grand strategy aimed at exploitation of American weakness and eventual Soviet control of the oil resources of the Persian Gulf.

Secretary of State Vance entertained both possibilities, but President Carter immediately assumed the worst and was strongly encouraged in his apocalyptic perceptions by Brzezinski. The National Security Adviser saw the Soviet invasion as an opportunity to convert the President completely to his view of the Soviets as a global threat. It matters little, he told the President (who had returned from Camp David to deal with the crisis), what "subjective motives" were behind Brezhnev's decision. What counted were the "objective consequences" of Soviet military power "so much closer to the Persian Gulf." Carter agreed. He used the hot line on December 27 to send Brezhnev the "sharpest message" of his Presidency. The Soviet invasion, said Carter, was "a clear threat to peace" which "could mark a fundamental and long-lasting turning point in our relations . . . Unless you draw back from your present course of action, this will inevitably jeopardize the course of United States–Soviet relations throughout the world."[33]

Secretary of Vance's long-standing efforts to keep the strategic-arms control agreement separate from other problems were now totally defeated. Brzezinski and his view of "linkage" prevailed. Three days after the Soviet invasion, Brzezinski advised Carter to blame the Soviets for blocking the SALT II treaty: "It will be less a political setback for us and will enable us to insist to the Europeans that we all proceed" with the installation of the Pershing II and cruise missiles in Europe.[34] In short, let SALT II go and shift the onus for failure to the Soviet Union.

On the last two days of the year, both Brzezinski and Carter used network television to communicate their grim views. On December 30, Brzezinski called the invasion "a qualitative new step involving direct invasion of a country outside the Warsaw Pact . . . It is an attempt to impose Soviet will on an independent foreign country."[35] The comment, repeated often throughout the crisis, ignored the question of whether Afghanistan had enjoyed any meaningful independence from the Soviet Union since the coup of April 1978. The next day, the President, in an interview with Frank Reynolds of ABC, called Brezhnev a liar for his response to the message of December 27. "He claimed that he had been invited by the Afghan government to come in and protect Afghanistan from some outside third nation threat. This was obviously false. Because the person that he claimed invited him in, President Amin, was murdered or assassinated after the Soviets pulled their coup." Then Carter said: "My opinion of the Russians has changed more drastically in the last week than even the previous two and one half years before that. It is only now dawning upon the world the magnitude of the action that the Soviets undertook in invading Afghanistan . . . What we will do about it, I cannot say. But, to repeat myself, the action of the Soviets has made a more dramatic change in my opinion of what the Soviets' ultimate goals are than anything they've done in the previous time I've been in office."[36]

RESPONDING TO THE INVASION

The Carter Administration's response to the Soviet invasion had four related parts: the request that the Senate suspend consideration of the SALT II treaty; the imposition of sanctions designed to make the Soviet Union realize that its action was not without cost; efforts to rally other nations into an anti-Soviet coalition; and the adoption of a primarily military approach to national security.

Taking Brzezinski's advice, the President on January 3, 1980, asked the Senate to put SALT II on the shelf. His letter to Senate majority leader Robert Byrd was brief:

> In the light of the Soviet invasion of Afghanistan, I request that you delay consideration of the SALT II Treaty on the Senate floor.
>
> The purpose of this request is not to withdraw the Treaty from consideration, but to defer the debate so that Congress and I as President can assess Soviet actions and intentions, and devote our primary attention to the legislative and other measures required to respond to this crisis.
>
> As you know, I continue to share your view that the SALT II Treaty is in the national security interest of the United States and the entire world, and that it should be taken up by the Senate as soon as these more urgent issues have been addressed.[37]

Hard-line critics of SALT II would have preferred to see the treaty abandoned, but Carter's tactic was designed to offer the

Soviets an incentive for ending their intervention in Afghanistan. Since they did not withdraw, the Senate had not resumed consideration by the time the Carter Administration came to an end a year later; however, the United States announced that since ratification was still officially pending, it would abide by the terms of the treaty as long as the Soviet Union did the same.

An array of sanctions was announced by the President in a public address on January 4. The most notable was an embargo on exports of grain from the United States to the Soviet Union in excess of existing contracts under a 1975 agreement (part of Kissinger's system of detente). This meant that eight million tons could go forward; but seventeen million additional tons were blocked. Vice President Mondale and other spokesmen for American farmers disagreed with the embargo, and so did all the leading candidates for the Republican nomination for President. Carter promised a variety of measures to find a market for the grain that would not be going to the Soviet Union and to otherwise insulate the American farmer from loss. Mexico and the People's Republic of China both bought some of the grain diverted from the Soviet Union. The President also pleaded with other grain-exporting nations not to increase their shipments to compensate for the American embargo. Canada, Australia, and France (which happened to have a small surplus) complied. Argentina did not. The grain embargo was potentially the most powerful of sanctions, because the Soviet Union had suffered a series of poor harvests. The Administration estimated that the Soviets purchased six million tons, mostly from Argentina, to make up for the blocked American tonnage, thus suffering a net loss of between ten and twelve million tons.[38]

Another food sanction involved fish. In 1976, the United States, following a practice initiated by other coastal states, proclaimed a two-hundred-mile fisheries zone from its coasts and thereafter regulated all foreign fishing within that zone. The Soviet Union, whose fleets of trawlers and giant factory ships had previously ravaged the fishing banks off New England, was allocated a small quota of fish of certain species which it could take from the American zone. Now President Carter revoked all Soviet fishing rights. This was a generally popular move, for no American interests were injured. But since Soviet fishing had already been drastically curtailed, its actual contribution to making the Soviets feel the cost of their aggression against Afghanistan was slight.[39] The President prohibited the sale of high technology to the Soviet Union. This meant primarily computers and other electronic devices. Brzezinski considered this sanction more important than the grain embargo—especially since it contrasted with growing exports of similar items to the People's Republic of China. Still another sanction was the cancellation of many, but not all, scientific and cultural exchange programs—a move noticed far more in the academic world than by the general public.

The most prominently discussed sanction was the cancellation of American participation in the 1980 summer Olympic Games in Moscow. In theory, the games were non-political, a competition of amateur athletes in a spirit of sportsmanship and peace. But since 1936, when Adolf Hitler had used the Berlin games to glorify Nazism, they had become increasingly political. The Munich games of 1972 had been shattered by the murder of Israeli athletes by Palestinian terrorists. The 1976 Montreal games had been boycotted by most black African nations because white countries had not done enough to ostracize South Africa. And, by every report, the Soviets were planning to make a public-relations spectacle of the Moscow games.

Vice President Mondale, compensating fervently for his opposition to the grain embargo, took the lead within the Administration in urging that the United States withdraw. Vance was initially opposed but soon became a convert. "I look back to the 1936 games, when I was in college, and I think in hindsight it was a mistake for us to attend," he said on January 15.[40] Thousands of American athletes, who had been training intensively for four years in anticipation of the games, were not enthusiastic about this development. Robert Kane, president of the U.S.

Olympic Committee, wrote President Carter and conferred with Vance and White House counselor Lloyd Cutler, whom Carter had assigned as coordinator of the issue. The Administration would not back down. Unless the Soviets withdrew their forces from Afghanistan within one month, Carter wrote Kane on January 20, no American team would go to Moscow. The President suggested that the U.S. committee try to get the games moved from Moscow or have them cancelled altogether: "This powerful signal of world outrage cannot be hidden from the Soviet people, and will reverberate around the globe. Perhaps it will deter future aggression."[41]

The Administration pretended the decision was up to the U.S. committee and lobbied hard with that group until, in April, it finally voted against participation. The committee, however, was powerless, because in March the President used his executive authority to block the shipment to the Soviet Union of all "goods and technology to be used in support of or in connection with" the games. It also barred all payments connected with television coverage. The NBC network had already announced it would not broadcast if there was no American participation.

Vice President Mondale drew the assignment of addressing the U.S. committee on the eve of its vote. His speech was an emotional exercise based on a revealing use of historical analogy. "As we meet today, the lesson of the Soviet invasion of Afghanistan still waits to be drawn," he said. "History holds its breath; for what is at stake is no less than the future security of the civilized world. If one nation can be subjugated by Soviet aggression, is any sovereign nation truly safe from that fate?" The decision would be "a referendum on America's character and fundamental values." The athletes of 1980 "may have been born a full generation after the Berlin Olympics. But as their advisers and trustees, you bear the responsibility of linking that history to their duty. For the story of Hitler's rise is more than an unspeakable tragedy, more than a study in tyranny. It is also a chronicle of the free world's failure—of opportunities not seized, aggression not opposed, appeasement not condemned."[42] Given such a choice and knowing that no Americans could participate in Moscow in any event, the committee voted as requested.

The American diplomatic effort was less successful. There was no significant support for cancelling or moving the games. The European Economic Community (Common Market) voted against boycotting the games. Individual European governments were split. A British team went; a German did not. Saudi Arabia led the boycott by many Islamic nations. The People's Republic of China, Japan, South Korea, and the nations of Southeast Asia in receipt of American aid did not go. Latin American and African nations were divided. In all, sixty nations did not attend because of Afghanistan (the number varies depending on how motive and participation are defined). Those who went were witness to what Secretary of State Edmund Muskie called "an East Germany–Russia bilateral track meet."[43] Four years later, when the summer Olympics were held in Los Angeles, the Soviet Union and nations aligned with it returned the compliment and did not come to the United States for the Los Angeles summer games.

THE CARTER DOCTRINE

Carter's Notre Dame speech of May 1977 was the fullest expression of his initial emphasis on human rights and of his call for non-military solutions to international problems. His State of the Union address before a joint session of Congress and television cameras on January 23, 1980, in the wake of the Soviet invasion of Afghanistan, marked his full conversion to military strength as the nation's highest priority and resistance to the Soviet Union as the dominant objective. The line which drew the strongest applause was his statement that "I am determined that the United States will remain the strongest of all nations."

He invoked history, not, as during the campaign of 1976, to list American wrongdoing for which repentance was necessary, but to celebrate the ways in which the United States had stood up to the Soviet Union. He also noted efforts at negotiation for arms control, but the emphasis on confrontation came first.

> In the 1940s, we took the lead in creating the Atlantic alliance in response to the Soviet Union's suppression and then consolidation of its East European empire and the resulting threat of the Warsaw Pact to Western Europe.
>
> In the 1950s, we helped to contain further Soviet challenges in Korea and in the Middle East, and we re-armed, to assure the continuation of that containment.
>
> In the 1960s, we met the Soviet challenges in Berlin and we faced the Cuban missile crisis, and we sought to engage the Soviet Union in the important task of moving beyond the cold war and away from confrontation.
>
> And in the 1970s, three American Presidents negotiated with the Soviet leaders to halt this growth of the nuclear arms race. We sought to establish rules of behavior that would reduce the risks of conflict, and we searched for areas of cooperation that could make our relations reciprocal and productive—not only for the sake of our two nations, but for the security and peace of the entire world.

But this effort, he suggested, had now been thwarted by the unconscionable Soviet invasion of Afghanistan, which "could pose the most serious threat to the peace since the Second World War . . . The Soviet Union must pay a concrete price for their aggression. While this invasion continues, we and the other nations of the world cannot conduct business as usual with the Soviet Union."

After listing the sanctions being imposed, the President described the strategic threat in the approved geopolitical manner. "The Soviet effort to dominate Afghanistan has brought Soviet military forces to within 300 miles of the Indian Ocean and close to the Straits of Hormuz—a waterway through which most of the world's oil must flow. The Soviet Union is now attempting to consolidate a strategic position, therefore, that poses a grave threat to the free movement of Middle East oil." Then the paragraph, deliberately echoing Harry S. Truman in 1947 and Dwight D. Eisenhower in 1957, which proclaimed the "Carter Doctrine":

> Let our position be absolutely clear: An attempt by any outside force to gain control of the Persian Gulf will be regarded as an assault on the vital interests of the United States of America, and such an assault will be repelled by any means necessary, including military force.

Some of Carter's critics ridiculed the speech as empty posturing. But the Administration proposed and implemented several measures to give the country more real and perceived military power. President Nixon had ended the military draft and draft registration back in 1973. Carter asked Congress to restore compulsory registration for men reaching their nineteenth birthday. Congress complied. He lamented the decline in defense spending which had occurred in the eight years before he became President, lauded his own efforts up to 1980, and now asked for a more rapid increase—at the rate of five percent per year in real terms over a five-year period, rather than the three percent which had been his goal since 1977.

In 1976, while campaigning for the Presidency, he had repeatedly warned against the nation's propensity to send troops into combat far from American shores. Now he declared that the Administration was "improving our capability to deploy U.S. military forces rapidly to distant areas" and that air and naval bases were being sought in "the region of northeast Africa and the Persian Gulf." At the outset of his Presidency, he had deplored the habit of supporting dictators and blatant violators of human rights because they were anti-communist. Now he described his efforts to forge an anti-Soviet military alignment with Pakistan, whose military ruler had deposed and executed his democratically elected predecessor. In 1976, he had criticized the CIA for its excesses. Now he said: "We need to remove unwarranted restraints on America's ability to collect intelligence."[44] But would all these measures give the United States the military means to turn back the Soviets should they actually seek control of the Middle East? Probably not, as Carter and Brzezinski fully understood. But they did not necessarily intend to meet a Soviet thrust on the scene. We would take action, Carter wrote later, "not necessarily confined to any small invaded area or to tactics and terrain of the Soviets' choosing."[45] Once before, an American leader had used almost the same words. Secretary of State John Foster Dulles, enunciating in 1954 what was known as the doctrine of "massive retaliation," had declared that it must be American policy "to depend upon a great capacity to retaliate instantly by means and at places of our own choosing."[46] "Means" meant any means, including nuclear weapons; "places" meant anywhere, including the Soviet Union itself.

"PEANUTS" FOR PAKISTAN

An immediate consequence of the Carter Doctrine and the perception of a direct Soviet threat to the oil resources of the Middle East was a reversal of American policy toward Pakistan, shifting from ostracism to courtship. This effort was accompanied by an unsuccessful attempt to enlist India in the ranks of nations opposed to the Soviet invasion of Afghanistan.

Until the end of 1979, the Carter Administration viewed the government of Pakistan with disapproval—for two principal reasons. In July 1977, the democratically elected Prime Minister Zulfikar Ali Bhutto was overthrown by a military coup headed by Mohammed Zia ul-Haq. The next year, a military court sentenced Bhutto to death, and in spite of international pleas for clemency, the sentence was carried out in 1979—a clear demonstration of disregard for human rights, perpetrated by a military regime. The second reason was Pakistan's open determination to acquire nuclear weapons, in defiance of American and international policies on non-proliferation. In April 1979, the United States announced it was withdrawing its aid programs to Pakistan, in conformity with the Non-Proliferation Act of 1978 barring aid to non-nuclear countries which refused to cooperate.[47] Pakistan was told by Secretary of Defense Brown, however, that substantial conventional military aid would be forthcoming from the United States if it abandoned the effort to become a nuclear power.[48] In November 1979, shortly after the hostages were seized in Teheran, relations between the United States and Pakistan were strained further when a mob invaded the American Embassy in Islamabad. The apparent reason was a rumor that the United States had been responsible for the attack by some Moslem extremists on the Grand Mosque in Mecca, Saudi Arabia. The Pakistani government, however, freed the embassy on the same day, and President Carter telephoned his thanks to President Zia.[49]

Then came the Soviet move into Afghanistan. Brzezinski recommended even before the Soviet invasion that the United States repeat a 1959 statement of American support for Pakistan's security and independence. After the invasion, Carter spoke to President Zia on the telephone, and early in January the United States offered Pakistan $400 million in military aid. Zia derided the amount as "peanuts." Brzezinski and Deputy Secretary of State Warren Christopher then flew to Pakistan—where Brzezinski was photographed gazing combatively in the direction of Afghanistan, with an automatic rifle in hand. They repeated the offer of aid, but Zia said no. The next step was to invite Zia to Washington for the standard state visit and flattery. "We are honored personally by his visit," said Carter of the man who had put Bhutto to death and imposed martial law on his country. "He's a military man who received part of his training in our country. He's familiar with our nation. His knowledge of the sensitivities and ideals of America make him particularly dear to us."[50]

Since the partition of British India into independent and mutually hostile India and Pakistan in 1947, the United States had learned that any move toward closer American relations with one of those countries would be resented by the other. Conversely, poor relations with one country usually meant better relations with the other. Thus, in the first part of the Carter Administration, the difficulties with Pakistan were balanced by relatively amicable contact with India. Another reason for the lack of difficulty was the defeat in India's March 1977 elections of Prime Minister Indira Gandhi, a strong-willed politician who had never refrained from criticizing the United States and who also, from the American point of view, was naïve about the Soviet Union. The new Prime Minister, Morarji Desai, was seen in Washington as pro-American.[51] President Carter, on a state visit to New Delhi in January 1978, called the victory of Desai's party a triumph for democracy after the two-year Emergency during which Gandhi had suspended the democratic process.[52]

But, as in Pakistan, there was the question of nuclear proliferation in India, a nation which as early as 1974 had tested a nuclear device. Now the problem was whether the United States should export enriched uranium for India's Tarapur generating station despite the fact that India had not accepted the stringent controls designed to prevent fuel from being diverted to weaponry.[53] The Nuclear Non-Proliferation Act of 1978, under which aid to Pakistan had been suspended, prohibited the uranium exports. And yet the Carter Administration engaged in some convoluted arguments why the law did not apply, and the exports continued.[54]

Prime Minister Desai resigned in July 1979 after accusations of corruption, and soon Indira Gandhi was back in power. President Carter tried to persuade her to condemn the Soviet invasion of Afghanistan and sent elder statesman Clark Clifford on a special mission to New Delhi—without positive result. According to Carter, India's speech in the United Nations on Afghanistan was "as supportive of the invasion as were those of Czechoslovakia and Vietnam. Even Cuba was more reticent in its praise than India."[55] Once again, as relations with Pakistan were improving, they began to deteriorate with India—but not to the point where the exports of uranium were cut off. In June 1980, Carter informed Congress that he was continuing to approve the exports, because the Soviet invasion of Afghanistan required that maintaining ties with India take precedence over the letter of the non-proliferation law. He did say that he was concerned over India's refusal to pledge not to conduct further nuclear tests or to abide by safeguards against proliferation. But the exports of uranium "will help us to maintain a dialogue with India in which we try to narrow our differences on these issues."[56] And so, for both India and Pakistan, the Soviet invasion of Afghanistan had turned a weak policy on non-proliferation into a dead letter. The effort to placate India, however, was a failure. In May 1980, India confirmed that she would acquire $1.6 billion worth of arms from the Soviet Union, and in December Gandhi received Leonid Brezhnev in New Delhi. The two leaders issued a statement condemning outside interference in the affairs of Southwest Asia.[57]

PLANNING FOR NUCLEAR WAR: PD-59

From 1945 until the early 1960s, the United States possessed either a monopoly of nuclear weapons (lost when the Soviet Union tested its first bomb in 1949) or superior ability to strike targets in the other country. American war doctrine through the 1950s postulated "massive retaliation" with nuclear weapons for Soviet misdeeds, whether or not the Soviets used nuclear weapons first.[58] The capacity for this retaliation was lodged in the intercontinental bombers of the Strategic Air Command. The United States also deployed a large number of nuclear land mines, artillery shells, and small bombs and rockets to be used in battle.

After the Cuban missile crisis of 1962, the Soviet Union accelerated the deployment of large intercontinental missiles and achieved a strategic balance of sorts. Either side henceforth had the theoretical ability to absorb a first strike and still in retaliation destroy the other as a functioning society. This was the balance of terror and the basis for the new doctrine of "mutual assured destruction." The SALT I treaty of 1972, forbidding both sides to attempt to defend more than limited areas with anti-ballistic missiles, was open recognition of the paradox that security was based on mutual insecurity.[59]

But no American leader has ever been completely comfortable with the doctrine of mutual assured destruction, and some, especially in the military and among the new breed of defense intellectuals, were strongly opposed. Given the supposed inferiority of the United States and its allies to the Soviet Union in non-nuclear weapons, mutual assured destruction seemed to provide only two terrible responses to Soviet aggression: surrender or destruction of the world. We must, said these critics, have the plans and the weapons to fight and win a nuclear war. The Soviets already have such plans. We must have them also.[60] The advocates of a war-fighting capacity were disdainful of the counterargument that the use of any nuclear weapon, no matter how small, would escalate into an all-out exchange, after which there would be few survivors and no meaningful distinction between winners and losers. On that grim question, no convincing proof, either way, could be offered.

Thus, two incompatible doctrines, like opposing theological beliefs, lived within a single government. From one year to another, the emphasis changed, but never did one doctrine eliminate the other. Mutually assured destruction was in vogue in 1972, but two years later Secretary of Defense James Schlesinger presided over the drafting of National Security Decision Memorandum 242, which called for planning to use nuclear weapons at different levels, against a range of targets, during the course of a war—not simply letting go with an end-of-the-world retaliatory strike.

There were two principal impulses behind the yearning for a capacity to fight a nuclear war. The professional military impulse was an understandable consequence of the need for the officers and civilian planners who devised and manned American weapons to plan for something other than efficient mass suicide. Thus, they scrutinized potential enemy targets, projected ways of cutting off the foe's command, control, communication, and intelligence faculties (known in the trade as C₃I), and designed precise and sophisticated weapons.[61] Then they sat in air-conditioned rooms and played war games with their computers.

The more important impulse was political. It rested on the assumption that the side which appeared to have the most fully developed capacity to wage nuclear war would be able to intimidate the other. Whether or not in an actual nuclear war this apparent superiority would produce "victory" could not be proved and was almost irrelevant. Power lay in the perception. Perceptions, however, could not be maintained for long with mere rhetorical flourishes, blue smoke, and mirrors. They had to be based on real programs—on command, control, and communications systems designed to function while the nation was under nuclear attack, on civil-defense schemes, on contingency planning for economic recovery, and on weapons and targeting strategies to attack the enemy's political, economic, and military structures in a discriminating, not a world-destroying, way.

Brzezinski was the foremost embodiment of the political motivation for the development of the capacity and doctrine for fighting a protracted nuclear war. Throughout the four years of the Administration, he gathered supporters. Secretary of Defense Brown was cool at first, but by the spring of 1979 Brzezinski was able to write in his journal that "Harold Brown has now become much more interested in greater flexibility and is clearly moving away from a rigid deterrence posture. Cy Vance remains concerned and skeptical." Brzezinski also ordered plans to be developed for enhancing the survival qualities of American C₃I and pressed the military to perfect their studies of Soviet targets. The crises over the hostages and the Soviet invasion of Afghanistan facilitated Brzezinski's campaign. By May 1980, he had a document approved by Secretary Brown and ready for the President's signature.[62]

This was Presidential Directive 59, or PD-59, signed by Carter in July. Although the text was highly classified, the existence and thrust of the document—like NSC-68 in the 1950s—was intentionally revealed in order to demonstrate the Administration's new tough line and to signal the Russians. A similar and connected revelation, with identical purpose, concerned the "Stealth" bomber. In August, Secretary Brown announced the successful development of a technique to make planes invisible to radar and thus virtually invulnerable to interception "with existing air defense systems . . . This achievement will be a formidable instrument of peace."

At the same news conference, Secretary Brown claimed that PD-59 was "not a radical departure from U.S. strategic policy over the past decade or so."[63] This was true only in the sense that thinking about fighting a nuclear war had always existed along with thinking about mutually assured deterrence. Furthermore, PD-59, like most doctrinal documents prepared by many hands, was filled with ambiguity reflecting different assumptions. "There were people in the government who believed in protracted nuclear war and even in prevailing in nuclear war," Brown told an interviewer in 1983. "The outcome was a rather uncomfortable compromise between those people and the people who believed mostly in deterrence."[64]

For Brzezinski, there was nothing uncomfortable about PD-59. He hailed it as the end of the paralyzing assumption that nuclear war would be "brief, spasmic, and apocalyptic"—similar, he believed, to attitudes that had prevailed before 1914. He celebrated the new preparations for protracted conflict "with flexible use of our forces, strategic and general-purpose, on behalf of war aims that we would select as we engaged in conflict." Only through such preparations could the Soviets be effectively deterred in the political as well as the strictly military sense and effectively engaged should deterrence fail. PD-59 was for Brzezinski the capstone of the foreign policy he had been seeking to shape since 1977.[65] In the fall of 1980, there remained only one more occasion for applying the new approach: a crisis in Poland.

POLAND

Poland—largest country in Eastern Europe and a nation whose incorporation within the Soviet sphere was an important cause of the Cold War—held an important place in the Carter Administration's foreign policy, for several reasons. Denouncing Soviet repression of Poland had been good politics in the United States since 1945, and during the 1976 campaign Gerald Ford gave Carter an easily exploited issue by foolishly remarking that he did not consider Poland under Soviet domination. Ford's blunder almost certainly helped elect Carter, and the new President was not going to relinquish a good issue. And lest Carter forget, there was Polish-born Zbigniew Brzezinski daily at his side. Once, Brzezinski drew Carter's attention to a passage in William Styron's novel *Sophie's Choice* describing "a surprising affinity between Poland and the [American] South, two peoples bred on a history that overcame defeat, on a code of chivalry and honor that proudly compensated for backwardness."[66]

At Brzezinski's urging, Carter decided that Poland would be the site of his first official state visit—in December 1977. That visit and generous economic aid were designed to encourage Poland to assert an increasing degree of independence from the Soviet Union. Poland, however, was experiencing serious economic problems caused by the inefficiency of the rigid communist bureaucracy and aggravated by the worldwide inflation and recession which were the consequence of soaring oil prices. In the summer of 1980, popular discontent with the Warsaw government led to a wave of strikes. Soon the strikers, led by the heroic Lech Walesa, had formed the movement and organization known as Solidarity and won concessions from the government.[67] American observers doubted, however, that Polish authorities would be able to control the situation. At the end of August, Carter wrote to his British, French, and German counterparts and to the Pope expressing American anxiety and urging a common

Western response to possible Soviet intervention in the style of Hungary in 1956 or Czechoslovakia in 1968.

The situation deteriorated rapidly through the autumn. In October, Brzezinski supervised the preparation of plans for punishing the Soviet Union should it intervene. In December, Carter sent Brezhnev a blunt warning letter—which was never acknowledged. Meanwhile, there were ominous signs of Soviet troops poised on the Polish border. The CIA said an invasion could be expected at any moment, with heavy bloodshed. But the invasion did not take place—neither then nor in 1981, when it was just as confidently expected by the Reagan Administration. Did the strong American warning make a difference? Perhaps, although without reliable internal Soviet sources, we cannot be sure; Soviet preoccupation with Afghanistan may have been a stronger deterrent. At least, the clarity of American and European statements was markedly different from the lack of attention before Czechoslovakia in 1968. The crisis was the last one to confront the Carter Administration before it left office. It was handled, as Brzezinski has observed, with firmness and a lack of internal dissent—although too late to be of political use to President Carter.

As the final days of the Carter Administration ran out in January 1981, the President and his foreign-policy advisers concentrated on the effort to secure the release of the hostages before Ronald Reagan took the oath of office. But Jimmy Carter did find time to prepare and deliver, on January 14, a farewell address. He made no mention of the Soviet Union, Afghanistan, Iran, MX missiles, war-fighting doctrines, or any of the confrontations and controversies which had marked the second half of his Presidency. "For a few minutes now," he began, "I want to lay aside my role as leader of one nation, and speak to you as a fellow citizen of the world about three issues—three difficult issues—the threat of nuclear destruction, our stewardship of the physical resources of the planet, and the preeminence of the basic rights of human beings." His words and delivery were quiet, moving, and sad—as if he were trying to recapture some of the larger vision expressed four years earlier, while regretting the narrow, nationalistic, dangerous jostling which had been his lot to witness as President. He accused no nation of particular fault, and appealed instead to all peoples to "see our Earth as it really is—a small, fragile, and beautiful blue globe, the only home we have. We see no barriers of race or religion or country. We see the essential unity of our species and our planet."[68]

The tragedy of his Presidency, of American foreign policy, and of international relations in the late twentieth century was that neither Jimmy Carter nor any other leader had ever been able to find a way to hold steadily to that vision and act upon it. Jimmy Carter had tried harder than most of his predecessors to transcend the normal combative, nationalistic character of foreign policy. He and his advisers had failed, not only to adhere to the broader vision of human interest, but also to avoid repudiation by the American people at the polls. Why that failure occurred requires some concluding reflections.

Reflections:
Why Carter Failed

American foreign policy—indeed, the foreign policy of any democratic state—must always pursue three broad objectives: security against the military power of present or potential enemies; the economic well-being of the population; and the preservation of democratic values. The degree to which these objectives have been attained at different times in American history has varied. Sometimes, American armed forces have been inadequate to deter an enemy. Sometimes, decisions in foreign policy have disrupted the domestic economy. Sometimes, democratic values have been compromised in the interests of perceived national security. Never have all three objectives been perfectly fulfilled. But no Presidential Administration has been able to sustain popular support and win reelection after it was perceived as failing egregiously to attain any one of these objectives. For example, Lyndon Johnson failed because entanglement in the Vietnam war seemed to undermine both military security and American values. Richard Nixon was forced from office primarily because his conduct at home and abroad seemed to mock morality.

Jimmy Carter entered office believing that the failure of his predecessors was moral. He promised a government and especially a foreign policy "as good as the people." He had the good luck to run in the only election since the days of Woodrow Wilson when such an emphasis would lead to victory. In 1972, George

McGovern tried something very similar and was easily defeated by Richard Nixon. But in 1976 the public—as confirmed by intuition and numerous surveys—was in favor of reform, disillusioned with recent leadership, and more opposed to a military emphasis in foreign policy than at any time since the 1930s.[1] Jimmy Carter did not create that mood. He was like a surfer who is in precisely the right position to catch the one wave of the day that will carry him all the way.

By 1977, the public mood was changing. Memories of Vietnam and Watergate were beginning to fade. Public opinion was beginning to shift in favor of more spending on defense and a more assertive foreign policy—in other words, it was returning to a normal condition. Jimmy Carter as the prophet assailing American wickedness was now out of step. By 1979, Carter had changed his approach, emphasizing American strength more than human values. But this did not bring him immunity from the earlier image of weakness or prevent him from acquiring a new image of inconsistency.

The policies of the Administration also were perceived as damaging the American economy. Here Carter was the victim of bad timing and conditions over which he had little control. The principal problem was double-digit inflation rooted in the deficit spending of the Vietnam years and the rise in oil prices since 1973, especially the 1979 increase connected with the Iranian revolution. The high interest rates which accompanied the inflation slowed the economy and led to rising unemployment. Carter was blamed. His Administration took remedial action, but the results did not begin to show until Carter was out of office.

Carter was the first President since Herbert Hoover not to have American soldiers die in combat during his term. He was proud of that. A case can be made that he served American military security well by refusing to intervene, as in Iran or Nicaragua, where intervention would have made a bad situation catastrophic. A nation's military security is also gained by reaching settlements and making peace rather than letting a conflict degenerate into war. On that score, the Carter Administration deserves credit for the Panama Canal treaties and the Camp David negotiations. But the Panama settlement was all too easily depicted as appeasement, and Camp David involved issues too remote and complex to capture the general imagination. The Administration made a good case that the SALT II treaty contributed to national security, but the treaty's provisions fell so short of Carter's original overly publicized objectives that critics charged that the United States had been defeated by the Soviet Union at the negotiating table. Even without the Soviet invasion of Afghanistan and Carter's request that the treaty be withdrawn from consideration, the Senate almost certainly would have voted against ratification. Ronald Reagan called it "fatally flawed," and the election of 1980 indicated that the majority of the American people were ready to accept Reagan's word.

Soviet actions also contributed to Carter's political failure in the United States. Suspicion, rigidity, and insensitivity are normal characteristics of the Kremlin's foreign policy, but in the waning years of Brezhnev, these qualities were particularly evident. Moscow automatically put the worst possible interpretation on every American gesture and thereby undercut those in the Administration who wanted accommodation while strengthening those who were eager for confrontation. Soviet policy could scarcely have been better designed to provide arguments for those who wanted to discredit Carter's initial emphasis on human rights and global issues. For example, the completion of SALT II in 1977 would have been a triumph for Carter. But SALT II in 1979, after the negotiations had wallowed along for thirty months and Soviet and American interests had collided on other issues, was an easy target for American hard-liners.

Sometimes Soviet misdeeds were exaggerated or invented by those who wanted to portray the Kremlin as viciously hostile. But on many occasions the Soviets did act crudely and provocatively. Soviet and Cuban behavior in Africa was just what Brzezinski needed to advance his point of view. Soviet deployment of SS-

20 missiles aimed at Europe stirred American and Western European fears and provided an excuse for introducing new American nuclear weapons. Soviet leaders always seemed to assume that the most hostile American voice was the real reflection of policy. This may have appeared prudent in Moscow, but the result was that the Soviets acted in ways which fulfilled their own predictions about the United States. The process, of course, was reciprocal—except that Soviet leaders had it in their power to react to conciliatory as well as to hostile American gestures at a time when Carter's approach was still fluid. By failing to respond to conciliation, they drove conciliation from the field.

Without access to Soviet archives or internal thinking, it is impossible to say if Brezhnev, Gromyko, and their colleagues wanted a lessening of tension. If they did want agreements with the United States, an excellent opportunity was at hand in 1977. They rejected it. Conversely, had the Soviets set out to ensure Carter's defeat in 1980, they could hardly have done better. Had they seized the opportunity for real settlements quickly reached, Carter would have been acclaimed in the United States as a successful peacemaker. If they had engaged in more blatant use of force by intervening in Iran, for example, they would have risked a major war but might have made Carter popular as a fighting President in the style of Truman.

Had there been no trouble in Iran, there might well have been a second Carter term. The Iranian revolution, product of three decades of the Shah's rule and American policies going back to the 1950s, happened to erupt on Carter's watch. Nothing the Carter Administration could have done would have prevented the revolution or squelched it. The direct use of American force to sustain the Shah would have had disastrous consequences for the security of the United States. Nor did the seizure of the hostages have an obvious solution. Carter's only large error in relation to Iran was the attempt to rescue the hostages by military means. The early inability of the mission to proceed prevented that error from having its worst probable consequences. But avoiding errors or even saving lives is not the same as winning popular support at home. Carter could have punished Iran within days of the seizure of the hostages if he had been willing to sacrifice their lives for American "honor." To his lasting credit, he did not take that course, even though he might have been more popular at home had he done so.

Bad luck and the uncooperative behavior of the Soviet Union are not the full explanation for Carter's failure. He selected Brzezinski and Vance as his two principal advisers on foreign policy. He knew they represented different viewpoints but did not appreciate how deep the incompatibility lay. He thought he could pick ideas now from one, now from the other, taking the best of each. Only a President with deep experience in foreign affairs and a grasp of the issues equal or superior to that of such contending advisers could have prevented crippling contradictions. Carter lacked such experience and grasp. His philosophy of repentance and reform was appropriate as criticism of past error, but it provided little guidance in dealing with new problems. Furthermore, it led to arrogance. The self-righteous reformer is easy prey to the argument that an adversary, in this case the Soviet Union, is the sole cause of all that is wrong. Carter thus was a ready convert to the world according to Brzezinski.

Carter's lack of experience and historical perspective also fed his penchant for alarmist, exaggerated rhetoric.[2] His description of the Soviet invasion of Afghanistan as the greatest threat to world peace since the Second World War is the most extreme example. But he used the same sort of rhetoric in discussing arms control, the energy shortage, the Panama treaties, and conflict in the Middle East. These were serious issues, but by discussing them all with apocalyptic rhetoric, Carter diluted the power of his words and diminished his ability to persuade. Every leader has to find a proper balance between seeming complacent in the face of danger and being overwrought. Carter was uncomfortable in seeking the balance. The uncertainties of the situations he faced produced in him the appearance of vacillation and inconsistency, and not the calm and serenity of more successful leaders.

Every triumphant President has commanded support from Congress. Carter, however, faced the double handicap of his own political style and a newly assertive, even abrasive mood in Congress. From the Second World War into the 1960s, Congress generally did the President's bidding on measures related to foreign affairs and national security. The Vietnam war, however, erased the automatic willingness of Congress to follow the Presidential lead. Old collaborationists, of whom J. William Fulbright was the most prominent, changed their minds. New, independent members were elected. Congress increased enormously the size of professional staffs, thus giving individual members and committees the capacity to challenge the old cliché that only the President possessed all the information necessary for decisions. In the 1970s, Congress enacted laws limiting the President's power in foreign affairs and giving Congress larger control over specific decisions.[3]

Carter's political history and personality made his task doubly difficult. He had won the nomination and been elected by making his inexperience and lack of connections in Washington an asset. The implication was that anyone who had been in Washington before the arrival of Jimmy Carter was tainted. Such a message and attitude were ill designed to win the trust and support of veterans in the House and Senate, most of whom had far more national and international experience than Carter. The President tried to cultivate Congress. He made the gestures—the obligatory letters, phone calls—but could not generate the impression of warmth and spontaneity. The result was that he never acquired a personal following. There were few in Congress on whom Carter could count for favors, and no leaders who would take on the task of getting a Carter proposal through.

Carter's personal relations with foreign leaders were uneven. His warmest feelings of friendship and his most successful working relations were with non-Europeans such as Sadat of Egypt, Torrijos of Panama, Deng of China, Ohira of Japan—all of whom knew how to flatter and stressed personal ties. Carter's relations with statesmen who, like congressional leaders, acted as his equals in power and his superiors in experience ranged from poor to atrocious. The worst relationship, by far, was with German Chancellor Helmut Schmidt. Carter considered him personally abusive, and the German made little effort to conceal his contempt for the former governor of Georgia. Whenever Schmidt and Carter were together, each reacted as if the other were dragging fingernails down a blackboard.[4] Again, as with Congress, Carter worked hard on his diplomatic chores, but in regard to Europe the outcome was increasing strain, not mutual understanding.

Finally and tragically, Carter failed because he asked the American people to think as citizens of the world with an obligation toward future generations. He offered a morally responsible and farsighted vision. But the clamor of political critics, the behavior of the Soviet Union, the discordant voices of his advisers, and the impossibility of seeing clearly what needed to be done—all combined to make Carter's vision appear naïve. In 1980, he fell back on an appeal to the combative, nationalistic instincts of the American people. "Never since World War II has there been so far-reaching a militarization of thought and discourse in the capital," observed George F. Kennan that winter. "An unsuspecting stranger, plunged into its midst, could only conclude that the last hope of peaceful, non-military solutions had been exhausted—that from now on only weapons, however used, could count."[5] This appeal was out of character for Carter. It was made in the belief that the Russians and the necessity of reelection left no alternative.

Ronald Reagan made the same appeal more convincingly and thereby brought the Carter Administration to its end.

Notes

The following abbreviations are used throughout for frequently cited sources:

AFP   Department of State, *American Foreign Policy: Basic Documents, 1977–1980* (Wash., D.C.: U.S. Government Printing Office, 1983). This is a superb 1,458-page selection of significant documents, compiled by the Historical Office of the department. Citations are given by document number.

Brzezinski   Zbigniew Brzezinski, *Power and Principle: Memoirs of the National Security Adviser, 1977–1981* (New York: Farrar, Straus and Giroux, 1983). This is a candid and richly detailed memoir. It is the most important single source for the present study.

Campaign 1976   *The Presidential Campaign 1976* (Wash., D.C.: U.S. Government Printing Office, 1978). One volume in two parts. Compiled under the direction of the Committee on House Administration, U.S. House of Representatives. Lengthy and well indexed; an important source.

Carter	Jimmy Carter, *Keeping Faith* (New York: Bantam Books, 1982). The President's memoirs treat some issues, such as Camp David, in great detail, while not mentioning others.
DSB	*Department of State Bulletin.* The monthly bulletin containing texts of statements, press conferences, articles.
Vance	Cyrus Vance, *Hard Choices: Critical Years in America's Foreign Policy* (New York: Simon and Schuster, 1983). Careful, discreet, comprehensive.

1. ECHOES OF HISTORY

1. John Lewis Gaddis, *Strategies of Containment: A Critical Appraisal of Postwar American National Security Policy* makes the useful analytical distinction between prescriptions calling for containing Soviet expansion wherever it was perceived to exist (symmetrical containment) and meeting it primarily in regions of vital interest to the United States (asymmetrical containment).

2. For an articulate example of the world-order approach, much admired by many members of the Carter Administration, see Stanley Hoffmann, *Primacy or World Order: American Foreign Policy Since the Cold War.* Robert C. Johansen, *The National Interest and the Human Interest: An Analysis of U.S. Foreign Policy* argues for a policy based on broad ethical principles.

3. Address to Congress, April 2, 1917, in Arthur S. Link, ed., *The Papers of Woodrow Wilson*, vol. 41 (Princeton: Princeton University Press, 1983), pp. 519–27.

4. Address to the Senate, Jan. 8, 1918, ibid., vol. 45, p. 537.

5. Address to the Senate, Jan. 22, 1917, ibid., vol. 40, p. 539.

6. The most powerful antagonist of Wilson and Wilsonian assumptions during the great debate of 1919 was Senator Henry Cabot Lodge. The best analysis of Lodge's thinking is William C. Widenor, *Henry Cabot Lodge and the Search for an American Foreign Policy.*

7. Charles A. Beard and co-author George H. E. Smith first explored how American political leaders had historically defined *The Idea of National Interest.* They discovered that "national interest" was often the interest of narrow economic groups, not the whole people, seeking to use the nation's power to perpetuate an open door for their markets around the world. In a companion volume, they argued that the government should avoid foreign entanglements and pursue *The Open Door at Home.*

8. Nicholas John Spykman, *America's Strategy in World Politics,* p. 18.

9. Reinhold Niebuhr, *The Irony of American History,* p. vii.

10. U.S. Department of State, *Foreign Relations of the United States,* 1950, vol. 1, p. 244.

11. Ibid., p. 254.

12. U.S. Department of State, *Foreign Relations of the United States,* 1950, vol. 2, p. 607.

13. David Halberstam, *The Best and the Brightest.*

14. Two excellent surveys are George C. Herring, *America's Longest War: The United States and Vietnam, 1950–1975* and Stanley Karnow, *Vietnam: A History.*

15. This important transformation is well described by Thomas M. Franck and Edward Weisband, *Foreign Policy by Congress.*

16. The best biography to date is Betty Glad, *Jimmy Carter: In Search of the Great White House.* Carter's campaign autobiography, *Why Not the Best?,* is thin.

17. This and subsequent quotations from Carter's campaign speeches come from the very useful *The Presidential Campaign 1976,* passim.

18. Carter, p. 19.

2. PEOPLE AND POLICIES

1. Rosalynn Carter, *First Lady from Plains* is a well-written memoir.

2. Zbigniew Brzezinski, *Between Two Ages: America's Role in the Technetronic Age.*

3. David Detzer, *The Brink: Cuban Missile Crisis*, 1962, p. 234.

4. Brzezinski, *Ideology and Power in Soviet Politics*, rev. ed., p. 227.

5. Coral Bell, *President Carter and Foreign Policy: The Costs of Virtue*, p. 23.

6. Brzezinski, p. xiv.

7. For Acheson's role, see his *Present at the Creation* and Gaddis Smith, *Dean Acheson.*

8. His criticism of Kissinger can be followed in a series of articles in *Foreign Policy*: "Half Past Nixon," 3 (Summer 1971); "The Balance of Power Delusion," 7 (Summer 1972); and "The Deceptive Structure of Peace," 14 (Spring 1974).

9. The power of the Trilateral Commission has been much exaggerated. See Holly Sklar, ed., *Trilateralism: The Trilateral Commission and Elite Planning for World Management.*

10. Hamilton Jordan, *Crisis: The Last Year of the Carter Presidency*, p. 45, recalls that Carter told him: "Those Trilateral Commission meetings for me were like classes in foreign policy— reading papers produced on every conceivable subject, hearing experienced leaders debate international issues and problems, and meeting the big names like Cy Vance and Harold Brown and Zbig."

11. Brzezinski, pp. 570-3, lists the officers who served on the National Security Staff during his four years.

12. Vance, p. 394.

13. Brzezinski, p. 400.

14. Ibid., pp. 42-3, 480-1.

15. Crane Brinton, *The Anatomy of Revolution*, rev. ed., p. 88.

16. Carter, *Why Not the Best?*, p. 147. Ambassadors, most of the time, had little importance in the formation of policy. George W. Ball, a distinguished diplomatist, declined an offer of an appointment from Carter. "I refrained from saying," he recalled in his memoirs, "what I really felt—that jet planes and telephones and the bad habits of Presidents, National Security Advisers and Secretaries of State had now largely restricted ambassadors to ritual public relations. I did not wish to end my days as an innkeeper for itinerant Congressmen." *The Past Has Another Pattern: Memoirs*, p. 452. For commentary by various ambassadors, see Martin F. Herz, ed., *The Modern Ambassador: The Challenge and the Search*.

17. His book, *Thinking About National Security: Defense and Foreign Policy in a Dangerous World*, is filled with sensible generalities and devoid of revelations or comment on personalities. It reflects the style of the man.

18. Brzezinski, pp. 44–7.

19. The appointment came as a surprise to Turner. See his *Secrecy and Democracy: The CIA in Transition*, pp. 9–20.

20. Stansfield Turner, "The Naval Balance: Not Just a Numbers Game," *Foreign Affairs* 55, no. 2 (Jan. 1977), p. 339.

21. Turner, *Secrecy and Democracy*, pp. 113–14.

22. Brzezinski, p. 400.

23. Public Law 94-329, Section 502(B).

24. The outstanding treatment of the subject is Sandy Vogelgesang, *American Dream, Global Nightmare: The Dilemma of U.S. Foreign Policy*. The author is an American diplomat with direct experience with human-rights policy, as well as a thoughtful scholar. A stimulating contemporary essay is Arthur Schlesinger, Jr., "Human Rights and the American Tradition," *Foreign Affairs: America and the World 1978* 57, no. 3, pp. 503–26.

25. The fullest report on the bureaucratic jostling within the

Administration over the human-rights question is Caleb Rossiter, "Human Rights: The Carter Record, the Reagan Reaction," *International Policy Report* (a publication of the Center for International Policy), Sept. 1984, pp. 1–27.

26. *AFP*, document 160.

27. Jeane Kirkpatrick, "Dictatorships and Double Standards," *Commentary* 68, no. 5 (Nov. 1979), pp. 34–45.

28. One result of President Carter's concern over the possible exhaustion of energy and other resources was an enormous interdepartmental study, *The Global 2000 Report to the President*, requested by him in 1977 and completed at the end of his Presidency. The philosophy of the report is expressed on its opening page with the observation that the world in 2000 will be in many ways worse than in 1980. "Barring revolutionary advances in technology, life for most people on earth will be more precarious in 2000 than it is now—unless the nations of the world act decisively to alter current trends." Council on Environmental Quality and the Department of State, *The Global 2000 Report to the President*, p. 1.

29. *AFP*, document 120.

30. *AFP*, document 124.

31. *AFP*, document 126.

32. Ann L. Hollick, *U.S. Foreign Policy and the Law of the Sea* is a comprehensive review of the subject. See also Jonathan I. Charney, "Law of the Sea: Breaking the Deadlock," *Foreign Affairs* 55, no. 3 (April 1978); and Richard G. Darman, "The Law of the Sea: Rethinking U.S. Interests," *Foreign Affairs* 56, no. 2 (Jan. 1979).

33. Noteworthy amid the vast literature on the subject are Lewis A. Dunn, *Controlling the Bomb: Nuclear Proliferation in the 1980s* and William C. Potter, *Nuclear Power and Nonproliferation: An Interdisciplinary Perspective*.

34. For criticism of the Administration's record, see Michael Brenner, "Carter's Nonproliferation Strategy: Fuel Assurances and Energy Security," *Orbis* 22, no. 2 (Summer 1978), and "Prolif-

eration Watch: Carter's Bungled Promise," *Foreign Policy* 36 (Fall 1979).

35. U.S. Department of State, *Foreign Relations of the United States*, 1947, vol. 2, pp. 725–6.

36. The most authoritative discussion of the subject is Andrew L. Pierre, *The Global Politics of Arms Sales*.

37. AFP, document 71.

38. Pierre, *The Global Politics of Arms Sales*, p. 57.

39. AFP, document 3.

3. NUCLEAR WEAPONS AND THE SOVIET UNION

1. Raymond L. Garthoff, *Détente and Confrontation: American–Soviet Relations from Nixon to Reagan* is a monumentally detailed and perceptive analysis of the ambiguities and mutually reinforcing misperceptions in the relationship during the years 1969–84, especially valuable for its insights into Soviet thinking. Also see Joseph S. Nye, Jr., ed., *The Making of America's Soviet Policy*.

2. *Public Papers of the Presidents: Jimmy Carter*, 1977, pp. 955–62.

3. Brzezinski, pp. 296–301.

4. Gregg Herken, *Counsels of War*, pp. 296–302.

5. Vogelgesang, *American Dream, Global Nightmare*, pp. 103–4.

6. *Current Digest of the Soviet Press*, March 13, 1977.

7. Carter, p. 220; Garthoff, *Détente and Confrontation*, p. 610.

8. *DSB*, July 1978.

9. Carter, pp. 259–60.

10. Marshall D. Shulman, "On Learning to Live with Authoritarian Regimes," *Foreign Affairs* 55, no. 2 (Jan. 1977), p. 333.

11. This is the thrust of "Dictatorships and Double Standards," the famous article by Kirkpatrick.

12. The two best books on the subject are Harold and Margaret Sprout, *Toward a New Order of Sea Power: American Naval Policy and the World Scene* and Roger Dingman, *Power in the Pacific: The Origins of Naval Arms Limitation, 1914–1922*.

13. Joseph I. Lieberman, *The Scorpion and the Tarantula: The Struggle to Control Atomic Weapons, 1945–1949*.

14. Glenn T. Seaborg, *Kennedy, Khrushchev, and the Test Ban*.

15. John Newhouse, *Cold Dawn: The Story of SALT*.

16. W. W. Rostow, *Open Skies: Eisenhower's Proposal of July 21, 1955*.

17. Strobe Talbott, *Endgame: The Inside Story of SALT II*, p. 43.

18. Paul Warnke, "Apes on a Treadmill," *Foreign Policy* 18 (Spring 1975), pp. 12–29.

19. Richard Pipes, "Why the Soviet Union Thinks It Could Fight and Win a Nuclear War," *Commentary* 54, no. 1 (July 1977). For a detailed discussion of the Committee on the Present Danger, see Jerry W. Sanders, *Peddlers of Crisis: The Committee on the Present Danger and the Politics of Containment*.

20. Quoted in Sanders, *Peddlers of Crisis*, pp. 206–7.

21. *Current Digest of the Soviet Press*, May 4, 1977.

22. Talbott, *Endgame*, pp. 81–2.

23. The texts of the treaty and accompanying documents are conveniently included in Talbott, *Endgame*, pp. 279–310. I am much indebted to this book for the material on which the above summary is based.

24. See the invaluable analyses in the annual volumes edited by Joseph A. Pechman, *Setting National Priorities*.

25. Carter, p. 83.

26. For the accounts, see Carter, pp. 225–9; Vance, pp. 92–7; and Brzezinski, pp. 301–6.

27. Statement of Feb. 2, 1978, quoted by Herbert Scoville, Jr., *MX: Prescription for Disaster*, p. 56.

28. Quoted by John Edwards, *Superweapon: The Making of MX*, p. 131.

29. Carter, p. 241.

30. Brzezinski, p. 335.

31. Quoted in Herken, *Counsels of War*, p. 291.

4. THE RETURN TO CONTAINMENT IN ASIA

1. Carter, p. 188.

2. Signed Dec. 2, 1954; ratified Feb. 11, 1955; entered into effect March 3, 1955.

3. *Campaign 1976*, p. 447.

4. Carter, p. 189.

5. Brzezinski, p. 200.

6. Vance, pp. 114–15.

7. Brzezinski, pp. 211–15.

8. Carter, p. 195.

9. AFP, document 506.

10. *Current Digest of the Soviet Press*, June 8, 1977.

11. Garthoff, *Détente and Confrontation*, pp. 598–600, 619–21, emphasizes the depth of Soviet dismay over American China policy and suggests that President Carter was not fully aware of the significance of Brzezinski's moves.

12. AFP, document 511.

13. *Time*, Jan. 15, 1979.

14. Ronnie Dugger, *On Reagan: The Man and His Presidency*, p. 276.

15. John Tierney, Jr., ed., *About Face: The China Decision and Its Consequences*, p. 24.

16. Goldwater et al. *v.* Carter, President of the United States, et al., 444 US 996.

17. Carter, p. 210.
18. *Congressional Quarterly Almanac* 1979, pp. 99–117.
19. Carter, p. 201.
20. AFP, document 515.
21. *Time*, Feb. 5, 1979.
22. Brzezinski, pp. 405–7.
23. Carter, p. 202.
24. AFP, document 520.
25. Brzezinski, p. 408.
26. AFP, document 519.
27. AFP, documents 530, 531.
28. AFP, document 527.
29. AFP, document 535.
30. For a powerful and controversial accusation that the United States caused the Cambodian tragedy, see William Shawcross, *Sideshow: Kissinger, Nixon and the Destruction of Cambodia*.
31. AFP, document 550.
32. AFP, document 592.
33. AFP, document 595.
34. AFP, document 551.
35. AFP, document 601.
36. AFP, document 605.
37. *The New York Times*, Feb. 14, 1977.
38. AFP, document 575.
39. News conference of April 7, 1979. AFP, document 580.
40. Quoted in Noam Chomsky, *Towards a New Cold War: Essays on the Current Crisis and How We Got There*, p. 466, footnote 2.
41. AFP, document 538.
42. Vance, p. 144. The crisis arose over North Korea's seizure of the *Pueblo*, a U.S. Navy vessel gathering electronic intelligence close to but probably outside of North Korea's territorial waters. The *Pueblo*'s crew was held prisoner for a year.
43. Ibid., p. 449.
44. *Public Papers of the Presidents: Jimmy Carter*, 1977, p.

1018. Franklin B. Weinstein, "The United States, Japan and the Security of Korea," *International Security* 2, no. 2 (Fall 1977), pp. 68–89, is a good contemporary discussion of the issues. Weinstein approved of Carter's decision. The decision and the Weinstein article are rebutted by Generals I. D. White and Richard G. Stilwell (both retired) in ibid., pp. 90–5.

45. Vance, pp. 127–30.

46. Andrew Nagorski, "East Asia in 1980," *Foreign Affairs: America and the World*, 1980 59, no. 3, p. 674.

47. See I. M. Destler and Hideo Sato, eds., *Coping with U.S.– Japanese Economic Conflicts*.

48. Elizabeth Drew, "Equations" [profile of Strauss], *The New Yorker*, May 7, 1979, pp. 50–127.

49. AFP, document 548.

5. PANAMA SUCCESS AND LATIN AMERICAN FAILURE

1. *Campaign 1976*, p. 372.

2. Brzezinski, p. 135.

3. *Campaign 1976*, p. 82.

4. David McCullough, *The Path between the Seas: The Creation of the Panama Canal, 1870–1914* is a classic account. President Carter admired the book and gained the author's support for the settlement.

5. William J. Jorden, *Panama Odyssey*, pp. 185–96. This book, by the American ambassador to Panama during the negotiations, is an indispensable source. An admirably succinct survey is Walter LaFeber, *The Panama Canal: The Crisis in Historical Perspective*.

6. Text in Jorden, *Panama Odyssey*, pp. 696–7.

7. Dugger, *On Reagan*, p. 362.

8. Commission on United States–Latin American Relations, *The United States and Latin America: Next Steps* (1976), p. 2.

9. *The New York Times*, Jan. 16, 1977.

10. Vance, pp. 143–5.

11. Brzezinski, p. 137.

12. Ibid., p. 136.

13. AFP, document 730.

14. Bernard Roshco, "The Polls: Polling on Panama–Si; Don't Know; Hell, No!" *Public Opinion Quarterly* 42, no. 4 (Winter 1978); and for a comprehensive study, see George D. Moffett III, *The Limits of Victory: The Ratification of the Panama Canal Treaties.*

15. Jorden, *Panama Odyssey*, p. 625.

16. Dugger, *On Reagan*, p. 276.

17. Carter, p. 184.

18. Vance, pp. 452–3.

19. *Campaign 1976*, p. 1023.

20. Statement by Terrence A. Todman, Oct. 18, 1977. *AFP*, document 688.

21. Barbara Walters, "An Interview with Fidel Castro," *Foreign Policy* 28 (Fall 1977), pp. 25–6.

22. Garthoff, "American Reaction to Soviet Aircraft in Cuba, 1962 and 1978," *Political Science Quarterly* 95 (Fall 1980).

23. This episode is discussed at greater length in chap. 9, below.

24. Neill Macaulay, *The Sandino Affair.*

25. LaFeber, *Inevitable Revolutions: The United States and Central America*, pp. 229–31.

26. Carter, p. 178.

27. Richard R. Fagen, "The Carter Administration and Latin America: Business as Usual?" *Foreign Affairs: America and the World* 1978 57, no. 3, pp. 662–3.

28. Interview with Daniel Ortega by Pedro Miranda in "Sandinista Perspectives: Three Differing Views," *Latin American Perspectives* (Winter 1979), pp. 114–18.

29. State Department news briefing, Feb. 8, 1979. *AFP*, document 697.

30. The journalist was Bill Stewart of ABC-TV news. Ac-

cording to *The New York Times*, June 21, 1979, "Mr. Stewart, 37 years old, was ordered to his knees and then told to lie down before a soldier fired a single shot into his head at close range." A television cameraman recorded the event.

31. Statement by Vance, June 21, 1979, before the Seventeenth Meeting Consultation of the OAS Foreign Ministers. AFP, document 698.

32. Carter, p. 585.

33. For a critique, see Arturo J. Cruz, "Nicaragua: The Sandinista Regime at a Watershed," *Strategic Review* (Spring 1984), pp. 11–23. Cruz originally supported the Sandinistas and served as Nicaraguan ambassador to the United States before parting with the revolution, which, in his opinion, had been betrayed.

34. Kirkpatrick, "Dictatorships and Double Standards."

35. For background, see James Dunkerley, *The Long War: Dictatorship and Revolution in El Salvador.*

36. Ibid., pp. 111–13.

37. Statement of Dec. 7, 1979, before the Senate Foreign Relations Committee. AFP, document 705.

38. These events are well chronicled in Robert Armstrong and Janet Shenk, *El Salvador: The Face of Revolution,* pp. 130–84.

39. *The New York Times*, March 13, 1980.

40. From President Carter's diary account of his conversation with the Rogers mission. Carter, p. 585.

41. I am indebted for most of the material in this section to Michael Massing, "Grenada Before and After," *The Atlantic Monthly*, Feb. 1984, pp. 75–87.

42. Ibid., p. 81.

43. Richard E. Feinberg, *The Intemperate Zone: The Third World Challenge to U.S. Foreign Policy,* p. 199.

44. Letter by Frank V. Ortiz in response to Massing article, *The Atlantic Monthly*, June 1984, p. 7.

45. Brzezinski, p. 128.

46. *The New York Times*, Feb. 25, March 1, March 18, Nov. 2, 1977.

47. Fagen, "The Carter Administration and Latin America," p. 659; Carter, p. 145.

48. *The New York Times*, Feb. 1, May 31, 1980; Carter, p. 477.

49. *Campaign 1976*, p. 954.

50. *The New York Times*, March 11, 1977.

51. Abraham F. Lowenthal, "Jimmy Carter and Latin America: A New Era or Small Change?" in Kenneth A. Oye et al., eds., *Eagle Entangled: U.S. Foreign Policy in a Complex World*, p. 294. Also see Albert Fishlow, "Flying Down to Rio: Perspectives on U.S.–Brazil Relations," *Foreign Affairs* 57, no. 2 (Winter 1978–79), pp. 387–405.

52. For her account of the trip to Brazil and other Latin American nations, see Rosalynn Carter, *First Lady from Plains*, pp. 185–214.

53. Memorandum of Sept. 13, 1979. AFP, document 723.

54. Carter, p. 468.

6. MAJORITY RULE AND THE COLD WAR IN AFRICA

1. For the nature and limits of the influence of American blacks on policy toward Africa, see Henry F. Jackson, *From the Congo to Soweto: U.S. Foreign Policy Toward Africa Since 1960*, pp. 142–68; and for opposition to apartheid as a liberal cause, see Andrew Young, "The United States and Africa: Victory for Diplomacy," *Foreign Affairs: America and the World*, 1980 59, no. 3, p. 652.

2. For representative criticism, see Bayard Rustin and Carl Gershman, "Africa, Soviet Imperialism and the Retreat of American Power," *Commentary* 64, no. 4 (Oct. 1977), pp. 33–43.

3. See Young's testimony in June 1977 in Subcommittee on African Affairs, Senate Foreign Relations Committee, *Hearings to Receive a Report from Ambassador Andrew Young* (Wash., D.C.: Government Printing Office, 1977).

4. AFP, document 608.

5. Brzezinski, pp. 139–50, 557.

6. An excellent account is Richard D. Mahoney, *JFK: Ordeal in Africa*.

7. For the text, see Mohamed A. el-Khawas and Barry Cohen, eds., *The Kissinger Study of Southern Africa: National Security Study Memorandum 39 (SECRET)*.

8. A critical account by a onetime CIA officer in Angola is John Stockwell, *In Search of Enemies: A CIA Story*.

9. See the description and criticism by Anthony Lake, *The "Tar Baby" Option: American Policy towards Southern Rhodesia*. Anthony Lake subsequently served as head of the State Department Policy Planning Staff in the Carter Administration and was an important influence on African policy.

10. *DSB*, May 31, 1976.

11. AFP, document 645.

12. Vance, pp. 266–70.

13. Brzezinski, p. 142.

14. Quoted in Study Commission on U.S. Policy Toward Southern Africa, *South Africa: Time Running Out*, p. 344.

15. Ibid., pp. 345–7.

16. *DSB*, Feb. 14, 1977.

17. Vance, p. 265; *DSB*, June 20, 1977.

18. AFP, document 608.

19. AFP, document 623.

20. Bell, *President Carter and Foreign Policy*, p. 72.

21. AFP, document 627.

22. In a speech in Oct. 1980, Assistant Secretary Moose summarized the actions taken. *AFP*, document 622. The code is known as the "Sullivan principles," in recognition of the Reverend Leon Sullivan, an American clergyman and their principal author.

23. AFP, document 617.

24. Vance, p. 313.

25. AFP, document 680.

26. AFP, document 674.

27. AFP, document 675.

28. Garthoff, *Détente and Confrontation*, pp. 626–7.

29. For more details, see Peter Mangold, "Shaba I and Shaba II," *Survival* 21 (May–June 1979), pp. 107–10; and William Leo-Grande, *Cuba's Policy in Africa, 1959–1980.*

30. AFP, document 677.

31. AFP, document 681.

32. Judith Miller, "When Sanctions Worked," *Foreign Policy* 39 (Summer 1980), pp. 118–29.

33. Carter, p. 410.

34. Robert Shaplen, "Eye of the Storm" [profile of David Newsom], *The New Yorker*, Oct. 22, 1979, p. 79.

35. AFP, document 252.

36. Brzezinski, p. 179.

37. AFP, document 662.

38. On Soviet policy and reactions, see Garthoff, *Détente and Confrontation*, pp. 630–53.

39. AFP, document 665.

7. SEARCHING FOR PEACE IN THE MIDDLE EAST

1. A good survey is Seth P. Tillman, *The United States in the Middle East.*

2. John Norton Moore, ed., *The Arab–Israeli Conflict: Readings and Documents*, pp. 1083–4.

3. Carter, p. 282.

4. Ibid., 288.

5. Moshe Dayan, *Breakthrough: A Personal Account of the Egypt–Israeli Peace Negotiations*, pp. 55–69.

6. Carter, p. 293.

7. Dayan, *Breakthrough*, p. 38.

8. Carter, p. 293.

9. Ibid., p. 302.

10. Carter (p. 310) says more than a thousand lives were lost; Dayan (p. 121) says three hundred.

11. AFP, document 386.

12. DSB, May 1978, pp. 46–7.

13. Carter, p. 313.

14. AFP, document 291.

15. Public Papers of the Presidents: Jimmy Carter, 1978, p. 1537.

16. Ibid., 1980–81, p. 427.

17. Jody Powell, The Other Side of the Story, pp. 114–17.

18. Carter, p. 546.

19. Campaign 1976, p. 837.

20. Vance, p. 205.

21. Hyman Bookbinder, Washington representative of the American Jewish Committee quoted in Tillman, The United States in the Middle East, p. 99.

22. AFP, document 246.

23. Robin Bidwell, The Two Yemens.

24. Brzezinski, p. 181.

25. AFP, document 250.

26. Garthoff, Détente and Confrontation, pp. 653–60.

27. Quoted in ibid., p. 660.

28. Laurence Stern, The Wrong Horse: The Politics of Intervention and the Failure of American Diplomacy. For a critical treatment of the influence of a Greek–American lobby in securing passage of the embargo, see Laurence Halley, Ancient Affections: Ethnic Groups and Foreign Policy.

29. Campaign 1976, pp. 690–1.

30. Memorandum of Oct. 1976, Vance, p. 447.

31. AFP, document 217.

8. IRAN, THE SHAH,
AND THE HOSTAGES

1. Vance, p. 447.

2. Arnold Raphel, "Media Coverage of the Hostage Negoti-

ations—From Fact to Fiction," U.S. Department of State, Foreign Service Institute, *Executive Seminar in National and International Affairs*, 24th sess. (1981–82), p. 14.

3. Bruce Kuniholm, *The Origins of the Cold War in the Near East: Great Power Conflict and Diplomacy in Iran, Turkey, and Greece*.

4. Benjamin Shwadran, *The Middle East, Oil and the Great Powers*, 3d ed.

5. Kermit Roosevelt, *Countercoup: Struggle for the Control of Iran*.

6. The Shah's grandiose concepts are sympathetically described in Shahram Chubin, "Iran's Security in the 1980s," *International Security* 2, no. 3 (Winter 1978), pp. 51–80.

7. For example, see the Shah's interview with Arnaud de Borchgrave, *Newsweek*, Nov. 14, 1977.

8. James A. Bill, "Iran and the Crisis of 1978," *Foreign Affairs* 57, no. 2 (Winter 1978–79), pp. 323–42. This is one of the most perceptive of the contemporary American efforts to explain the crisis, but even it underestimates the power of the fundamentalist Islamic clergy.

9. 1977 *Congressional Quarterly Almanac*, pp. 387–8; Carter, p. 434.

10. Rosalynn Carter, *First Lady from Plains*, p. 306.

11. Carter, p. 437.

12. Jordan, *Crisis*, p. 89.

13. Pierre Salinger, *America Held Hostage: The Secret Negotiations*, pp. 1–5.

14. AFP, document 328.

15. William H. Sullivan, *Mission to Iran*, pp. 80–1.

16. Shaplen, "Eye of the Storm," *The New Yorker*, June 2, 1980, p. 50.

17. The best and most recent account, by the member of the National Security Council staff responsible for Iranian matters, is Gary Sick, *All Fall Down: America's Tragic Encounter with Iran*.

18. In the view of Gary Sick, ibid., p. 71.

19. Sullivan, *Mission to Iran*, pp. 154–63.

20. Mohammed Reza Pahlavi, *Answer to History*, p. 164.

21. For a description and criticism of Sullivan's cable, see Sick, *All Fall Down*, pp. 81–7.

22. Sullivan, *Mission to Iran*, pp. 199–226.

23. Ball, *The Past Has Another Pattern*, pp. 453–62.

24. Rosalynn Carter, *First Lady from Plains*, p. 308.

25. Mohammed Reza Pahlavi, *Answer to History*, p. 171.

26. Sullivan, *Mission to Iran*, p. 253.

27. Ibid., p. 258.

28. Jordan, *Crisis*, p. 29.

29. A National Security Council report to the President on March 6 noted the possibility that, after the Shah came to the United States, a "guerrilla group could retaliate against the remaining Americans, possibly taking one or more Americans hostage and refusing to release them until the Shah was extradited." Quoted in Sick, *All Fall Down*, p. 178.

30. Conditions at the time are dramatically described by Ken Follett, *On Wings of Eagles*.

31. Warren Christopher et al., *American Hostages in Iran: The Conduct of a Crisis*, pp. 54–5.

32. Shaplen, "Eye of the Storm," *The New Yorker*, June 9, 1980, p. 61.

33. Christopher, *American Hostages in Iran*, pp. 56–8.

34. Barry Rubin, *Paved with Good Intentions: The American Experience and Iran*, pp. 297–8.

35. Christopher, *American Hostages in Iran*, pp. 35–44.

36. Jordan, *Crisis*, p. 60.

37. Ibid., p. 44.

38. Sick, *All Fall Down*, chap. 13, and an earlier version of the same material in Christopher, *American Hostages in Iran*, pp. 144–72.

39. Jordan, *Crisis*, p. 52.

40. AFP, document 353.

41. Jordan, *Crisis*, p. 246.
42. Vance, pp. 409–11.
43. Christopher, *American Hostages in Iran*, p. 281.
44. Ibid., p. 295.

9. CONFRONTING THE SOVIETS: FROM VIENNA TO AFGHANISTAN

1. Quoted in Talbott, *Endgame*, p. 5.
2. Arkady N. Shevchenko, *Breaking with Moscow*, p. 302.
3. Brzezinski, p. 340.
4. Carter, p. 241.
5. Ibid., p. 245.
6. For an extended analysis of the Vienna summit, see Garthoff, *Détente and Confrontation*, pp. 728–40.
7. Carter, p. 253.
8. U.S. Senate, Committee on Foreign Relations, 96th Cong., 1st sess., "The SALT Treaty," part 1, p. 82. The hearings are conveniently summarized in 1979 *Congressional Quarterly Almanac*, pp. 412–36.
9. Ibid., p. 97.
10. Ibid., part 5, p. 143.
11. AFP, document 94.
12. Gaddis Smith, "The Legacy of Monroe's Doctrine," *The New York Times Magazine*, Sept. 9, 1984.
13. DSB, Oct. 1979, p. 63.
14. Brzezinski, pp. 346–9.
15. AFP, document 711.
16. Brzezinski, p. 565, weekly reports of Sept. 13 and 21, 1979.
17. *Public Papers of the Presidents: Jimmy Carter*, 1979, pp. 1802–5.
18. AFP, document 713.
19. R. Jeffrey Smith, "Missile Deployments Roil Europe," *Science* 223 (Jan. 27, 1984), pp. 371–6.

20. For an illuminating description of how the Soviets perceived the SS-20s as legitimate modernization and not as an attempt to gain a new advantage, see Garthoff, *Détente and Confrontation*, pp. 870–86.

21. Quoted by Brzezinski, p. 290.

22. Brussels communiqué. *AFP*, document 199.

23. *DSB*, May 1978, p. 58.

24. *AFP*, document 400.

25. Vance, p. 385.

26. For an excellent general account of these events, including the Soviet invasion, see Nancy Peabody Newell and Richard S. Newell, *The Struggle for Afghanistan*; and for detail, see Henry S. Bradsher, *Afghanistan and the Soviet Union*.

27. Shaplen, "Eye of the Storm," *The New Yorker*, June 2, 1980, p. 55.

28. Brzezinski, p. 427.

29. *DSB*, Dec. 1979, pp. 53–4.

30. *AFP*, document 405.

31. *Current Digest of the Soviet Press* 31, no. 51, p. 4.

32. Garthoff believes the Soviets perceived themselves as acting defensively, not as intending a challenge to the United States. *Détente and Confrontation*, pp. 915–37.

33. Carter, p. 472.

34. Brzezinski, p. 566.

35. *AFP*, document 408.

36. *AFP*, document 409.

37. *Public Papers of the Presidents: Jimmy Carter*, 1980–81, p. 121.

38. President Carter at a news conference, April 19, 1980. *AFP*, document 449.

39. For conditions in the last years of unregulated fishing, see William W. Warner, *Distant Water: The Fate of the North Atlantic Fisherman*.

40. *AFP*, document 427.

41. *AFP*, document 428.

42. *AFP*, document 447.

43. *AFP*, document 458.

44. *Public Papers of the Presidents: Jimmy Carter,* 1980–81, pp. 194–9. The budgetary implications of the response to Afghanistan are analyzed in Joseph A. Pechman, ed., *Setting National Priorities: Agenda for the 1980s*, chaps. 9–15.

45. Carter, p. 483.

46. Speech of Jan. 12, 1954. *DSB*, Jan. 25, 1954.

47. *AFP*, document 475.

48. *AFP*, document 476.

49. *AFP*, document 477.

50. *AFP*, document 484.

51. Seymour Hersh in *The Price of Power: Kissinger in the White House*, p. 450, asserts that, during the Johnson Administration, Desai received an annual retainer of $20,000 from the CIA as an informer.

52. *AFP*, document 468.

53. Dunn, *Controlling the Bomb*, pp. 44–8.

54. *AFP*, document 471.

55. Carter, p. 479.

56. *AFP*, document 473.

57. "Chronology 1980," *Foreign Affairs: America and the World,* 1980 59, no. 3, p. 733.

58. For an excellent history of American thinking about nuclear war, see Herken, *Counsels of War.*

59. Newhouse, *Cold Dawn.*

60. Pipes, "Why the Soviet Union Thinks It Could Fight and Win a Nuclear War," pp. 21–44.

61. An outstanding study is Paul Bracken, *The Command and Control of Nuclear Forces.*

62. Brzezinski, pp. 454–9.

63. *The New York Times*, Aug. 23, 1980.

64. Herken, *Counsels of War*, p. 301.

65. Brzezinski, pp. 459–60.

66. Ibid., pp. 20–1.

67. Timothy Garton Ash, *The Polish Revolution: Solidarity.*

68. *Public Papers of the Presidents: Jimmy Carter,* 1980–81, pp. 2889–93.

REFLECTIONS: WHY CARTER FAILED

1. Shifting public attitudes, as revealed by extensive polls, are described and tabulated in John E. Reilly, ed., *American Public Opinion and U.S. Foreign Policy 1983,* especially pp. 28–32. The divided opinions of American leaders, strikingly similar to the disagreements within the Carter Administration, are analyzed by Ole R. Holsti and James N. Rosenau, *American Leadership in World Affairs: Vietnam and the Breakdown of Consensus.*

2. Hedley Donovan, who served as a senior adviser in the White House during Carter's final year, remarks on the President's "odd lack of a sense of history." Donovan also notes that "Carter didn't seem to recognize instinctively when ideas are in collision, when two sets of facts cannot be equally pertinent, when desirable objectives are in conflict." *Roosevelt to Reagan: A Reporter's Encounters with Nine Presidents,* pp. 233–5.

3. The best account of these changes is Franck and Weisband, *Foreign Policy by Congress.*

4. See Carter, pp. 536–8, for a representative encounter.

5. *The New York Times,* Op Ed page, Feb. 1, 1980, reprinted in George F. Kennan, *The Nuclear Delusion: Soviet–American Relations in the Atomic Age,* p. 164.

Bibliography

Dean Acheson, *Present at the Creation*. New York: W. W. Norton, 1969.

Robert Armstrong and Janet Shenk, *El Salvador: The Face of Revolution*. Boston: South End Press, 1982.

Timothy Garton Ash, *The Polish Revolution: Solidarity*. New York: Charles Scribner's, 1984.

George W. Ball, *The Past Has Another Pattern: Memoirs*. New York: W. W. Norton, 1982.

William J. Barnds, ed., *Japan and the United States: Challenges and Opportunities*. New York: New York University Press, 1979.

Richard J. Barnet, *The Alliance—America, Europe, Japan: Makers of the Postwar World*. New York: Simon and Schuster, 1983.

R. P. Barston and Patricia Birnie, eds., *The Maritime Dimension*. London: George Allen and Unwin, 1980.

John H. Barton, *The Politics of Peace: An Evaluation of Arms Control*. Stanford: Stanford University Press, 1981.

Charles A. Beard and George H. E. Smith, *The Idea of National Interest*. New York: Macmillan, 1934.

———, *The Open Door at Home*. New York: Macmillan, 1934.

Coral Bell, *President Carter and Foreign Policy: The Costs of Virtue*. Canberra: Department of International Relations, The Australian National University, 1980.

Robin Bidwell, *The Two Yemens*. Singapore: Longman/Westview Press, 1983.

273

Richard E. Bissell, *South Africa and the United States: The Erosion of an Influence Relationship*. New York: Praeger, 1982.

Paul Bracken, *The Command and Control of Nuclear Forces*. New Haven: Yale University Press, 1983.

Henry S. Bradsher, *Afghanistan and the Soviet Union*. Durham, N.C.: Duke University Press, 1983.

Crane Brinton, *The Anatomy of Revolution*, rev. ed. New York: Vintage Books, 1965.

Harold Brown, *Thinking about National Security: Defense and Foreign Policy in a Dangerous World*. Boulder, Colo.: Westview Press, 1983.

Seyom Brown, *The Faces of Power: Constancy and Change in United States Foreign Policy from Truman to Reagan*. New York: Columbia University Press, 1983.

Zbigniew Brzezinski, ed., *Africa and the Communist World*. Stanford, Cal.: Hoover Institution Publications, Stanford University Press, 1963.

———, *Between Two Ages: America's Role in the Technetronic Era*. New York: The Viking Press, 1970.

———, *Ideology and Power in Soviet Politics*, rev. ed. New York: Praeger, 1967.

———, *Power and Principle: Memoirs of the National Security Adviser, 1977–1981*. New York: Farrar, Straus and Giroux, 1983.

Claude A. Buss, *The United States and the Republic of Korea: Background for Policy*. Stanford, Cal.: Hoover Institution Press, 1984.

Joseph A. Califano, Jr., *Governing America: An Insider's Report from the White House and the Cabinet*. New York: Simon and Schuster, 1981.

Jimmy Carter, *The Blood of Abraham*. Boston: Houghton Mifflin, 1985.

———, *A Government as Good as Its People*. New York: Simon and Schuster, 1977.

———, *Keeping Faith: Memoirs of a President*. New York: Bantam Books, 1982.

———, *The Presidential Campaign 1976*. One volume in two parts. Compiled under the direction of the Committee on House Administration, U.S. House of Representatives. Wash., D.C.: U.S. Government Printing Office, 1978.

————, *Why Not the Best?* Nashville: Broadman Press, 1975.

Rosalynn Carter, *First Lady from Plains.* Boston: Houghton Mifflin, 1984.

Leon H. Charney, *Special Counsel.* New York: Philosophical Library, 1984.

Noam Chomsky, *Towards a New Cold War: Essays on the Current Crisis and How We Got There.* New York: Pantheon, 1982.

Warren Christopher, Harold H. Saunders, Gary Sick, et al., *American Hostages in Iran: The Conduct of a Crisis.* New Haven: Yale University Press, 1985.

Duncan L. Clarke, *The Politics of Arms Control: The Role and Effectiveness of the U.S. Arms Control and Disarmament Agency.* New York: Free Press, 1979.

Richard W. Cottam, *Nationalism in Iran.* Pittsburgh: University of Pittsburgh Press, 1979.

Moshe Dayan, *Breakthrough: A Personal Account of the Egypt–Israeli Peace Negotiations.* London: Weidenfeld and Nicolson, 1981.

Lloyd deMause and Henry Ebel, *Jimmy Carter and American Fantasy: Psychological Explorations.* New York: Two Continents/Psychohistory Press, 1977.

I. M. Destler, *Making Foreign Economic Policy.* Wash., D.C.: The Brookings Institution, 1980.

I. M. Destler, Leslie H. Gelb, and Anthony Lake, *Our Own Worst Enemy: The Unmaking of American Foreign Policy.* New York: Simon and Schuster, 1985.

I. M. Destler and Hideo Sato, eds., *Coping with U.S.–Japanese Economic Conflicts.* Lexington, Mass.: Lexington Books, 1982.

David Detzer, *The Brink: Cuban Missile Crisis, 1962.* New York: Crowell, 1979.

Roger Dingman, *Power in the Pacific: The Origins of Naval Arms Limitation, 1914–1922.* Chicago: University of Chicago Press, 1976.

Martin Diskin, ed., *Trouble in Our Backyard: Central America and the United States in the Eighties.* New York: Pantheon Books, 1983.

Hedley Donovan, *Roosevelt to Reagan: A Reporter's Encounters with Nine Presidents.* New York: Harper and Row, 1985.

Elizabeth Drew, *Portrait of an Election: The 1980 Presidential Campaign.* New York: Simon and Schuster, 1981.

Ronnie Dugger, *On Reagan: The Man and His Presidency.* New York: McGraw-Hill, 1983.

James Dunkerley, *The Long War: Dictatorship and Revolution in El Salvador.* London: Junction Books, 1982.

Lewis A. Dunn, *Controlling the Bomb: Nuclear Proliferation in the 1980s.* New Haven: Yale University Press, 1982.

John Edwards, *Superweapon: The Making of MX.* New York: W. W. Norton, 1982.

Mohammed el-Khawas and Barry Cohen, eds., *The Kissinger Study of Southern Africa: National Security Study Memorandum 39 (SECRET).* Westport, Conn.: Lawrence Hill, 1976.

Philip J. Farley, Stephen S. Kaplan, and William H. Lewis, *Arms Across the Sea.* Wash., D.C.: The Brookings Institution, 1978.

Richard E. Feinberg, *The Intemperate Zone: The Third World Challenge to U.S. Foreign Policy.* New York: W. W. Norton, 1983.

Michael M. J. Fischer, *Iran: From Religious Dispute to Revolution.* Cambridge, Mass.: Harvard University Press, 1980.

Ken Follett, *On Wings of Eagles.* New York: William Morrow, 1983.

Gerald R. Ford, *A Time to Heal: The Autobiography of Gerald R. Ford.* New York: Harper and Row, 1979.

Thomas M. Franck and Edward Weisband, *Foreign Policy by Congress.* New York: Oxford University Press, 1979.

John Lewis Gaddis, *Strategies of Containment: A Critical Appraisal of Postwar American National Security Policy.* New York: Oxford University Press, 1982.

Raymond L. Garthoff, *Détente and Confrontation: American–Soviet Relations from Nixon to Reagan.* Wash., D.C.: The Brookings Institution, 1985.

Marvin E. Gettleman et al., eds., *El Salvador: Central America in the New Cold War.* New York: Grove Press, 1981.

Betty Glad, *Jimmy Carter: In Search of the Great White House.* New York: W. W. Norton, 1980.

Colin Gray, *Strategic Studies and Public Policy: The American Experience.* Lexington: University of Kentucky Press, 1982.

Ernst B. Haas, *Global Evangelism Rides Again: How to Protect*

Human Rights without Really Trying. Berkeley, Cal.: Institute of International Studies, 1978.

David Halberstam, *The Best and the Brightest.* New York: Random House, 1972.

Laurence Halley, *Ancient Affections: Ethnic Groups and Foreign Policy.* New York: Praeger, 1985.

Paul Y. Hammond, David J. Louscher, Michael D. Salomone, and Norman A. Graham, *The Reluctant Supplier: U.S. Decision-making for Arms Sales.* Cambridge, Mass.: Oelgeschlager, Gunn and Hain, 1983.

Gregg Herken, *Counsels of War.* New York: Alfred A. Knopf, 1985.

Alfred O. Hero, Jr., *The American People and South Africa.* Lexington, Mass.: D. C. Heath, 1982.

George C. Herring, *America's Longest War: The United States and Vietnam, 1950–1975.* New York: Wiley, 1979.

Seymour Hersh, *The Price of Power: Kissinger in the White House.* New York: Summit Books, 1983.

Martin F. Herz, ed., *The Modern Ambassador: The Challenge and the Search.* Wash., D.C.: Institute for the Study of Diplomacy, 1979.

Stanley Hoffmann, *Primacy or World Order: American Foreign Policy since the Cold War.* New York: McGraw-Hill, 1978.

Ann L. Hollick, *U.S. Foreign Policy and the Law of the Sea.* Princeton: Princeton University Press, 1981.

Henry F. Jackson, *From the Congo to Soweto: U.S. Foreign Policy Toward Africa Since 1960.* New York: William Morrow, 1982.

Robert C. Johansen, *The National Interest and the Human Interest: An Analysis of U.S. Foreign Policy.* Princeton: Princeton University Press, 1980.

Haynes Johnson, *In the Absence of Power: Governing America.* New York: The Viking Press, 1980.

Loch K. Johnson, *A Season of Inquiry: The Senate Intelligence Investigation.* Lexington: University of Kentucky Press, 1985.

Hamilton Jordan, *Crisis: The Last Year of the Carter Presidency.* New York: G. P. Putnam's Sons, 1982.

William J. Jorden, *Panama Odyssey.* Austin: University of Texas Press, 1984.

Stanley Karnow, *Vietnam: A History*. New York: The Viking Press, 1983.

Nikki R. Keddie, ed., *Religion and Politics in Iran: Shi'ism from Quietism to Revolution*. New Haven: Yale University Press, 1983.

———, *Roots of Revolution*. New Haven: Yale University Press, 1981.

George F. Kennan, *The Nuclear Delusion: Soviet–American Relations in the Atomic Age*. New York: Pantheon Books, 1982.

Sidney Kraus, ed., *The Great Debates: Carter vs. Ford, 1976*. Bloomington: Indiana University Press, 1979.

Michael Krepon, *Strategic Stalemate: Nuclear Weapons and Arms Control in American Politics*. New York: St. Martin's Press, 1984.

Bruce Kuniholm, *The Origins of the Cold War in the Near East: Great Power Conflict and Diplomacy in Iran, Turkey, and Greece*. Princeton: Princeton University Press, 1980.

Walter LaFeber, *Inevitable Revolutions: The United States and Central America*. New York: W. W. Norton, 1983.

———, *The Panama Canal: The Crisis in Historical Perspective*. New York: Oxford University Press, 1978.

Anthony Lake, *The "Tar Baby" Option: American Policy towards Southern Rhodesia*. New York: Columbia University Press, 1976.

Anthony Lake, ed., *The Vietnam Legacy: The War, American Society and the Future of American Foreign Policy*. New York: New York University Press, 1976.

Michael Ledeen and William Lewis, *Débacle: The American Failure in Iran*. New York: Alfred A. Knopf, 1981.

William LeoGrande, *Cuba's Policy in Africa, 1959–1980*. Berkeley, Cal.: Institute for International Studies, 1980.

Joseph I. Lieberman, *The Scorpion and the Tarantula: The Struggle to Control Atomic Weapons, 1945–1949*. Boston: Houghton Mifflin, 1970.

Neill Macaulay, *The Sandino Affair*. Chicago: Quadrangle, 1967.

David McCullough, *The Path between the Seas: The Creation of the Panama Canal, 1870–1914*. New York: Simon and Schuster, 1977.

David S. McLellan, *Cyrus Vance*. Totowa, N.J.: Rowman and Allenheld, 1985.

Richard D. Mahoney, *JFK: Ordeal in Africa*. New York: Oxford University Press, 1983.

Bruce Mazlish and Edwin Diamond, *Jimmy Carter: A Character Portrait*. New York: Simon and Schuster, 1979.

George D. Moffett III, *The Limits of Victory: The Ratification of the Panama Treaties*. Ithaca, N.Y.: Cornell University Press, 1985.

Clark R. Mollenhoff, *The President Who Failed: Carter out of Control*. New York: Macmillan, 1980.

John Norton Moore, ed., *The Arab–Israeli Conflict: Readings and Documents*. Princeton: Princeton University Press, 1977.

Nancy Peabody Newell and Richard S. Newell, *The Struggle for Afghanistan*. Ithaca, N.Y.: Cornell University Press, 1981.

John Newhouse, *Cold Dawn: The Story of SALT*. New York: Holt, Rinehart and Winston, 1973.

Reinhold Niebuhr, *The Irony of American History*. New York: Charles Scribner's, 1952.

Joseph S. Nye, Jr., ed., *The Making of America's Soviet Policy*. New Haven: Yale University Press, 1984.

Bernard H. Oxman, David D. Caron, and Charles L. O. Bruderi, eds., *Law of the Sea: U.S. Policy Dilemma*. San Francisco: ICS Press, 1983.

Kenneth A. Oye, Donald Rothchild, and Robert J. Lieber, eds., *Eagle Entangled: U.S. Foreign Policy in a Complex World*. New York: Longman, 1979.

Mohammed Reza Pahlavi, *Answer to History*. New York: Stein and Day, 1980.

Sir Anthony Parsons, *The Pride and the Fall*. London: Jonathan Cape, 1984.

Herbert Passin and Akira Iriye, eds., *Encounter at Shimoda: Search for a New Pacific Partnership*. Boulder, Colo.: Westview Press, 1979.

Joseph A. Pechman, ed., *Setting National Priorities: The 1978 Budget*. Wash., D.C.: The Brookings Institution, 1977.

———, *Setting National Priorities: The 1979 Budget*. Wash., D.C.: The Brookings Institution, 1978.

———, *Setting National Priorities: Agenda for the 1980s*. Wash., D.C.: The Brookings Institution, 1980.

————, *Setting National Priorities: The 1982 Budget*. Wash., D.C.: The Brookings Institution, 1981.

Andrew J. Pierre, *The Global Politics of Arms Sales*. Princeton: Princeton University Press, 1982.

Andrew J. Pierre, ed., *Arms Transfers and American Foreign Policy*. New York: New York University Press, 1979.

Alan Platt and Lawrence D. Weiler, *Congress and Arms Control*. Boulder, Colo.: Westview Press, 1978.

William C. Potter, *Nuclear Power and Nonproliferation: An Interdisciplinary Perspective*. Cambridge, Mass.: Oelgeschlager, Gunn and Hain, 1982.

Jody Powell, *The Other Side of the Story*. New York: William Morrow, 1984.

John Prados, *The Soviet Estimate: U.S. Intelligence Analysis and Russian Military Strength*. New York: Dial, 1982.

Robert D. Putnam and Nicholas Bayne, *Hanging Together: The Seven-Power Summits*. Cambridge, Mass.: Harvard University Press, 1984.

Parviz C. Radji, *In the Service of the Peacock Throne: The Diaries of the Shah's Last Ambassador to London*. London: Hamish Hamilton, 1983.

John E. Reilly, ed., *American Public Opinion and U.S. Foreign Policy 1983*. Chicago: The Chicago Council on Foreign Relations, 1983.

Kermit Roosevelt, *Countercoup: Struggle for the Control of Iran*. New York: McGraw-Hill, 1979.

James N. Rosenau and Ole R. Holsti, *American Leadership in World Affairs: Vietnam and the Breakdown of Consensus*. Boston: Allen and Unwin, 1984.

W. W. Rostow, *Open Skies: Eisenhower's Proposal of July 21, 1955*. Austin: University of Texas Press, 1982.

Barry Rubin, *Paved with Good Intentions: The American Experience and Iran*. New York: Oxford University Press, 1980.

————, *Secrets of State: The State Department and the Struggle over U.S. Foreign Policy*. New York: Oxford University Press, 1985.

Barry Rubin and Elizabeth P. Spiro, eds., *Human Rights and U.S. Foreign Policy*. Boulder, Colo.: Westview Press, 1979.

Pierre Salinger, *America Held Hostage: The Secret Negotiations*. New York: Doubleday, 1981.

Jerry W. Sanders, *Peddlers of Crisis: The Committee on the Present Danger and the Politics of Containment*. Boston: South End Press, 1983.

Martin Schram, *Running for President 1976: The Carter Campaign*. New York: Stein and Day, 1977.

Herbert Scoville, *MX: Prescription for Disaster*. Cambridge, Mass.: MIT Press, 1981.

Glenn T. Seaborg, *Kennedy, Khrushchev, and the Test Ban*. Berkeley: University of California Press, 1981.

William Shawcross, *Sideshow: Kissinger, Nixon and the Destruction of Cambodia*. New York: Simon and Schuster, 1979.

Arkady N. Shevchenko, *Breaking with Moscow*. New York: Alfred A. Knopf, 1985.

Laurence H. Shoup, *The Carter Presidency and Beyond: Power and Politics in the 1980s*. Palo Alto, Cal.: The Ramparts Press, 1980.

Benjamin Shwadran, *The Middle East, Oil and the Great Powers*, 3rd ed. New York: Wiley, 1973.

Gary Sick, *All Fall Down: America's Tragic Encounter with Iran*. New York: Random House, 1985.

Holly Sklar, ed., *Trilateralism: The Trilateral Commission and Elite Planning for World Management*. Boston: South End Press, 1980.

Gaddis Smith, *Dean Acheson*. New York: Cooper Square, 1972.

South Africa: Time Running Out. The Report of the Study Commission on U.S. Policy Toward Southern Africa. Berkeley: University of California Press, 1981.

Harold and Margaret Sprout, *Toward a New Order of Sea Power: American Naval Policy and the World Scene*. Princeton: Princeton University Press, 1940.

Nicholas John Spykman, *America's Strategy in World Politics*. New York: Harcourt, Brace, 1942.

John Bryan Starr, ed., *The Future of U.S.–China Relations*. New York: New York University Press, 1981.

John D. Stempel, *Inside the Iranian Revolution*. Bloomington: Indiana University Press, 1981.

Laurence Stern, *The Wrong Horse: The Politics of Intervention and the Failure of American Diplomacy*. New York: Times Books, 1977.

John Stockwell, *In Search of Enemies: A CIA Story*. New York: W. W. Norton, 1978.

Kandy Stroud, *How Jimmy Won: The Victory Campaign from Plains to the White House*. New York: William Morrow, 1977.

William H. Sullivan, *Mission to Iran: The Last U.S. Ambassador*. New York: W. W. Norton, 1981.

Strobe Talbott, *Endgame: The Inside Story of SALT II*. New York: Harper and Row, 1979.

John Tierney, Jr., ed., *About Face: The China Decision and Its Consequences*. New Rochelle, N.Y.: Arlington House, 1979.

Seth P. Tillman, *The United States in the Middle East*. Bloomington: Indiana University Press, 1982.

Stansfield Turner, *Secrecy and Democracy: The CIA in Transition*. Boston: Houghton Mifflin, 1985.

U.S. Council on Environmental Quality and the Department of State, *The Global 2000 Report to the President*. New York: Penguin Books, 1982.

U.S. Department of State, *Foreign Relations of the United States*. Wash., D.C.: U.S. Government Printing Office, 1947, vol. 2 (1973); 1950, vol. 1 (1977); 1950, vol. 2 (1977).

Cyrus Vance, *Hard Choices: Critical Years in America's Foreign Policy*. New York: Simon and Schuster, 1983.

Sandy Vogelgesang, *American Dream, Global Nightmare: The Dilemma of U.S. Human Rights Policy*. New York: W. W. Norton, 1980.

William W. Warner, *Distant Water: The Fate of the North Atlantic Fisherman*. Boston: Atlantic–Little, Brown, 1983.

Robert Wesson, *Communism in Central America and the Caribbean*. Stanford, Cal.: Hoover Institution Press, 1982.

William C. Widenor, *Henry Cabot Lodge and the Search for an American Foreign Policy*. Berkeley: University of California Press, 1980.

James Wooten, *Dasher: The Roots and Rising of Jimmy Carter*. New York: Summit Books, 1978.

Index

97–9; American people and, 52, 68; China and, 52, 105; Philippines and, 54, 100–1; Eastern Europe and, 55; Indonesia and, 102–3; Pakistan and, 55, 231; Vietnam and, 97; ASEAN and, 100; Somoza and, 119; Carter and Nicaragua and, 119, 122; El Salvador and, 123–4; ABC powers and, 127; Argentina and, 127–9; Brazil and, 129–30; Mexican workers and, 131; U.S. and Africa and, 134, 136; Mobutu and, 149; Uganda and, 150–1; Eritreans and, 154; Shah and Iran and, 185, 189, 195; Soviet Union and, *see* Soviet Union
Humphrey, Hubert, 26
Hussein, King, 163, 167–9
Huyser, Robert, to Iran, 193

Ibn Saud, King, 169
ICBMs, 72–3, 76, 81–2
Iklé, Fred, and SALT II, 212–13
India, 60–1, 231–4; U.S. and, 233–4
Indonesia, 100, 102–3; U.S. and, 102–3
internalists, *see under* foreign policy
International Court of Justice, 199
Iran, 54, 181–2, 184–6, 199; revolution in, 8, 10, 48, 56–7, 156, 167, 180, 187, 189, 193, 196–7, 200, 244; attack on American Embassy in, 10, 180, 194, 197; Brzezinski and Vance and, 42, 46, 49, 181, 188–91, 193–5; "loss" of, 55, 188, 196; war of, with Iraq, 172, 205; U.S. and, 181–2, 184, 187–91, 193–7, 242, *see also* hostages; Soviet Union and, 181–2, 190, 196, 202, 244; U.S. arms sales to, 182–4, 186, 196; Americans in, 183, 186, 192, 194–5, 197, *see also* hos-

tages; students of, in U.S., 184, 196; terrorists and rioting in, 187, 191; economy of, 191–2; Afghanistan and, 219–20; hostage crisis in, *see* hostages; *see also* Iran, Shah of
Iran, Shah of, 8, 55, 122, 132, 134, 152, 183, 193, 195, 201–2; fall of, 10, 172–3, 178, 187, 191–3; and human rights, 54, 185, 189–90; Brzezinski and, 152, 189–91, 195; with King Hussein and Carter, 163; and U.S., 180, 183–5, 187–91, 193, 195–7; removal of Mossadegh by, 182, 189; Islamic clergy and, 183, 186; and AWACS, 183–4; change in character of, 189–90; European leaders and, 192; and Guadeloupe summit, 192–3; death of, 205; wealth of, and hostage crisis, 206–7; *see also under* Carter
Iraq, 169, 171–2, 205
Irony of American History, The, 20
isolationists (ism), 14, 17–18, 116
Israel, 56, 158, 164, 169; and Egypt, 7–9, 30, 157, 159, 166–7, 170, 178; v. Arab states, U.S. and, 157–8, 160–1; Palestinians and, 157, 160, 162, 169, 178; U.S. and, 157, 164, 168, 171; and conquered territories, 158, 163–6; and West Bank and Gaza, 161, 163–4, 166–8; *see also* Begin, Camp David, *and names of leaders*
Izvestia, and Vance proposals, 76–7

Jackson, Henry M., and SALT II, 208–9, 213
Jackson-Vanik resolution, 94–5
Japan, 19, 60–1, 85, 104–5; U.S. and, 30, 85, 106–8
Javits, Jacob, 171, 195, 213
Johnson, Lyndon, and Vietnam,